LESSONS ON AGING FROM THREE NATIONS

Volume II

The Art of Caring for Older Adults

Edited by:

Sara Carmel

Ben-Gurion University of the Negev, Beer-Sheva, Israel

Carol A. Morse

Monash University, Melbourne, Australia

Fernando M. Torres-Gil

University of California, Los Angeles (UCLA), United States

Coeditors:

JoAnn Damron-Rodriguez

University of California, Los Angeles (UCLA), United States

Susan Feldman and Terence Seedsman

Victoria University, Melbourne, Australia

Society and Aging Series

Jon Hendricks: Series Editor

CRC Press

Taylor & Francis Group

Boca Raton London New York

CRC Press is an imprint of the

Taylor & Francis Group, an **informa** business

First published 2007 by Baywood Publishing Company, Inc.

Published 2018 by CRC Press
Taylor & Francis Group
6000 Broken Sound Parkway NW, Suite 300
Boca Raton, FL 33487-2742

First issued in paperback 2018

ISBN-13: 978-0-89503-369-7 (v. 1)

VOLUME 2: The Art of Caring for Older Adults
ISBN-13: 978-0-415-78396-5 (pbk)
ISBN-13: 978-0-89503-370-3 (hbk) (v. 2)

Visit the Taylor & Francis Web site at
http://www.taylorandfrancis.com

and the CRC Press Web site at
http://www.crcpress.com

Library of Congress Catalog Number: 2006047507

Library of Congress Cataloging-in-Publication Data

Lessons on aging from three nations / edited by Sara Carmel, Carol A. Morse, and Fernando M. Torres-Gil ; coeditors, JoAnn Damron-Rodriguez, Susan Feldman, and Terence Seedsman.
p. cm. -- (Society and aging series)
ISBN-13: 978-0-89503-369-7 (v. 1 : cloth)
ISBN-13: 978-0-89503-370-3 (v. 2 : cloth)
ISBN-10: 0-89503-369-0 (v. 1 : cloth)
ISBN-10: 0-89503-370-4 (v. 2 : cloth)
1. Older people--United States. 2. Older people--Israel. 3. Older people--Australia. 4. Aging--United States. 5. Aging--Israel. 6. Aging--Australia. I. Carmel, Sara, 1943- II. Morse, Carol A., 1942- III. Torres-Gil, Fernando M. IV. Series.

HQ1064 . U5L477 2006
305.2609172'2--dc22 2006047507

Dedication

To Dr. Samuel Aroni, Professor Emeritus of UCLA, who, through his initial enthusiasm and motivation for a worthwhile project on global aging, brought together some of his well-known colleagues from the United States, Israel, and Australia. His faith, encouragement, and support make him, in essence, the godfather of this book. This book affirms the philosophical belief that people joining forces can achieve great things that one person acting alone cannot do.

The Editors also wish to acknowledge all the remarkable and diverse older people who, in so many ways, provided the essential data and insights that enabled the respective contributors to present their cases. In a very real way, this book is a testimony to the fact that people of any age share so much with each other, regardless of nationality, race, religion, cultural heritage, or status.

Table of Contents

Prologue

The world is undergoing a demographic transformation unprecedented in human history. The aging of nations and increases in life expectancy among most developed and developing countries will fundamentally influence how governments and societies address the needs of individuals and families. Global aging presents a set of challenges, concerns, and problems that will require the attention of all sectors of society. This growing awareness has led to various international dialogues about the implications of this phenomenon, including initiatives of the World Health Organization, numerous professional conferences in a variety of disciplines, and the World Congress on Aging held every four years. Yet, the depth and breadth of what we know and how this phenomenon affects societies and governments is relatively limited. What are the pressing issues facing nations around the world as their populace lives longer? How should we respond to the needs and expectations of older persons and their families? What is the "art" of caring for older adults in an environment where governments and their nonprofit and voluntary sectors are hard-pressed to address the needs of all citizens, particularly the young? This book addresses these fundamental questions through the prism of three key concerns: Caregiving, family care, and the end-of-life stage. Together, these issues reflect the complexity and importance of responding proactively; and the extent to which nations handle these successfully may well demonstrate their level of compassion and greatness as a country and a civilization. There are few comparative studies that examine the art of caregiving and the policies and services needed by caregivers and their families; and there are very few willing to examine the art of letting go and the end-of-life reality. This book uses the experiences of Australia, Israel, and the United States to address issues of responsibility, consumer-directed care, residential choices, family-based caregiving, dementia care, advance directives, palliative care, and end-of-life decision making as a foundation from which to draw lessons that other nations might use as they address the demographic imperative.

THREE NATIONS: SHARED EXPERIENCES

This book draws on case studies from selected countries to begin the process of a multifaceted and substantive understanding of the concerns, challenges, and opportunities facing global aging. The journey begins with the study of three nations—the United States, Israel, and Australia. Together, these countries form the basis for identifying the insights, indicators, and trends that may affect the developed and developing world as it faces its inevitable demographic destiny. Why these three nations? The world is complex, and no two nations are alike. Yet the United States, Israel, and Australia share certain similarities in history and experiences that ferret out the issues of global aging.

First, there is the serendipitous opportunity of these three countries sharing multilateral partnerships among their universities and having a cadre of gerontologists with a long-standing history of collaboration that affords them the ability to become intimately involved in the lives of their communities. The coeditors and contributors to this book share long-standing professional ties, which allow them to coordinate and collaborate in their studies of aging phenomena. More importantly, each country is relatively well aware of its aging issues and has established infrastructures of programs, services, and public benefits for its older citizens. Each has stable political and governmental systems and a pluralistic democracy that allows for contentious debates about public policy. In addition, they face an even more important commonality: The tension of coping with dramatic social and demographic change and the growing nexus of aging and diversity. Each of these countries faces continued immigration and the arrival of refugee groups while its minority groups grow in population.

Globalization, political events, and technological and social developments add to this complexity and put enormous stress on families, individuals, and local communities. As each country ages, its citizens and public policymakers wonder how they will face the future, when its older and retiree populations double in size. Clearly, there are differences. The United States remains the behemoth in global affairs, while Israel is one of the smallest nations. Australia is relatively remote geographically and is caught between its Western-oriented heritage and the growing prominence of its Asian neighbors.

By examining their unique experiences, we can highlight the potential issues affecting the developed and the developing world as they age. Notwithstanding these commonalities and differences, the shared demographic experiences of the United States, Israel, and Australia provide an opening to understanding the many concerns of aging in a global community.

CHALLENGES AND OPPORTUNITIES

What we have found in our study of these three nations is that each is committed to addressing the needs of caring for older adults and in many respects has developed innovative and compassionate solutions. Yet, each faces a series of problems and challenges to their continued ability to address the art of caring for their eldest citizens. Volume II examines policies, services, and interventions that enable families and caregivers to care for their own. This volume explores how Australia, Israel, and the United States address the manpower needs for health and social-service professionals in gerontology and geriatrics, as well as the clinical and programmatic interventions that best serve those elders with dementias, and chronic and terminal illnesses. It explores caregiving and long-term care policies, the needs of families, and death and dying. Whereas Volume I of this series examined The Art of Aging Well and the successful examples of how these three nations respond to the various needs of older and diverse populations, this volume delves into an issue generally avoided but inevitable: The end of life. Perhaps no other topic in the life span of humans is a better illustration of the fundamental intimacy that all of us must face than, how we prepare to die, and how we treat those at this stage with dignity and compassion. Volume II faces squarely the art of letting go and how we can and must provide quality services and support for those who are least empowered and able to exercise control in the last stages of life. The authors fundamentally believe that if nations and societies resolutely address the last stage in the life cycle, then how they do so will permeate all other aspects of serving older citizens and those who are aging in their respective communities. Perhaps no other barometer of a compassionate and great nation can so effectively measure and demonstrate this commitment. Thus, though this volume addresses a set of sobering concerns, it ultimately gives direction, suggestions, and a promise of resolution to policymakers, advocacy groups, governments, and the private and voluntary sectors. Volume I and II are intended as companion pieces, yet each provides a coherent and comprehensive set of lessons that can be drawn from these three nations.

GLOBAL AGING

The demographic challenges facing the world and each of these three nations make a compelling case for moving toward a more in-depth understanding of the myriad issues likely to face all nations. The world's population added 20 years in average life expectancy at birth between 1950 and 2000 (Andrews, 2001). Simultaneously, fertility rates have dropped dramatically, from 6.54 to 5.54 children per woman to well below 2.1 children in many developed countries. According to Professor Gary Andrews, between 2000 and 2050, the number of people who are 65 and older could increase by 218%, and the number of people 80 and older may increase by 386%. In addition, the number of centenarians is projected to increase 15-fold during that period.

As Tables 1, 2, and 3 illustrate, all nations or regions of the world will need to address the challenge of individual and population aging. Even the developed world has seen dramatic increases in its life expectancy. While Europe, the United

States, and Asia currently represent the greatest number of persons over age 65, Latin America and Southeast Asia will join the ranks of aging nations by 2050. Perhaps only Africa faces diminished pressures, tragically because of the lack of public health and the prevalence of communicable diseases.

THE TRILOGY OF DEMOGRAPHIC REALITIES: UNITED STATES, ISRAEL, AND AUSTRALIA

The demographic reality for the trilogy of nations in this book makes a similar compelling statement. Table 4 illustrates aspects of these trends.

While the population size of each country differs dramatically, they are all facing similar life expectancies at birth as well as similar gender differences. The dependency ratios differ somewhat, with Israel and the United States having higher ratios.

All three societies are considered relatively young among the developed countries. They are in the second-tier populations, which also includes Canada and New Zealand, the so-called "younger" group of countries with a combined older proportion of the population of approximately 12%. This group is ranked behind the first-tier, or "older" group of countries—European nations including Scandinavia—in which approximately 17% of their population were aged 65 and older in 2000. The third-tier, or "late initiation" countries, includes Korea, Mexico, and Turkey, which, with approximately 4.1% to 5.6% of their populations aged 65 and older, are just beginning to identify their population growth projections.

Examining each of the three countries in turn reveals the commonalities and diversity in their demographic realities.

THE CHANGING DEMOGRAPHIC PROFILE OF OLDER AUSTRALIANS

Australia's proportion of people aged 65 and older will be larger in the first decade of the 21st century than in the 10 years of the previous decade. The total

Table 1. Average Life Expectancies (years)

	1970-75	1997	2025
More developed countries	71.0	74.5	79.2
Less developed countries	55.5	63.6	71.1
World	59.5	65.8	72.4

Source: World Health Organization (1998). *World Atlas of Ageing.* Kobe, Japan: Centre for Health Development.

Table 2. Top 10 Countries with the Highest Proportion of Persons Above Age 65

1997 (%)		2025 (%)		2050 (%)	
Monaco	19.6	Japan	26.7	Spain	34.7
Sweden	17.2	Italy	25.1	Italy	34.2
Italy	17.0	Finland	24.5	Greece	33.8
Belgium	16.4	Monaco	24.1	Portugal	33.1
Greece	16.4	San Marino	23.9	Germany	32.8
Spain	16.1	Greece	23.7	Slovenia	32.7
United Kingdom	15.7	Belgium	23.5	Austria	32.2
Norway	15.7	Slovenia	23.5	Japan	32.0
France	15.6	Switzerland	23.4	Switzerland	31.3
Japan	15.4	France	23.4	Netherlands	31.2

Source: International database, U.S. Bureau of Census; WHO Kobe Centre, Ageing and Health.

Table 3. Top 10 Countries with the Highest Absolute Number of Persons Above Age 65

1997 (millions)		2025 (millions)		2050 (millions)	
China	77.9	China	199.3	China	344.5
India	40.2	India	108.2	India	239.8
United States	34.1	United States	62.0	United States	78.9
Japan	19.4	Japan	32.2	Indonesia	55.3
Russia	18.0	Russia	25.0	Brazil	42.3
Germany	12.9	Indonesia	24.8	Russia	34.1
Italy	9.8	Brazil	21.1	Japan	32.6
United Kingdom	9.2	Germany	20.4	Mexico	29.8
France	9.1	France	14.3	Bangladesh	29.3
Indonesia	8.0	Italy	13.6	Pakistan	28.8

Source: International database, U.S. Bureau of Census; WHO Kobe Centre, Ageing and Health.

Table 4. Sociodemographic Characteristics of Australia, Israel, and the United States

	Total population	Percent 60+	Percent 65+[a]	Life expectancy at birth			Expectation of disability at birth		Dependency ratio (per 100)
				Men	Women	Both	Men	Women	
Australia	19,544,000	16.7	12.8	77.9	83.0	80.4	7.0	8.7	48
Israel	6,304,000	13.1	9.9	77.3	81.4	79.4	6.9	9.0	61
United States	291,038,000	16.2	12.4	74.6	79.8	77.3	7.4	8.5	51

[a]Percentages of elderly aged 65+ were drawn from: cia.gov/cia/publications/factbook.
Source: The World Health Report: Changing History, 2004, World Health Organization.

older population is projected to grow at the same rate (3.2% over the coming 20 years as during the previous 20 years). Even so, this rate is above the OECD average of 2.0% to 2.2% and above the projected rates of growth for the United States, which are 1.8% to 2.6% (Australian Institute of Health & Welfare, 2002).

Australia's population is also changing in terms of age, gender, and ethnicity categories. The oldest old, aged 85 and older, has been the fastest growing age group to date, with an estimated increase of approximately 69%, to account for 11% of the total population in 2001. Comparatively, the country has seen smaller increases of 36% among the 75- to 84-year-olds and just 10% for those aged 65 to 74. Between 2011 and 2021, these profiles are expected to reverse. During that decade, the rates of increase in the older population are projected to decrease to less than 50% for those who are 85 and older and to 17% for those who are 75 to 84. The rate is expected to increase to 28% for those aged 65 to 74. Thus, instead of the usual "aging" of Australia's society, where the numbers of older people continue to expand, with the anticipated reduction in the absolute numbers of those aged 75 to 90, a "younging" of the population is predicted.

An important issue for Australia is its ethnic diversity, with more than 204 different cultural groups. The total number of people born overseas was approximately 33% in 2001. Of these, 39% were from English-speaking countries, and the remainder were from culturally and linguistically diverse (CALD) societies (e.g., Poles, Italians, Greeks, Indians, Maltese, Egyptian, and Chinese). The population of older people from culturally and linguistically diverse origins currently accounts for about 18% of the total population and is projected to increase to 23% by 2011. These groups, including those of second and third generations of migrant heritage and parentage, are also expected to age more rapidly than the Australian-born population. By the end of the first decade of the

21st century, the number of people aged 85 years and older from CALD backgrounds is expected to increase by 165% compared with an increase of about 47% in the Australian-born population (Gibson, Braun, Benham, & Mason, 2001). These trends are attributed to the aging of the migrants who arrived during the 1950s and 1960s and is expected to continue in waves, depending on the arrival points of people from particular ethnic origins to the present time and subsequently followed by sharp declines.

The indigenous population of Australia is composed of Aboriginals and Torres Strait Islanders in a ratio of approximately 6:1. Together, they account for 2.4% of the total Australian population (Australian Bureau of Statistics, 2002). Among these people, those aged 65 and older account for only 2.8% of all indigenous Australians, compared with 12% of nonindigenous elderly Australians. Thus, beyond the age of 45, the numbers of indigenous people declines more sharply than among the nonindigenous. Life expectancy rates for those born from 1998 to 2001 is 63 years for females and 56 years for males, revealing a difference of about 20 years between the indigenous and the total population, which is attributed to poorer health status and higher mortality rates.

Among all older Australians, an important consideration is the gender differential that operates in each age group and culture. The ratio of older women to older men is projected to decrease from 57% in 1991 to 53% in 2021.

All of these projected changes in populations will inevitably present economic and social challenges as well as opportunities. Dang, Antolin, and Oxley (2001) propose that the expected increases in expenditures on age pensions and health care over the next two decades will be counterbalanced by decreased expenditures on child and family benefits and education in most developed countries. In Australia, the present GDP (Gross Domestic Product) expenditure on age-related needs is comparable with that of other OECD countries at approximately 16.9%. This is expected to increase to 17.6% of GDP by 2020, stronger than of some countries such as New Zealand, but behind that of the United Kingdom and the United States.

THE CHANGING DEMOGRAPHIC PROFILE OF OLDER ISRAELIS

Similar to the situation in other developed nations, the absolute number and percentage of elderly persons in Israel is increasing, while the percentage of younger persons is decreasing. In 2002, life expectancy at birth in Israel was relatively high, at 79.4–81.4 years for women, and 77.3 years for men (World Health Organization, 2004).

However, Israel differs from other developed countries in the pace of these demographic changes. Compared with the United States, where the percentage of elderly aged 65 and older doubled over the twentieth century, this demographic change in Israel occurred within only four decades, from 4.8% in 1955 to 9.5% in

1995. When the state of Israel was established in 1948, it was a relatively young society with elderly people accounting for less than 4% of its total population. Currently, the proportion is 9.9%. Furthermore, since 1955, while Israel's total population has grown 3.7-fold, the population of elderly people has grown 7.7-fold. The highest rate of growth occurred from 1960 to 1970, with an annual average rate of 6.7%. This proportion decreased to 3.2% from 1990 to 2000. The population of the old-old (75+) grew even faster. By the end of 1998, the old-old group accounted for 42.5% of people aged 65 and over, and increased to 45% by the end of 2002. From 1980 to 1990, the average annual rate of growth was 6.3% for people aged 80 and older, 5.5% for those aged 75 and older, and only 2.7% for those aged 65 and older. This trend of a rapid growth of the oldest-old is also expressed in the increased percentages of this sector in the elderly population. For example, in 1980, about 33% of the total population of elderly were 75 and older, and 14% were 80 and older. By the end of 2002, this increased to 45%, and 23% respectively (Mashav–National Database, 2004).

These developments are due to both a natural growth and the absorption of immigrants from more than 100 countries. Most of the immigrants came to Israel in large numbers during relatively short periods of time, as some countries opened their gates for emigration. Israel's open-door policy, under which every Jew is eligible to immigrate to Israel and receive immediate citizenship, has periodically brought about unexpected changes in the age structure of Israel (Carmel, 2002). For example, the last wave of immigrants, which came from the former Soviet Union beginning in 1989, significantly increased both the absolute number of elderly people in Israel and their proportion in the general population. At the end of 2002, those aged 65 and older accounted for 17% of this wave of new immigrants, while Israelis in this age group constituted only 9.9%. At the end of 2002, the Israeli population reached 6.6 million, with 655,000 aged 65 and older. In 2020, elderly people are expected to account for close to 12% of the general population (Mashav, 2004).

Considering that the population of the old-old is the heaviest consumer of health and social services in Israel and elsewhere, one of the most significant implications of these demographic trends is an increased need for such services, which must be designed to meet the special needs of the various groups of elderly persons in Israel.

Heterogeneity is one of the dominant characteristics of Israel's older population. For example, until 1960, Jewish, native-born elderly accounted for only 3% of the elderly population. That proportion increased to 11% in 2002. In the same year, the largest group of elderly persons, 61%, was composed of those born in European or American countries; 15% were of Asian origin and 13% were of North-African origin. In the 75-and-older age group, people of European and American origin accounted for 53%, compared with 39% of people born in Asian countries and 35% of people born in North African countries.

In general, Israeli-born and European- and American-born elderly persons are apt to be more highly educated and have higher levels of income than elderly people of Asian or African origin. However, the elderly immigrants who arrived in Israel in the early and mid-1990s from the former Soviet Union have become an even weaker group than people of Asian and African origin, in terms of their economic status, health, and subjective well-being, despite being younger and more educated than the Israeli elderly (Carmel, 2001; Carmel & Lazar, 1998).

Over the years, there has been a clear increase in the elderly population's level of education. For example, in 1970, 40.1% of elderly persons aged 65 and older had poor education—up to four years of formal education. This number decreased to 26.7% in 1990 and to 18.4%, in 2002. Also, the percentage of elderly Israelis who receive pensions from their previous workplaces has increased over the years. These trends indicate that, in the future, the socioeconomic status of elderly people will significantly improve.

In 2002, elderly Arabs accounted for only 3.2% in the Israeli population. Elderly Arabs and Jews of Ethiopian origin are the most disadvantaged groups in the Israeli aged population in terms of education, health, and economic status (Carmel, 2002). For example, in 2002, among the non-Jews, 40% of the men and 65% of women reported having up to four years of formal education only, while among the Jews; the numbers were 11% among men and 19% among women. In addition, 30.5% of elderly Arabs reported difficulties in activities of daily living, compared with 14.7% of elderly Jews (Mashav, 2004). The percentage of elderly Arabs in the total population of elderly Israelis is expected to increase rapidly over the next two decades, from 6% to as much as 10%.

Women comprise 58% of Israel's population of persons aged 65 and older. This percentage is lower among the Arabs (54%), and significantly higher among the new immigrants (62%). The percentage of women in this population increases with age. Elderly women are disadvantaged compared with men in terms of indicators of well-being, such as education, income, and health status (Carmel & Bernstein, 2003). For example, in 2002, 33% of elderly men had 13 or more years of formal education, compared with 25% of elderly women. Also, 15% of men reported being employed, compared with 5% of women. Furthermore, 52% of elderly men received pensions from their workplaces on a regular basis, as opposed to only 28% of elderly women (Mashav, 2004), since women of all ages earn less than men in Israel. Gender differences are also prominent in terms of life expectancy. The life expectancy for Jews aged 65 today is 81.8 years for men and 84 years for women, although it is quite similar for both genders among the Arabs (81.3 for men and 81.7 for women) (Mashav, 2004).

Holocaust survivors form a special group of elderly people in Israel. They account for 40% of the total population aged 65 and older. About 55% of them are 75 and older, and 60% are women. By 2020, the number of people in this group will significantly decrease (Mashav, 2004).

The rapid increase in the population of elderly people, with its special physical and psychosocial needs and social diversity, has presented a challenge of significant dimensions to Israeli society. It has required addressing the needs of special groups of elderly, such as Jews and Arabs, veterans and new immigrants, religious and secular, Holocaust survivors, and other immigrants of different ethnic origins and cultural backgrounds.

Awareness of the needs of this large and rapidly growing population group intensified in the 1980s. Israeli society has addressed this new need by passing welfare laws and developing a wide range of community services. The basic orientation that has guided Israel's health and welfare policies in tending to the needs of frail and disabled elderly persons has been to enable them to continue living in their own homes and communities as long as possible. Accordingly, a wide network of welfare and long-term health services has been established throughout the country by public and private agencies. Social clubs and sheltered housing units have opened for independent elderly persons and for those who require limited services. Disabled elderly persons' needs have been addressed in part by the Long-Term Insurance Law, enacted in 1988. Under this law, people who need assistance in performing activities of daily living receive personal and domestic help in their homes by home-care workers and in community day-care centers for disabled elderly that offer a variety of personal and social services. Long-term institutional care is provided in public and private old-age homes and in nursing homes.

However, significant difficulties in the continuity of care have been a major weakness of this wide and impressive network of health and social services. The multiplicity in public and private services in terms of responsibility, ownership, provision of different kinds of services, entitlement criteria, and financing, creates duplications and fragmentation in the continuity of care. These are confusing to disabled persons, their families, and formal caregivers and are also a factor in the inefficient provision of services (Clarfield, Paltiel, Gindin, Morginstin, & Dwolatzky, 2000). Israel is attempting to change its financing arrangements, establish coordinating mechanisms, and is considering centralizing the services for elderly people under one ministry. Such structural changes, should they occur, will ensure access to comprehensive and continuous care for all and enhance the efficiency and effectiveness of current services.

THE CHANGING DEMOGRAPHIC PROFILE OF OLDER AMERICANS

Along with many other countries around the world, the U.S. population is aging and being driven by declining fertility and mortality rates. The increase in the older adult population in the United States is driven by the aging of the population born during the "baby boom" after World War II (1946 to 1964). In 1994, about 30% of the elderly population was born during the baby-boom generation (Cheeseman, 2001). As this population ages, the median age will rise. People born during the baby boom were between 36 and 54 years old at the turn of the twentieth century (Hollmann, 2000). In 2011, the first members of the baby boom generation will reach age 65 and according to the U.S. Census Bureau, between 2011 and 2030, the number of elderly will rise from 40.4 million (13% of the population) to 70.3 million (20% of the population). The last of the baby-boom population will reach age 65 in the year 2029. By that time, the "baby boom" population is projected to be only about 16% of the total population (Hollmann, 2000).

Due to better medical knowledge and technological advancements in health care, more and more people are living longer. Although the United States is considered to be a part of the "younger" group of countries, it has seen a 12% (35 million people) increase in its 65+ cohort between 1990 and 2000 (Hetzel & Smith, 2001). In the year 2000, the older population between the ages 75–84 comprised 35% of the entire older population as reported by the U.S. Census. The growth in the number of the oldest old (aged 85+) is of greater public concern. It is estimated that between the years 1995 and 2010, the "oldest old" population will grow by 56%, as compared with 13% for the age group between 65 and 84 years of age (Administration on Aging, 2004). This means that a larger share of the elderly will be over age 85. In fact, in the decades that follow, the 85+ age group will grow sharply as the baby-boom generation ages. The projected increase from 2030 to 2050 is 116%. The cumulative growth of the 85+ population between the years 1995 and 2050 is expected to be more than 400%, and the proportion of this cohort in the total population is anticipated to increase from the 1.4% in 1995 to 4.6% in 2050 (Administration on Aging, 2004).

In 1990, 37,306 centenarians (people age 100 or over) were living in the United States, while in 2000, there were 50,454 (National Center for Health Statistics, 2003). According to the 2000 Census, the greatest number of centenarians (5,341) lived in California, followed by 3,997 centenarians in New York (U.S. Bureau of the Census, 2000). Internationally, the United States has one of the highest proportions of centenarians among people aged 85 and older. This finding is in line with research indicating that life expectancy after 80 is higher in the United States than in a number of other developed countries.

The American population is also changing in its internal structure by age categories, gender, and ethnicity. According to the 2000 U.S. Census, the male-female ratio has been dropping steadily among older age groups. In fact, most of today's elderly, and especially the older aged, are women. Four out of five centenarians were reported to be women in 1990 (Krach, 1999). Overall, the elderly population in 1995 included "45% more women than men, and the older the age group, the lower the proportion of men in the group" (Administration on Aging, 2004). For example, there were 158% more women than men aged 85+ in 1995. It is expected that in 2050, women in this age group will outnumber men aged 85 and over by more than 4 million, and women will make up 61% of the population aged 85 and over (U.S. Department of Commerce, Economics and Statistics Administration, 1995).

The United States faces a nexus of aging and diversity with the U.S. older adult population. Currently, 7.9% of this population is African American, 5.1% is Hispanic, 1.2 is Caucasian and 7.2% is Asian/Pacific Islanders (Administration on Aging, 2004).

The demographic profile of older persons will change by 2050. In this year, 17% of the elderly population is projected to be Hispanic, in comparison with 4.5% in 1995 (Administration on Aging, 2004). The proportions of blacks and "other races" in the elderly population are also expected to increase. The shift in the percentages of the non-Hispanic white population is expected to decrease from 85% to 66%, with one third of elderly in that group encompassing either black, Hispanic, or "other races" in 2050 (Administration on Aging, 2004). Yet, as the society ages, the United States is witnessing a unique phenomenon: The diversification of its population. Census 2000 data make this point more vivid than ever before. Nearly one in every three Americans is a member of a minority group, reflecting the immigration surge of the 1990s (Rosenblatt, 2001). Not since the early 1900s have we seen such a dramatic growth of immigrant and minority groups. From 1990 to 2000, the nation's non-Latino white population dropped from 75.6% to 69.1% (U.S. Bureau of the Census, 1990, 2000b). Latinos are now roughly equal to African Americans as two of the nation's largest minority groups. Latinos accounted for 9% of the U.S. population in 1990 (22.4 million) and increased to 12.5% (35.3 million) in 2000. African Americans showed a more modest increase from 12.1% (30 million) to 12.3% (34.6 million). In the same period, the population of Asians and Pacific Islanders increased from 2.9% to 3.7%. In addition, there are sizable numbers of other immigrant groups, including Armenians, Persians, Slavs, and Russians, reflecting the world's trouble spots and a continued propensity to see America as a refuge and a land of opportunity. There is greater diversity in the United States today than at any time in its history; about 10% (more than 25 million) of Americans today are foreign-born.

ISSUES FACING POPULATION AGING

The preceding data point out that these three nations, with elderly people comprising 10%–12% of their population, are facing unprecedented rates of aging, heterogeneity within their older populations, pressures and challenges of immigration, refugee groups, and the growth of minority populations. Furthermore, all three nations anticipate significant changes in the demographic structure of their old populations in terms of age groups, gender, and ethnicity. All of these developments are forcing governments to confront the nexus of aging and diversification of their populations and the need for services, programs, and policies that respond to these changes.

These challenges present a host of questions about how each nation will respond to its particular population aging. Among them:

- To what extent are their governments prepared to respond to individual and population aging?
- How will longevity and population aging alter their demographic profiles and the impact on their political, social, and economic institutions?
- What role and responsibilities do the various sectors of their societies—public, private, nonprofit, voluntary, and religious—have in preparing for a longer life span?
- What values should be exercised, promulgated, and integrated into the approaches they use in caring for older adults, and how do diverse cultures address the needs of older persons?
- What role do technological and biomedical advances play in addressing the needs of the chronically and terminally ill, and how might this influence how governments and society prepare for demographic changes?
- To what extent will the elderly be empowered to make their own choices and determine their own destinies, and will these lead to a politics of aging where older persons become influential constituents?
- Where and how should they educate, train, and prepare the workforce that will require gerontological and geriatric skills for the expanded population of elders?
- What are the legal, social, emotional, and professional concerns in addressing death and dying?

This book (Vol. II) and its companion volume (Vol. I) fill an important niche in the growing interest in global aging and seek to identify the issues, challenges, and opportunities of aging. The editors of the text for these three nations draw upon their own unique knowledge and perspectives to present a series of themes and topics to answer the above questions. In doing so, they suggest that there is an "art" in responding to aging, and that art requires a proactive, educated, and insightful set of skills, adaptability, and planning. How well we learn this art determines the positive and problematic aspects of individual and population aging. Developing policies and providing services, enhancing family caregiving, and responding compassionately to the end of life and developing examples of how to let go represent the art of understanding, responding, and incorporating these themes and topics into our response to the future of global aging.

The editors explore these arenas and offer the art of caring for older adults as a framework for connecting the disparate issues of aging and presenting a set of lessons for these three nations. Here, in Volume II, the authors present the challenges and concerns regarding caregiving that involve families, professional providers of care, governments, and policymakers. Volume I, entitled *Lessons*

On Aging From Three Nations: The Art of Aging Well examines the positive side of aging and the successful adaptations. In this way we hope these two volumes provide clues and suggestions for further research, policies, and practices in the comparative study of global aging.

REFERENCES

Administration on Aging. (2004). *Aging into the 21st century.* Retrieved from http://www.aoa.gov/prof/Statistics/future_growth/ageing21/demography.asp.

Administration on Aging. (2004, September). *Aging into the 21st century.* Retrieved from http://www.aoa.gov/prof/Statistics/future_growth/future growth.asp.

Andrews, G. (2001). Community health care in ageing societies: The past, present, and future. In *Community health care in ageing societies* (pp. 26-34). The proceedings of the WHO KOBE Centre, International Meeting on Community Health Care in Ageing Societies, Shanghai, China, 12-14 June, 2000. World Health Organization.

Australian Bureau of Statistics. (1998). *Disability, ageing and carers survey: Summary of findings,* Catalogue No. 4430.0. Canberra, Australia: Author.

Australian Bureau of Statistics. (2002). *Population distribution: Aboriginal and Torres Strait Islander Australians,* Catalogue No. 4705.0. Canberra, Australia: Author.

Australian Institute of Health & Welfare. (2002). *Older Australia at a glance.* Canberra, Australia: Author.

Carmel, S. (2001). Subjective evaluation of health in old age: The role of immigration status and social environment. *International Journal of Aging and Human Development, 53,* 91-105.

Carmel, S. (2002). Israel. In D. J. Ekerdt, R. Applebaum, K. C. A. Holden, S. G. Post, K. Rockwood, R. Schulz, R. L. Sprott, & P. Uhlenberg (Eds.), *Encyclopedia of ageing.* New York: Macmillan.

Carmel, S., & Bernstein, J. (2003). Gender differences in physical health and psychosocial well-being among four age groups of elderly people in Israel. *International Journal of Aging and Human Development, 56*(2), 113-131.

Carmel, S., & Lazar, A. (1998). Health and well-being among elderly persons: The role of social class and immigration status. *Ethnicity & Health, 3,* 31-43.

Cheeseman, J. (2001). *National population projections.* U.S. Census Bureau. Retrieved November 19, 2004 from http://www.census.gov/population/www/pop-profile/natproj.html.

Clarfield, A. M., Paltiel, A., Gindin, Y., Morginstin, B., & Dwolatzky, T. (2000). Country profile: Israel. *Journal of the American Geriatrics Society, 48,* 980-984.

Dang, T. T., Antolin, P., & Oxley, H. (2001). *Fiscal implications of ageing: Projections of age-related spending.* Paris: Organization for Economic Cooperation and Development.

Gibson, D., Braun, P., Benham, C., & Mason, F. (2001). *Projections of older immigrants: People from culturally and linguistically diverse backgrounds, 1996–2026.* Canberra, Australia: Australian Institute of Health & Welfare.

Hetzel, L., & Smith, A. (2001). *The 65 years and over population: 2000.* Washington, DC: U.S. Census Bureau Brief.

Hollmann, F. W. (2000). *Census Bureau projects doubling of nation's population by 2100.* Retrieved November, 2004 from http://www.census.gov/Press-Release/www/2000/cb00-05.html.

Krach, C. (1999). *Centenarians in the United States.* Washington, DC: U.S. Census Bureau. Retrieved November 19, 2004 from http://www.census.gov/prod/99pubs/p23-199.pdf

Mashav—National Database. (2004). *The elderly in Israel: Statistical abstract 2003.* Jerusalem, Israel: JDC-Brookdale Institute & Eshel.

Meyers, J. (2001, October). *Age 2000-Brief.* Catalogue No. C2KBR/01-12, Washington, DC: U.S. Census Bureau.

National Center for Health Statistics. (2003). *National Vital Statistics Reports, 52*(3). Retrieved from www.cdc.gov/nchs.

Rosenblatt, R. (2001). Census illustrates diversity from sea to shining sea. *The Los Angeles Times,* A1-16.

U.S. Bureau of the Census. (1990). *Profile of general demographic characteristics for the United States: 1990,* Table DP-1. Washington, DC: Author.

U.S. Bureau of the Census. (2000a). *The 65 years and over population: 2000.* Retrieved from http://www.census.gov/mso/www/pres_lib/65yrs/tsld024.htm.

U.S. Bureau of the Census. (2000b). *Census 2000: Profile of general demographic characteristics for the United States,* Table DP-1. Retrieved from http://www.census.gov/Press-release/www/2001/tables/dp_us_2000.PDF.

U.S. Department of Commerce, Economics and Statistics Administration. (1995). *Sixty five plus in the United States.* Retrieved from http://www.census.gov/population/socdemo/statbriefs/agebrief.html.

World Health Organization. (1998). *World Atlas of Ageing.* Kobe, Japan: Centre for Health Development.

World Health Organization. (2004). *World Health Report: Changing History.* Geneva: Author.

Acknowledgments

We would like to offer acknowledgments and great appreciation for invaluable assistance to Ms. Amber Richards for editing and research in the United States; to Ms. Stella Sarkisyan for compiling demographic information in the United States; to Ms. Claudette Butler for the multiple liaison tasks with the Australian contributors and the international editors; and to Mrs. Odelia Chorin for all her work and efforts with the publishers, the editors, and the Israeli contributors.

SECTION 1

THE ART OF CAREGIVING: POLICIES AND SERVICES

Introduction

Carol A. Morse

During the twentieth century, the developed nations experienced significant gains in disease controls and the development of effective and accessible medications and interventions for a wide range of diseases, disorders, and disabilities. There have been significant advances in the emancipation of women and informed public-health measures and standards through universal education and training. This social revolution has been aided for forty years by accessible and increasingly effective means of fertility control, resulting in reduced fecundity during the young adult years and the enhanced general health and concomitant increase in life expectancy.

Throughout the industrialized countries, the expectation is of a longer life span to the late 70s for men and the low 80s for women. As well, more people aged 65 and over anticipate aging well rather than poorly with minimal serious morbidity or disability and remaining in their own home and community, able to pursue their older years as positively as possible.

In each of the three nations considered in this book, the picture is very similar. While more people are living to around or beyond four score years, and more women than men reach their older years, the number of people achieving a healthy and well older life increases over time. The burden of disease, of all known causes of mortality, morbidity, and disability accounts for a dramatic increased rate from the age of 70 years for both men and women.

During the past decade, recognition has emerged of the need to improve and expand on caregiving services and attempts are being made by governments to provide better and flexible improved home and community care systems that can alleviate the immediate and long-term burdens of caregiving. In the years ahead, governments must also find different ways to provide financial compensation for caregivers through tax relief, income support, and indexed pension benefits. In the coming years, it is predicted that fewer people will willingly take on the family-based caregiver role, especially as more mid-aged women continue in paid employment for longer periods of time. The questions raised are: Who will care in the future? Where and how will that care occur? How will that care be funded? What choices and options exist currently and in the future?

The four chapters in this section seek to address these major issues and provide illuminating examples of the challenges and opportunities that each nation faces. The choices that are examined include state care-provisions in Israel, consumer-driven care services in the United States, and residential care facilities in Australia. The final chapter explores the new demands on the education and training of formal-care providers from the perspective of Israel.

Iecovich examines the interface of family and state responsibility for the care of Israeli older people. This focus also has universal resonance for all countries, not least, for both Australia and the United States. The key traditional duty of care for aging parents' needs among family members (filial responsibility) is proposed as an expression of family solidarity and positive feelings of "giving back." Yet today's young and mid-aged populations perceive a weakening of filial ties and the sense of intergenerational responsibility with a concomitant expectation that the state should provide the necessary support for its older populations through the provision of formal services. In keeping with similar changes in Australia and the United States, governmental financing has shrunk, forcing a greater reliance on family care for elderly people at home.

Recent researchers and policymakers have proposed that care provisions should not be seen as a dichotomy but rather a continuum, with an integrated model of family care that is supplemented by state care when the needs of the elderly exceed the availability of the family and its resources. It is also revealed that attitudinal differences exist among the various ethnicities regarding what is deemed proper attitudes and practices. Thus, in the traditional groups (e.g., Arabs), care for the elderly and the disabled is regarded as the proper domain of the family; contemporary emancipated groups (e.g., Jews) regard the government as the required provider of care needs and services.

Who will be available to provide the necessary care within the family is a key issue. The rising divorce rate, increases in single-mother families, and greater workforce participation by women indicates that fewer female caregivers are or will be available compared with previous times. While the accepted tradition within Israeli society is that family care of the elderly is the societal norm, exceeding that found in other European countries, the tension between family and state-responsibility acceptance remains.

Given the changing shape of population demographics, the "sandwich generation," the mid-aged children of older parents, will not be available to sustain caregiving demands. Therefore, it is proposed that the adult grandchildren of future elderly people will be required to contribute to the care role. From the state's perspective, while it is predicted that community care services will become more significant to caregiving, the older people who are expected to have greater disposable assets than the current older cohorts will be required to contribute more in order to purchase formal services. For the younger age groups, there should be schemes introduced of employer-based contributions for this purpose as well as tax incentives and long-term care insurance to enable workers to prepare for their own old age and the necessary needs in their later years. Two interesting suggestions to assist in overcoming the anticipated caregiver deficits are to mobilize and train long-term unemployed people and to increase the utilization of prepared volunteers.

The situation of caregiving in the United States, as analyzed by Benjamin, indicates that long-term care concerns receive a lower place on the government's policy agenda, while public pensions and health insurance preoccupy many Americans. While informal, family-based care and agency-based care services provide the "twin pillars of support," the reality is that families are a resource of diminishing viability due to a gradual reduction in the numbers of available and willing caregivers. As well, a range of dissatisfactions with agency services has been identified for some time.

An innovative alternative to both of these types of services is referred to as Consumer Directed Care (CDC) which provides greater control for the care recipients to self-direct the choices of caregiving services, the particular providers who attend, when, and where. There is not just one model of this innovative reversal of care provision where the recipient is the one determining what is received rather than an agency deciding what an individual requires and shall be given. At one end of the spectrum is a model of expanded decision making that involves no financial control; the other is of total control by the recipient who takes on the role of employer. A middle model provides for an agency to operate as a case manager, while, in consultation with the care recipient, services are arranged, worker eligibility, qualifications, capabilities, and probity checks are determined, and the extent of service hours and wages are determined. This interesting departure from the usual agency-based service common in most places has already appeared in different states in the United States, and in several European countries. There are several benefits from this initiative, not least being the empowerment and flexibility that emerges through tailoring services to an individual's needs at any given time. A needed aspect is for research to be carried out on the experiences of consumers, the impact of such a service, and the true costs to both care recipient and the service providers before any definitive statements can be made about the feasibility of this innovative development. The abiding issues of choice, the facilitating aspects for and barriers against it in the Australian residential care industry are the focus of the chapter provided by Tilse, Wilson, and Setterlund. The authors discuss consumer sovereignty, individuals' rights, and citizenship discourses in relation to making informed decisions about existing choices of entering and remaining in an aged-care facility. Three major options exist under the Aged Care Principles to emerge in recent years that increase consumer choices. These include a wider range of community care "packages" that provide alternatives to residential care, emerging policies of aging in place with security of tenure, and stated outcome standards regarding resident lifestyles underpinned by consumer rights and responsibilities.

While there is evidence of aging in place occurring to a greater level than previously with increased capacity for consumers to enter and remain in the home of choice, choices are still limited by few alternatives, especially for those with high care and specialized needs. As well, limitations remain in the capacity and willingness of consumers and their representatives to exercise their rights and participate in decision making. Part of this can be explained by the unchanging attitudes and beliefs of care workers toward the older person as able and entitled to self-determination, the practical task-focused approaches to care, the hierarchical nature of residence administration, and a still pervasive negative ageism.

These regulatory practices serve to constrain real choices for residents, families, and staff as not only are residential facilities places to live and work in but also now, a great emphasis is placed on the profit margins. For present barriers to true choice to be overcome, the authors argue for changes in a whole of community approach that will require different leadership styles in residential-care facilities. A key question concerns who will train the managers to achieve a democratic community-focused model of supported aged care. From the perspective of Israel, the final chapter by Galinsky examines the new demands on the education and training of workers for the aged-care industry. The author identifies that the "new" older person lives in their community for longer with a gradual onset in medical and social losses over time that lead to increasing levels of dependency (the compression and expansion of morbidity phenomena). The current system of formal care is outdated, based on earlier custodial models of care that do not meet the contemporary demands and expectations of today's elders, and therefore the training needs should be rethought and modernized.

Key concepts for consideration include the ways and means to maintain individuals' functional independence for as long as possible, the necessity of integrating and coordinating community services, and the provision of a multidisciplinary team approach from medical, allied-health, and social disciplines that can more ably respond to and address the complex array of issues affecting people as they age.

To effect these changes, the training programs of medical and allied health personnel (e.g., aged-care workers, nurses, social workers, psychologists, occupational therapists, physiotherapists) should be exposed to enhanced curricula in psychosocial gerontology and geriatric medicine, with internships or fieldwork placements in community aged-care services and facilities and primary-care settings. These proposals are placed against a backdrop of fragmented, uncoordinated services that remain seriously underresourced in spite of the growth in the older-aged segments of the populations of these three countries. Clearly, the need for enhanced education and training programs is urgently required so that the aged-care and support workforce can meaningfully provide and respond to the changing expectations of older people. These issues are universally recognized in countries throughout the world as the aged-care sector has traditionally remained the "Cinderella" poor relation in most health-care systems. The care of frail elderly people has usually been undertaken by minimally trained people, the career path has been unclear, and the remuneration has been low. Thus, the attraction of keen and committed workers has been difficult to start and sustain over time. It is only during the present decade that recognition has been increasingly given to the complex nature of such care requirements which has seen the concomitant rise in education requirements.

The four chapters in this section concerned with "The Art of Caregiving: Policies and Services" have all identified common themes. These include emerging desires for empowerment and right to decision making and control by the older consumers themselves; the struggles by family members to continue to provide support for their older relatives by a gradually diminishing group of younger adults; and the increasing mismatch between the style of formal caregiving that is based on old traditional models of care and the different sort of older person needing a range of care *supports* that do not infantilize nor diminish their rights. The characteristics of the older persons that emerge in these chapters indicate desires for self-determination, a strong voice in what is provided and available, and demands for flexibility in the provision of services that can be adapted to the individual's changing needs over time.

Interestingly, the gaps and shortfalls in services, practices, and attitudes among many in the industry of aging provisions are very similar across all three nations under consideration here and can be identified in many other countries. A pressing need is for an enlightened contemporary education and training of the current and future workforce. This requires a move towards a collaborative approach between consumers and workers to replace the paternal custodial model that is still apparent in many places and in several guises.

CHAPTER 1

The Interface between Family Responsibility and State Responsibility in Caring for the Elderly in Israel

Esther Iecovich

The elderly population in Israel is constantly growing, and longevity in Israel is among the highest in the world as a result of a highly developed system of health care, improvements in nutrition and quality of life, and a decrease in fertility rates. According to census data, from 1948 (year of the establishment of the State of Israel) to 2001, the Israeli elderly population increased from 4% to 9.8%, of which elderly Jews constituted 92.4% and elderly Arabs 6.3%, and is expected to reach 11.6% in 2020 (Brodsky, Shnor, & Beer, 2004). These demographic trends have resulted in an increased number of elderly people who are infirm, disabled, and dependent upon others. To date, for example, 15.7% of the elderly persons are functionally dependent in terms of ability to perform basic activities of daily living (Brodsky et al., 2004). In terms of economic status, approximately 30% of the elderly are defined as poor, with many more only slightly above the poverty line. Consequently, the length of time that elderly people are dependent on others is increasing. The rapid aging of society and the significant rise in the numbers of frail and disabled elderly persons have raised the question of what solutions family and society are able to provide to meet the growing needs of this population.

In parallel to the increase of the elderly population—and in particular the increase in the number of those who are functionally dependent—families have undergone a multiplicity of changes. First, rates of divorce and of the participation of women in the labor force have been increasing, resulting in more single-parent families, in most of which mothers have to rear their children and work outside of their homes. This results in less time available to personally care for elderly family members. During the years 1986–2002, for example, the proportion of women aged 15 and over in the labor force increased from 43% to 53% (Israel Bureau of Statistics, 2003). Second, since rates of fertility have been constantly decreasing, nuclear families have become much smaller: Among the Jewish population, the average number of children per woman decreased from 4 children in 1950 to 2.3 in 2002, while among the Moslems, the average decreased from 9.8 in 1965 to 4.6 in 2002 (Israel Bureau of Statistics, 2003). Third, there are more families with two generations of elderly people still living, and it is expected that the number of such families will continue to grow. This suggests a substantial reduction in the ability of adult children to provide care to their elderly parents, an increased caregivers' burden, and more responsibility imposed on other kin. These data suggest also that the more elderly there are who need care and assistance, the less the family will be able to meet their needs and the fewer potential family caregivers who will be available to provide care.

Furthermore, Israel is a multicultural society. Although the vast majority of the elderly population is Jewish, most of them came from different countries and continents; for example, 27.5% of elderly Jews were born in Asian or African countries (Sephardim), 61.2% were born in European or American countries (Ashkenazim), and only 11.2% were born in Israel (Brodsky et al., 2004). This means that there is a wide range of norms, expectations, and patterns of family relationships within the Israeli Jewish population. The Sephardim, more than the Ashkenazim, tend to lead a traditional way of life in terms of religiosity and family relationships, (i.e., they tend to live in extended families). Elderly Arabs, most of them Moslems, tend to live in traditional extended families (*hamulas*) in which the elderly person is highly revered. As an immigration country, Israel has absorbed many new immigrants since its establishment, of which one million arrived to Israel during the past decade. New immigrants tend to preserve and maintain their cultures and traditions and speak their mother languages. All these factors create a mosaic of family structures in terms of expectations, roles, and filial commitments and responsibilities.

Given this information, it is important to know who should be—and who actually is—responsible for meeting the growing needs of this elderly population and what role the state of Israel should play in this issue. State and family responsibilities in caring for elderly people, in particular those disabled and dependent, and the balance between these responsibilities, are a major issue in welfare policy. The major goals of this chapter are therefore three-fold:

1. To review the literature on family responsibility and the utilization of formal services and present research findings on these issues.
2. To describe and analyze the policies in Israel with respect to responsibility for elder care and the extent to which families and the state share this responsibility.

3. To appraise the extent to which the needs of elderly persons are met, to point out the gaps between policies and service provision, and to address the implications for future policies and practice.

LITERATURE REVIEW

Filial Responsibility: Theoretical Approaches and Research Findings

Filial responsibility is conceptualized as a general societal attitude toward adult children's duty to care for their aging parents' needs as well as what their appropriate behavior should be. This might include their duty to provide assistance to their elderly relatives and to maintain contact with them, although the extent of their responsibilities may differ as a function of geographical proximity to parents, residential location, gender, and ethnicity (Stein, Wemmerus, Ward, Gaines, Freeberg, & Jewell, 1998).

Filial responsibility should be considered in two different perspectives: Personal and social. First, filial commitment is an attitude that reflects personal acceptance for the care and well-being of the elderly parents. This attitude relates to the feelings of adult children about performing this duty and to the expectations that elderly parents have in relation to their adult children. Exchange theory suggests that filial responsibility stems from the feeling of gratitude the adult children feel toward their parents for rearing and caring for them along the years (Sung, 1994). Second, from a social perspective, filial commitment is an expression of family solidarity and positive feelings that exist between the generations. This is part of a normative system between family members regarding intergenerational relationships and expectations of support and assistance when necessary (Bengtson & Roberts, 1991). The actual expression of commitment occurs when adult children provide services and assistance to their parents (Litwin, 1994).

For many generations, the family has been the core welfare institution for older persons. Although attitudes toward filial responsibility are positive and family members provide substantial help to their elderly family members, demographic and modernizing changes, such as those noted above, have altered the ability and willingness of families to sustain this role. Furthermore, studies conducted in various countries across the globe show that norms of filial responsibility have substantially weakened during the past decades, and most people perceive that families are less willing to care for their older relatives than they used to be. They perceive that it is the state's responsibility to support its older population and to strengthen the family in its functions by utilizing formal services (Adamchak, 1996). Moreover, elderly people feel uncomfortable receiving help from their children (Twigg & Grand, 1998). In China, for example, these changes made it necessary for the government to pass the Law on Welfare for the Elderly, which defines the roles of government, community, and family (Leung, 1997). On the other hand, evidence from other countries, such as Sweden and Canada, show that state expenditures for elder care have shrunk during the past years, and there has been a return to greater reliance on family care for elderly people at home, with family members increasingly called upon to shoulder the bulk of the care of their elderly relatives (Sundstrom, Johansson, & Hassing, 2002; Ward-Griffin & Marshall, 2003). Thus, state versus filial responsibility should be looked at as a continuum rather than a dichotomy.

Studies of attitudes toward filial obligations have found that there is consensual agreement that adult children should provide help to their elderly parents if it is necessary (Hamon & Blieszner, 1990). Sons tend to be more responsible for providing financial assistance, while daughters are more often expected to provide care and instrumental assistance (Finch, 1997). Attitudes toward filial responsibility were found to be positive among young caregivers and noncaregivers alike (Dellmann-Jenkins & Brittain, 2003; Franks, Pierce, & Dwyer, 2003).

The Interface between Filial and State Responsibility: Theoretical Approaches

There is a considerable debate over whether care provided by formal caregivers complements, parallels, competes with, or substitutes the informal care provided by family members (Davey & Patsios, 1999; Ward-Griffin & Marshall, 2003). There are, however, two major approaches to understanding relationships between these two systems of caregiving and the interaction between them. The first includes the hierarchical substitution model, which implies that there is a hierarchy of support providers who may be replaced by others as needed (Cantor, 1979; Cantor & Brennan, 2000). According to this model, kin are the primary source of support, followed by nonkin. Formal support systems are a last resort when assistance from a spouse or children is unavailable. These patterns of governing the selection process of care providers are normatively defined and dependent on the cultural values of a society, an issue that will be broadly addressed later on.

The second approach includes the complementary or task-specific model of care (Litwak, 1985), which postulates that different primary groups (family, friends, and neighbors) provide different types of support for different needs, and therefore both systems, formal and informal, are necessary. Within this model, family members are best suited to provide everyday care, whereas the formal system is more suited to perform other tasks, which are of a more technological nature. According to this model, the nature of the task determines the source of care.

Based on Litwak's work (1985), the policies adapted by many Western countries show that the formal and informal support systems complement each other and are both necessary to meet the needs of elderly persons. Some scholars (Chappell & Blandford, 1991) propose an integrated model that would include both models, suggesting that formal care supplements informal care when the care needs of an elderly individual exceed the abilities or affordability of the latter. Various interchangeable models, however, have been suggested and adopted in different countries that reflect their policies in respect to these issues (Davey & Patsios, 1999).

The Cultural Context of Filial Responsibility

With the increased recognition of the diversity of the elderly population, attempts have been made to understand the impact of ethnicity, culture, and social class on availability and utilization of formal and informal support for the elderly (Cantor & Brennan, 2000). These ethnic differences derive from tradition and values that encourage filial responsibilities and foster positive attitudes and respect toward the older generation, as well as such things as patterns of living arrangements (i.e., living in multigenerational households, which are more prevalent among specific ethnic groups than in others). These characteristics increase the likelihood and availability of informal support to those elderly persons belonging to specific ethnic groups (Lee, Peek, & Coward, 1998; Peek, Coward, & Peek, 2000).

Ethnicity also affects institutionalization rates, which are significantly higher in Western countries than in traditional societies. It is therefore expected that, in traditional societies, more disabled elderly persons live in their homes and need more extensive domiciliary services. The same can be said with regard to countries that are multicultural, that disabled elderly persons from Asian or North African origin who live in Western countries tend to prefer care provided at their homes and underutilize institutionalization compared to their counterparts who are of Western origin. In Israel, for example, elderly Arabs and Jews of Asian-African origin are least represented among the residents of long-term care facilities. Altogether, approximately 4.1% of the Jewish elderly people live in long-term facilities, compared with 0.7% among their Arab counterparts (Brodsky et al., 2004).

Studies conducted in Israel show that social norms and expectations of adult children to support their elderly parents are still high and common. In a cross-cultural study conducted in several European countries and in Israel (Daatland & Herlofson, 2003), filial norms and policy opinions about the proper role of the family and the welfare state in the care of elderly persons were examined. The findings showed that levels of support for filial norms varied between countries, with Spain and Israel being the highest and Norway, England, and Germany being the lowest. National differences regarding policy opinions were also substantial and in congruence with traditions of family and social policy. Nevertheless, many of those who were surveyed who scored high on positive attitudes toward filial responsibility also believed that the welfare state should be the main source of care provision to its older adults.

A study that examined the relationship of filial responsibility and formal support among Jewish family caregivers found that future expectations of support of caregivers were explained by perceptions of filial responsibility, which were affected by caregivers' religiosity (Litwin, 1994). In another study (Iecovich & Lankri, 2002), attitudes of elderly Jews toward filial responsibility tended to differentiate between various conditions that justify provision of assistance to elderly parents. The majority, however, viewed assistance to elderly parents as an obvious and undebatable commitment that should not be contingent upon quality of relationships between them. These unequivocal attitudes toward filial responsibility were manifested by most of the elderly people regardless of their ethnic origin, although gender and living arrangements were found to be significantly associated with elderly persons' attitudes. This perspective is somewhat different from that evidenced in some other Western countries, where various surveys and studies confirm that there is a shift in attitudes among elderly people that responsibility for care for the aged should tend to be the responsibility of the state (Phillipson, 1991).

Arab society maintains a patriarchal social tradition, although it has undergone many social changes during the past decades. The pattern of multigenerational households (*hamula*) is a unique pattern of living that is very prevalent among the Arab population in Israel (which mainly inhabits rural regions and small towns) and has considerable informal support (Litwin & Haj-Yahia, 1996). Values of filial commitment are carefully adhered to; thus, whenever an older person becomes functionally dependent, the family automatically takes care of that person. Institutionalization is not common in this society and admission of an elderly Arab to a nursing home is still considered a stigma upon his or her family. Elderly Arabs who live in nuclear, one-generation households, however, are likely to become more dependent upon formal services when they become functionally dependent compared with those who live in extended, multigenerational households (Azaiza, Lowenstein, & Brodsky, 1999; Lowenstein & Katz, 2000). Furthermore, since institutionalization rates are significantly lower among the Arabs, greater proportions of frail and severely handicapped elderly persons remain in their homes and need help.

In other words, research shows that filial responsibility in Israel is still greater than that evidenced in some other Western countries. Perceptions and attitudes toward filial responsibility show that both the Israeli elderly and family caregivers alike consider filial responsibility as an important and undebatable norm, regardless of their ethnicities. Nevertheless, among some ethnic groups, this responsibility is more strongly manifested in actual help provided to elderly parents and in lower institutionalization rates.

Policy and Practice in Israel

Filial obligation to elderly parents and caring for them is an important religious and moral commandment in both Judaism and Islam, the two religions that encompass the vast majority of the population in Israel. This religious commandment includes the provision of material assistance, instrumental help whenever the elderly person needs help, and respect (Linzer, 1986). These norms of filial obligation are anchored in several laws that reflect Israel's policies regarding family versus state responsibilities for the care of elderly persons.

The first law is the Welfare Services Law, enacted in 1958, which determines that a needy person is entitled to receive formal help—financial, instrumental, or social—if he or she meets specific income test criteria. Furthermore, whenever a needy person has family members who are responsible for meeting his or her needs, but who do not fulfill their duties although they are financially able to do so, the local welfare department can appeal to the court and ask that the welfare department be reimbursed for its expenditures for assistance it has provided to the needy person. This law relates to any family of a needy person, including elderly persons.

The second law is the Alimony Law, enacted in 1959, which postulates that the family is the predominant source of assistance for elderly relatives. Unlike other countries, in which alimony laws are supposed to specifically ensure the sustenance of spouses and minor children (Shehan, Berardo, Owens, & Berardo, 2002), Israeli law is much broader in terms of the types of kinships it covers. For example, the law postulates that adult children, grandchildren, and their spouses are responsible for the care of their elderly relatives and must provide them with subsistence. This law, however, has only been enforced in a few cases: Either because elderly people feel ashamed to ask for support from their children or kin and would rather avoid making a claim against them, or because their adult children support them whenever support is necessary (Iecovich, 1983-4). Although family members are not required to share the expenditures for formal community services provided to elderly people who cannot afford purchasing these necessary services privately (e.g., domiciliary services, day-care centers), adult children and their spouses are obliged to share the costs of institutional care whenever this is necessary and have to undergo income tests, according to which their share will be determined.

A third law is the Long-Term Insurance Law, enacted in 1986, which enables disabled elderly persons to receive home-care services, which include personal care, housekeeping, and surveillance. The rationale that underlies this law is that family members are primarily responsible for care provision for their elderly family members. The role of the state is to help their families cope with the care burden by supporting them and supplementing the care provided by the family. Thus, according to this law, older adults are entitled to receive in-kind home-care services if they are functionally disabled and meet income tests. Cash benefits are provided only to those who live with their families and live in remote places where in-kind services are unavailable or inaccessible. In case a person is childless and has no family who cares for him or her, the elderly person will be offered placement in a long-term care facility. To date, approximately 114,000 elderly persons (60 and over for women and 65 and over for men), which cover almost all those who are mentally or physically dependent, receive home-care services under this law (National Insurance Institute, 2004). It is not surprising that the recent economic crisis that Israel has been undergoing—predominantly due to the prolonged conflict with the Palestinians—and the budgetary cutbacks, which reflect policy trends of withdrawal from the welfare state, have not skipped the elderly population. These new trends may have a tremendous impact on the welfare of older adults and the provision of formal services in the future.

Several studies examined the extent to which the long-term insurance law has succeeded in meeting the elderly persons' needs and alleviating family burden. Based on a national census, Iecovich and Nir (2001) found that elderly Jews and Arabs, who received long-term home-care services, differed in their perceptions of unmet needs for help. The majority of elderly Arabs reported more unmet needs than elderly Jews, although more Arabs than Jews reported receiving help from their adult children on a regular basis. Among the elderly Jews, those from Asian-African origin expressed more unmet needs for help than those from European-American origin. In other words, in spite of the Israeli law being universal and enabling elderly persons who meet objective eligibility criteria to receive long-term care services, in reality there are specific ethnic groups whose needs are inadequately met. Furthermore, cultural values regarding filial commitment and negative attitudes toward institutionalization may account for the higher rate of elderly persons of specific ethnicities who receive insufficient care from their families and from the formal support system altogether and especially those who are severely disabled and need care around the clock.

A more recent study (Brodsky et al., 2004) examined the extent to which social changes and state support during the past 15 years affected assistance patterns among family members of disabled elderly persons. The findings show that the volume of family care had not changed along the years since the long-term care insurance law was enacted, but patterns and domains of help had changed (i.e., family members provide more help with arrangements and housekeeping). The findings indicate, however, that both systems—formal and informal alike—play a major role in caregiving, with those elderly persons who are severely dependent receiving the greatest amount of care from both support systems. The study also found that, in spite of formal assistance, family caregivers experience significant emotional and physical burden, which hinders their social functioning.

To conclude, the current social policies regarding elder care, as they are reflected in the three laws, indicate that the primary responsibility for elder care lies on the family's shoulders; this responsibility is however, shared by the state and replaced by the state only for childless elderly persons.

CONCLUSIONS AND IMPLICATIONS FOR POLICY AND PRACTICE

Similar to other Western countries, the age structure of Israel has been changing during the past decades and is projected to continue to change in the future. Thus, from a pyramid with a large base progressively tapering into a narrow group of those aged 65 and over, the situation is gradually changing into a more rectangular shape characterized by similar numbers of people in each age category, starting from infancy through old age, with more family generations alive, but with fewer members in each generation. The rapid demographic and aging processes and the economic crises that the Israeli society has been undergoing during the past years, as well as various policy reforms such as the adoption of more stringent entitlement criteria to receive income insurance benefits for those who are unemployed in order to force them to participate in the labor force, are consequently expected to reduce the family's capacity to provide care to their elderly family members. Furthermore, political philosophies about the roles of the government alongside governmental deficits and cutbacks threaten the availability of funds for formal services and raise questions about the feasibility of expanding services to meet the mounting needs of the aging population. Thus, policymakers are simultaneously required to reduce governmental expenditures and face the increasing needs of elder care and its costs. It is therefore assumed that these needs will have to be met by greater reliance on the family. Greater reliance on family caregivers has the potential for greater caregiver stress and burden, which may become a precursor of elder abuse and neglect.

The higher life expectancy increased the requirement from family members to economically and emotionally support older adults for longer durations. Therefore, multigenerational bonds are becoming more important, and they are expected to replace nuclear family functions that are no longer able to provide the necessary services (Bengtson, 2001). This means that adult grandchildren will have to play a more active role in caring for elderly grandparents and aging parents. Furthermore, since the nuclear family is decreasing in size, other kin and nonkin will be called upon to accept a greater share of elderly care responsibilities. Community care, in which informal care is a key component, will become a more significant factor in challenging these deficits. Social networks and formal services alike, of which community and neighborhood volunteers are integral parts, will have to extensively and intensively supplement and complement the support provided by family members.

Undoubtedly, more formal services will be necessary to complement and supplement the informal care provided by family members, in particular by adult children. The dilemma is, who should pay for these services—the state, the family, or the elderly persons themselves. Furthermore, what should be defined as the "right" balance between the roles of the formal and informal support systems? Should family members be encouraged to provide care and be paid for it? These issues have to be faced and addressed by policymakers, and current policies will need to be reassessed and modified.

It is expected that future generations and new cohorts of elderly people and those who are close to retirement age will be wealthier and have higher real incomes following retirement. Thus, they may also be more able to afford purchasing formal services, either through private long-term-care insurance policies or other saving schemes, that will enable them to cover long-term-care services that can ensure them a decent quality of life. Furthermore, employer-based programs should be developed, in which collective policies will be sold to younger people and to those who are close to retirement. For this purpose, governmental involvement is required on two levels: First, to encourage people to save for their old age through tax incentives and other economic benefits; and second, long-term-care insurance schemes should be regulated and monitored by the government to ensure reasonable premiums and prevent fraudulent practices.

More targeting policies may be required with respect to the two most vulnerable groups of elderly people: (1) Those who live alone, are childless, and have no other siblings. This group, which tends to also be the poorest, may be most likely to need public formal long-term-care services; and (2) Elderly persons of specific ethnicities, including new immigrants, who cannot afford to purchase formal care. The differences found across ethnic groups suggest that ethnic criteria and cultural norms should be taken into account when dealing with eligibility and entitlement criteria for receiving formal long-term services.

As noted above, the reduced ability of family members to provide care and the cutoffs of public funding suggest that more responsibility will be transferred to the community where elderly people live. This suggests that more volunteers will be necessary to alleviate family burden and to some extent replace paid formal services. Voluntary work is a well-developed tradition in the Israeli society. Nevertheless, there are three significant sources from which many more volunteers can be recruited and channeled to elder care: (1) The elderly people themselves. The current retirement age in Israel is 62 for women and 67 for men. Most of the retired people are healthier and wealthier than past generations of the elderly and may look for some employment and social roles, including voluntary work. In most cities in Israel, there are local associations of elderly people whose major role is to provide community services to elderly people in their area. Unfortunately, insufficient attention is currently given to voluntary work; thus the number of volunteers utilized by these associations is very small (Iecovich & Katan, 2003). These associations will need, however, to reevaluate their goals and adopt new strategies according to which voluntary work will become their core mission. (2) To date there are approximately 145,000 chronically unemployed people—most of whom are nonprofessionals and women—who receive monthly income insurance benefits. Some incentives, such as increased income insurance benefits or municipal tax discounts or exemptions might be used to motivate at least part of these people to provide a certain amount of weekly hours for elder care. (3) In Israel there is a mandatory military service for youngsters aged 18 and over. This military service includes three years for boys and two for girls. In addition, a certain percentage of these up to age 45 are recalled every year for reserve service. Nevertheless, significant numbers of people are not recruited into the military services for various reasons (e.g., there are limits to the number of people that are necessary for the army at a given time, ultra orthodox people, etc.). Some of these people voluntarily replace military service by several years of civil service and volunteer work in various public services, including hospitals and nursing homes. Enforcing a civil service for all those not serving in the army would be socially justified and could provide more solutions to various social needs such as home care and surveillance services for elderly people.

To encourage and enable family caregivers to provide care to their elderly family members for prolonged periods of time, respite care, as a source of relief for caregivers, should be given more attention. For this purpose, day-care centers should be rearranged to provide care six days a week, instead of five days a week at present, and operate 8–10 hours or more a day, instead of 5–6 hours a day in order to enable family caregivers to work as well as to care for their other family members. Furthermore, these community day-care centers should be accommodated to provide respite care to those care recipients whose families need some relief or vacation. Undoubtedly, this might be cheaper than institutionalization.

In sum, Israel is a rapidly aging society in which elder care is increasingly becoming a national agenda. The extent to which families can sustain prolonged periods of care are now questioned due to sociodemographic trends as noted previously. Current policies and budgetary curtailment and cutbacks are also causing questions about the probability of the governmental responsibility for elder care in the future. All these suggest that the younger generations will have to provide care for themselves through various private policies and savings programs, and that community care will become the core of elder care. All these necessitate the adoption of new policies, including amendments to existing laws, to create alternative reservoirs of labor that can be channeled into elder care. Furthermore, community services—in particular daycare centers—will have to be modified to accommodate the growing and changing needs of elderly persons and their families.

REFERENCES

Adamchak, D. J. (1996). Population ageing: Gender, family support and the economic condition of older Africans. *Southern African Journal of Gerontology, 5*(2), 3-8.

Azaiza, F., Lowenstein, A., & Brodsky, J. (1999). Institutionalization for the elderly is a novel phenomenon among the Arab population in Israel. *Journal of Gerontological Social Work, 31*(3-4), 65-85.

Bengtson, V. L. (2001). Beyond the nuclear family: The increasing importance of multigenerational bonds. *Journal of Marriage and Family, 63*(1), 1-16.

Bengtson, V. L., & Roberts, T. E. L. (1991). Intergenerational solidarity in ageing families: An example of formal theory construction. *Journal of Marriage and the Family, 53,* 856-870.

Brodsky, J., Shnor, Y., & Beer, S. (2004). *The elderly in Israel.* Jerusalem: Joint-Brookdale Institute of Gerontology (in Hebrew).

Brodsky, J., Naon, D., Resnizky, S., Ben Noon, S., Morgenstin, B., & Graa, R. (2004). *Recipients of long-term care insurance benefits: Characteristics, formal and informal assistance patterns and unmet needs.* Jerusalem: JDC-Brokdale Institute, RR-440-04.

Cantor, M. (1979). The informal support system of New York's inner city elderly: Is ethnicity a factor? In D. Gelfand & A. Kutzik (Eds.), *Ethnicity and ageing* (pp. 153-174). New York: Springer.

Cantor, M. H., & Brennan, M. (2000). *Social care of the elderly: The effects of ethnicity, class and culture.* New York: Springer.

Chappell, N., & Blandford, A. (1991). Informal and formal care: Exploring the complementarity. *Ageing and Society, 11,* 299-317.

Daatland, S. O., & Herlofson, K. (2003). "Lost solidarity" or "changed solidarity": A comparative European view of normative family solidarity. *Ageing and Society, 23*(5), 537-560.

Davey, A., & Patsios, D. (1999). Formal and informal community care to older adults: Comparative analysis of the United States and Great Britain, *Journal of Family and Economic Issues, 20*(3), 271-299.

Dellmann-Jenkins, M., & Brittain, L. (2003). Young adults' attitudes towards filial responsibility and actual assistance to elderly family members. *Journal of Applied Gerontology, 22*(2), 214-229.

Finch, J., & Mason, J. (1997). Filial obligations and kin support for elderly people. In J. Barnet, J. Johnson, C. Pereira, D. Pilgrim, & F. Williams (Eds.), *Community Care* (pp. 96-106), London: Macmillan.

Franks, M. M., Pierce, L. S., & Dwyer, J. W. (2003). Expected parent-care involvement of adult children. *Journal of Applied Gerontology, 22*(1), 104-117.

Hamon, R. R., & Blieszner, R. (1990). Filial responsibility expectations among adult child older parent pairs. *Journal of Gerontology, 45,* P110- P112.

Iecovich, E. (1983-4). Filial responsibility for their parents' support. *Gerontologia,* 25-26, 28-38 (in Hebrew).

Iecovich, E., & Katan, Y. (2003). *Elderly associations in Israel: Organizational and managerial aspects.* Beer-Sheva, Israel: Ben-Gurion University (in Hebrew).

Iecovich, E., & Lankri, M. (2002). Elderly persons' attitudes towards receiving financial support from adult children. *Ageing Studies, 16*(2), 121-133.

Iecovich, E., & Nir, M. (2001). Perceived needs for home help services among Jewish and Arab elderly recipients of long-term care benefits. *Social Security, 60,* 171-190 (in Hebrew).

Israel Bureau of Statistics. (2003). *Yearbook of Statistics in Israel* (p. 54). Jerusalem: Israel Bureau of Statistics (in Hebrew).

Lee, G. R., Peek, C. W., & Coward, R. T. (1998). Race differences in filial responsibility expectations among older parents. *Journal of Marriage and the Family, 60,* 404-412.

Leung, J. C. B. (1997). Family support for the elderly in China: Issues and challenges. *Journal of Ageing and Social Policy*, *9*(3), 87-101.

Linzer, N. (1986). The obligation of adult children to aged parents: A review from Jewish tradition. *The Journal of Ageing and Judaism*, *1*(1), 34-48.

Litwin, H. (1994). Filial responsibility and informal support among family care givers of the elderly in Jerusalem: A path analysis. *International Journal of Aging and Human Development*, *8*(2), 137-151.

Litwin, H. (1997). Network shifts of elderly immigrants: The case of Soviet Jews in Israel. *Journal of Cross-Cultural Gerontology*, *12*(1), 45-60.

Litwin, H., & Haj-Yahia, M. M. (1996). Informal support networks among ageing populations in transition. *Bold*, *7*(1), 2-7.

Litwak, E. (1985). *Helping the elderly: The complementary role of informal networks and formal systems*. New York: Guilford.

Lowenstein, A., & Katz, R. (2000). Rural Arab families coping with care giving. *Marriage and Family Review*, *31*(1-2), 179-197.

National Insurance Institute. (2004). *Statistical Quarterly*, *33*(3). Jerusalem: Author, The Administration of Research and Planning.

Peek, M. K., Coward, R. T., & Peek, C. W. (2000). Race, ageing, and care. *Research on Ageing*, *22*(2), 117-142.

Phillipson, C. (1991). Inter-generational relations: Conflict or consensus in the 21st century. *Policy & Politics*, *19*(1), 27-36.

Shehan, C. L., Berardo, F. M., Owens, E., & Berardo, D. H. (2002). Alimony: An anomaly in family social science. *Family Relations*, *51*(4), 308-316.

Stein, C. H., Wemmerus, V. A., Ward, M., Gaines, M. E., Freeberg, A. L., & Jewell, T. C. (1998). "Because they're my parents": An intergenerational study of felt obligation and parental care giving. *Journal of Marriage and the Family*, *60*, 611-622.

Sundstrom, G., Johansson, L., & Hassing, L. B. (2002). Shifting balance of long-term care in Sweden. *Gerontologist*, *42*(3), 350-355.

Sung, K. T. (1994). A cross-cultural comparison of motivations for parents care: The case of Americans and Koreans. *Journal of Ageing Studies*, *8*(2), 195-209.

Twigg, J., & Grand, A. (1998). Contrasting legal conceptions of family obligation and financial reciprocity in the support of older people: France and England. *Ageing and Society*, *18*, 131-146.

Ward-Griffin, C., & Marshall, V. W. (2003). Re-conceptualizing the relationship between "public" and "private" elder care. *Journal of Ageing Studies*, *17*(2), 189-208.

CHAPTER 2

Consumer-Directed Services at Home for Older People in the United States

A. E. Benjamin

There is widespread interest in expanding and reforming the ways in which nations provide for the needs of older people and others with disabling chronic conditions, although this interest has emerged slowly. The twin challenges of public pensions and health insurance have preoccupied policymakers and advocates in the United States and other developed countries and have relegated "long-term care" to lower on the policy agenda. As nations turn their attention more decisively to addressing the complex needs of their burgeoning older populations, this policy myopia is beginning to change. Nearly every top policy priority is encouraging home and community-based services rather than institutional care for people of all ages with disabling conditions who require longer-term support and assistance.

While the risk of utilizing institutional care rises steadily with advancing age, across developed countries at any given time 4% to 5% of older people are residing in institutional settings. (Damron-Rodriguez & Lubben, 2001). Consequently, most persons who need assistance with daily living activities are living in the community and most at home. In the United States, an estimated twelve million Americans of all ages need some kind of long-term services, and about one-third of these require supportive assistance from another person to function in their daily lives (Tilly, Goldenson, & Kasten, 2001; U.S. General Accounting Office, 1999). For many, the extended family is often the primary source of care. With some variation across industrialized nations, policy attention has shifted to enabling older persons to remain in their homes and assisting them in maintaining their independence (World Health Organization & Milbank Memorial Fund, 2000). Living at home with assistance is touted as the preference of the people affected and as a means to utilize resources judiciously by containing the costs of care (Benjamin, 1993; Damron-Rodriguez & Lubben, 2001).

The informal care network (or "social network") and agency-based care remain the twin pillars of most discussions about maintaining older people in the community. Many governments are promoting home care by shifting the burden of care to families. This is occurring just at the point in history when families are becoming smaller and when more members, notably women, are participating in the workforce. Much research has been devoted to how the family (or informal care network) copes with these growing demands and what consequences this has for the well-being of older persons. There is mounting evidence that many people with assistance needs live apart from their families and that many families are not able to manage the care demands they confront. Public policy debate about expanded home care now includes considering various alternatives for supporting the family in its continuing and more complex role as the care network.

The home-care industry has expanded and changed over the last three decades in response to growth in demand for its services and changes in public policies. Home-care agencies represent the "formal care" side of the service equation and in developed countries are the primary providers of publicly funded home and community-based services for people with chronic impairments (Lubitz, Greenberg, Gorina, Wartzman, & Gibson, 2001). These services typically are provided by home-care agencies that send nurses, therapists, and aides into the home to deliver both medically related home health services and more supportive personal-care assistance. Personal-care assistance includes help with activities of daily living (ADLs) such as bathing, dressing and eating, and with instrumental activities of daily living (IADLs) such as cooking, shopping, and housekeeping.

THE EMERGENCE OF CONSUMER DIRECTION

Discussions about care planning for older people typically include the preferences of older people and the importance of incorporating these into any decisions about supportive services at home. Both the family and the home-care agency are expected to elicit recipient preferences and to integrate them into decisions about supportive services. However, there is growing evidence that recipient preferences may vary considerably from those of family members and service providers (Degenholtz, Kane, & Kivnik, 1997), suggesting that no other party truly speaks for the recipient.

Industrialized countries have traditionally relied upon agency-based services and the judgments of professionals in planning and implementing publicly-funded supportive services. By most accounts, professional judgments about appropriateness and quality have outweighed recipient preferences in making service decisions (Geron, 2000). It is commonplace to ascribe specialized knowledge and skills to home-care professionals (i.e., physicians, nurses, and social workers) and to delegate authority to them, even when the services provided involve fairly prosaic tasks far removed from medical science and technology. These include routine tasks such as help with bathing and dressing and assistance with housekeeping and chores. Only in the marketplace, where people purchase private services, have recipients had extensive discretion in designing services.

Since the early 1970s, representatives of younger people with disabilities in the United States and Europe have suggested an alternative approach to organizing long-term services in the community. Rather than invest further in agency-based services run by professional nurses and social workers, advocates urge that society should channel resources directly to people with disabilities so that they might determine, design, and direct whatever home-based supportive services they require. This argument, which draws from both the civil rights and consumer movements of the 1960s, suggests that we are mistaken to think that people with disabilities primarily need medical services at home, since most of their needs are supportive and do not require medical supervision. Therefore, it may be unnecessary to organize supportive services through medically oriented, professionally run, and expensive home care agencies. In this view, what is needed is not a home-health program but a supportive services program that relies more on the strengths and preferences of the people receiving services (DeJong, Batavia, & McKnew, 1992).

Over the past decade, there has been a steady increase in the number of publicly funded programs in the United States that allow recipients to independently arrange and supervise personal-assistance services at home. This approach is known as consumer direction. First tested in public programs in the 1970s, various forms of consumer-directed home care are now offered in several European systems and in about thirty U.S. states. Consumer-directed services in the United States are typically authorized under Medicaid, the medical assistance program for low-income populations, or under individual, state-funded programs.

Several forces have stimulated the recent expansion of consumer direction. First, aggressive advocacy by younger people with disabilities has increased political pressure to expand publicly funded personal-assistance services that give recipients more autonomy to direct their own services. Second, consumer movements have called for the "de-medicalization" of conditions like old age, disability, and pregnancy, and services like supportive home care and childbirth (Glover & Hartman, 2000).

Third, concerns about the costs of long-term care have made policymakers receptive to home-care services believed less costly than institutional ones (Feder, Komisar, & Niefeld, 2000; Wiener & Stevenson, 1998). Because consumer direction reduces or eliminates the roles of agencies and case managers from service delivery, costs are expected to be lower. Fourth, the U.S. Supreme Court's 1999 Olmstead Decision mandated that people with disabilities have options to live in the community rather than isolated in institutions. This has put additional pressure on states to consider diverse approaches to providing community placements and services (Rosenbaum, 2000). Fifth, the recent shortage of frontline workers has increased receptivity to new strategies for recruiting long-term-care providers. For example, if recipients can hire family and friends as workers, as in many consumer-directed programs, this may attract new workers to low-paying jobs in home care.

Expanded interest in consumer direction poses challenges for policymakers. The first is simply to understand how these alternative approaches differ from traditional professional/agency-managed home-care models. Second, on both ideological and pragmatic grounds, provider and professional opposition to consumer-directed approaches remains persistent and strong. Third, public officials face some specific programmatic issues that continue to provoke debate, including who should be permitted to self-direct, whether family members should be hired by consumers, how quality can be assured, and whether costs are truly lower when consumers self-direct. This chapter will first explore the rationale for consumer direction; next, describe the range of approaches now being implemented in the United States and Europe; summarize what research and analysis have told us thus far about the impact of these new approaches on recipients; and assess issues that may continue to provoke debate as various nations consider consumer-directed approaches.

THE RATIONALE FOR CONSUMER DIRECTION

Disability advocates in the United States argue that throughout the long-term-care system, in all types of settings (e.g., home, congregate housing, nursing home), people with disabilities have insufficient opportunities to shape and direct their own supportive services. Most home care is delivered by formal organizations, or agencies, typically licensed and certified by the state. When an applicant is deemed eligible for supportive services at home, he or she is referred to an authorized agency that assigns a worker and schedules service visits. The agency also defines allowable tasks, monitors worker performance, receives any recipient complaints, arranges back-up as needed, and otherwise manages service delivery.

Critics of the agency model argue that service decisions are based more on agency interests than consumer ones. Workers are assigned to recipients, whose input about who will work with them is often limited. Workers are rotated when agency scheduling demands require, disrupting existing service relationships. Scheduling is done by the agency, often with little regard for recipient preferences (e.g., a consumer needing assistance in going to bed must go to bed when the worker is there, even if she prefers earlier or later). For liability reasons, agencies carefully define allowable tasks for workers, whatever recipient needs and preferences may be. Workers are trained to provide assistance the agency way, which may conflict with consumer priorities about services (Batavia, DeJong, & McKnew, 1991; DeJong et al., 1992).

In consumer-directed approaches, most choices and responsibilities are shifted to the recipient or consumer. This approach is based on the premise that people with disabilities of all ages should be empowered to live as independently as possible and that physical (and even cognitive) limitations should not be barriers to expressing preferences and making decisions about services and community living. Consumer direction assumes that most supportive services are essentially nonmedical, with an emphasis on low-technology services not requiring extensive training or monitoring. This approach shifts control from home-care agencies to the consumer over which personal assistance services are received and who, when, and how those are delivered. Consumers can and should self-manage their personal care rather than rely on professional case management (Stone, 2000).

A Range of Models

In the United States and elsewhere, consumer direction is not a single approach but a range of models that vary in terms of how much decision making, control, and autonomy are shifted from home-care professionals and agencies to the consumer of services (see Table 1). At one extreme is a professionally monitored approach that expands the decisional authority of the recipient but provides little direct control over resources. In Oregon's Medicaid program, for example, service recipients are able to hire (and fire) workers of their choice with guidance from case managers. A case manager assists the consumer at start-up and monitors services over time. Roughly "in the middle" are models that assign a case manager to determine eligibility and approve service hours, while shifting all service decisions about hiring, scheduling, supervision, and so forth to the recipient. These programs vary in terms of the amount of assistance they give to consumers as they initiate services, and most make some provision to support consumers as they arrange their own services (Doty, Kasper, & Litvak, 1996).

In Maine, for example, those needing home care are referred to a consumer-run center, where trained peers assess their preferences and ability to self-direct, train them (as needed) on hiring and supervising, and provide a list of available workers. Those recipients not considered good candidates for self-direction are referred to a home-care agency. In a few places, most notably California, consumer direction is widely available but with little training or assistance for consumers, who make all service arrangements while a fiscal agent handles worker payments.

At the other extreme is the cash model, which has been implemented in Germany and other European nations and has been the subject of formal experimentation in the United States. Several European nations provide recipients with cash payments to buy services or support informal caregivers. Germany and Austria place no significant restrictions on the use of cash benefits and do not monitor recipient spending. France provides cash allowance, limits the use of most of it to paying workers for services, and has a small amount set aside that can

Table 1. Key Features of Agency and Consumer-Directed Home-Care Models in United States

		Consumer-directed model		
	Agency model	California	Maine	Arkansas
Range of benefits?	Authorized agency hours	Authorized service hours	Authorized service hours	Cash: goods and services
Consumer screening?	No	No	Yes	Yes (financial only)
Who hires worker?	Agency	Consumer	Consumer, with support	Consumer, with support
Family members as paid workers?	No, only employees of licensed-certified agencies	Yes, there are no limits (state-only funds)	Yes, there are no limits (state-only funds)	Yes, there are no limits (waiver)
Who supervises worker?	Agency	Consumer	Consumer, with support	Consumer, with support
Who counsels/assists consumer?	Home care agency/ case manager	Little or none from program	Contracted intermediary	Contracted counseling service
Who handles financial tasks?	Home care agency	County-state program	Contracted intermediary	Consumer of fiscal agent
Degree of consumer choice?	Variable	Low	High	High

Source: Interviews by the author with federal, state, and county program representatives, including those in the states of California, Maine, and Arkansas (U.S.).

be spent on any kind of service or equipment (Tilly, Wiener, & Cuellar, 2000). Countries vary as to whether eligibility is based on means testing (France and the United States) or is universal (Germany, Austria, the Netherlands).

In the United States, the cash model has recently been tested in a federal demonstration program in three states (Arkansas, Florida, and New Jersey), known as the Cash and Counseling Demonstration and Evaluation (Mahoney, Simone, & Simon-Rusinowitz, 2000). In this experiment, fielded in 1998, low-income recipients (more than half over age 65) were randomly assigned to receive either (1) a monthly cash allotment and the discretion to purchase any services *or* goods they considered essential (the treatment group), or (2) conventional agency services (the control group). Consumers receiving cash sometimes make creative spending choices, especially for home modifications and furniture that facilitate mobility, but are not covered by public medical assistance. Cash recipients have had the option to manage the cash directly or pay a small fee to have a certified fiscal agent manage the funds; most have opted for the latter. The counseling part of the program makes peer-professionals available to provide information and advice about organizing and implementing a spending plan.

The Impact of Consumer Direction

Results from the evaluation of the Cash and Counseling program have been very encouraging about the feasibility and promise of this approach. Program enrollees have been assessed on a number of measures, and those receiving cash have reported either more positive results or results no worse than those receiving agency services. Compared with agency clients, cash recipients are more satisfied with the performance of the workers they hire, more likely to find them capable and reliable, and less likely to report having unmet needs. Cash recipients reported fewer adverse events like bedsores and muscle contractures. Overall, cash recipients indicate higher satisfaction with their worker relationship, care arrangements, and life overall (Foster, Brown, Phillips, Schore, & Carlson, 2003). These outcomes were strikingly similar to those from an earlier study of a natural experiment in California, involving both consumer-directed (but not cash) and agency-based home-care services (Benjamin, Matthias, & Franke, 2000).

The careful design and testing of cash alternatives as opposed to agency-provided services continues in the United States with at least ten new states being funded in late 2004 to develop cash models for those needing home care. In a country that has been wary of "deregulating" services in ways that shift authority to lower-income populations, this is a dramatic development. This new support also demonstrates public willingness to address several issues confronting consumer-directed approaches, especially those involving cash.

Issues and Challenges

Consumer-directed programs are now established in many Western European countries and in more than half of the United States. Skeptics about the feasibility and impact of consumer direction are not confined to the home-care industry, which is critical of approaches that minimize the role of agencies and reduce public funds to them. Policymakers have also raised more substantive concerns. These involve, first, who should appropriately be included in these programs? Should not careful screening of candidates occur? Are not older persons and people with cognitive limitations unlikely candidates? Second, should there be limits on who can be hired as a worker? In particular, should family members be paid to care?

Third, how should quality be assured in the absence of an agency employer? How can public programs meet accountability expectations when the recipient becomes the judge of service quality? Given the potentially blurry line between nonmedical and medical services, how do we assure that consumer-directed workers are properly trained? Fourth, is consumer direction less costly than agency-delivered care? Supporters argue that this model is cheaper and delivers more services within a fixed budget. Is available evidence convincing?

For each of these, the issues will be defined, available research will be summarized, and the challenges for policymakers will be considered.

Who Should Self-Direct?

As discussed earlier, consumer direction initially emerged as the model of choice for working-age disabled persons, especially younger adults in wheelchairs with physical disabilities. Because consumer direction is understood to require substantial energy, awareness, and judgment, some programs insist that applicants be screened. Only those who prefer and can manage self-direction are expected to take it on, while others are assigned to the traditional agency model. However, there is growing support for providing a consumer-directed option to anyone eligible for personal assistance services, regardless of age or other characteristics (Doty, 2000; Stone, 2000). In the United States, several states have rejected screening and have chosen to offer all eligible recipients the option to self-direct. In the extreme case, California assigns nearly everyone (paradoxically, regardless of preference) to that model. Where cash is involved, recipients may be asked to demonstrate their ability to manage their funds and tasks related to unemployment insurance and benefits. Controversy also persists about the place of the elderly and those with cognitive limitations in consumer direction.

Age Issues

Skeptics in the United States continue to question whether consumer direction is appropriate for frail older people. The preferences and experiences of those over 65 are believed to differ significantly from those of younger disabled. Older people may be accustomed to services arranged by case managers and delivered by medically oriented home-care agencies. The old may have more unstable medical conditions and need more professional monitoring at home. For elderly people, the focus of supportive services has been to maintain current levels of functioning at home and to slow what is seen as inevitable decline. In contrast, younger recipients tend to view home-based services not as an end in themselves but as a means to a better life. Younger people with disabilities are seen as more grounded in "independent living" ideals and as having stronger preferences for directing their own lives (Eustis & Fischer, 1992; Simon-Rusinowitz & Hofland, 1993).

Recent research indicates that while older people are somewhat less enthusiastic about consumer-direction, their expectations and experiences generally mirror those of younger people. A higher percentage of younger disabled prefer self-direction, but a significant minority of older people shares the same preference (Simon-Rusinowitz, Mahoney, Desmond, & Shoop, 1997). Like others, older persons prefer to have a significant say in what is done, when, and how. On average, however, older recipients may need more outside support in getting started and making consumer direction work. They are also more likely to prefer hiring family members as workers (Benjamin & Matthias, 2001). In sum, consumer-directed options can be marketed to older consumers and tailored to their specific support needs.

Cognitive Impairment

An obvious challenge in shifting service decisions away from professionals and to consumers is the prevalence of cognitive limitations among people with disabilities. This challenge goes well beyond older people with Alzheimer's disease. In the United States, about 200,000 people with mental retardation and related developmental disabilities (MR/DD) receive supportive services through Medicaid (Brown, Lakin, & Burwell, 1997). A growing number of younger adults with traumatic brain injuries survive and need supportive services in the community. Advocates long ago recognized this issue and proposed a modified consumer-directed model using a guardian or surrogate for those with limited cognitive capacity (DeJong, 1992).

Other advocates for MR/DD populations have argued not for surrogacy but for supported self-determination. In this approach, the person with cognitive limitations actively participates in decisions not only about services but also about broader resource allocation (e.g., housing, education, and recreation). The recipient chooses a support team of family members, advocates, and professionals to assist in making these decisions. Various methods have been developed to facilitate the clarification and expression of personal preferences by those with cognitive impairments. These have been applied in many state programs, first through the federal Community Supported Living Arrangements demonstration program in the 1990s, and more recently through a program funded by the Robert Wood Johnson Foundation called Self-Determination for Persons with Developmental Disabilities (Benjamin, 2000).

Other research has examined consumer direction for older people with mild to moderate cognitive impairment. A recent study found that cognitively-impaired older persons answered factual questions accurately and consistently across several interviews and expressed specific preferences about their lifestyle and service needs. Differences were identified between what family members thought persons with cognitive impairment valued and what the persons themselves expressed. Echoing a growing body of other research, this study concluded that persons with mild to moderate cognitive impairments could express their preferences clearly and consistently and that family members as surrogates only imperfectly echo these views (Degenholtz et al., 1997; Feinberg & Whitlach, 2001). Research continues to investigate ways to expand the roles of people with cognitive limitations in defining their own service priorities and determining their own futures.

Who Can Be Hired as Provider?

Implementing consumer direction also provokes controversy over hiring family members as paid providers. Federal Medicaid regulations proscribe federal payment to "legally responsible" family members (i.e., spouses or parents of minors), and states vary in the extent to which other family members may be reimbursed with public funds. By contrast, recipients in California's Medicaid personal-assistance program may hire anyone as their workers, including immediate family members such as a spouse, parent, or child. California (like Maine) complies with federal regulations by using state funds to pay immediate family members hired by program recipients. Why? In a program that requires recipients to recruit their own workers, it is argued that choice about hiring should not be limited and that recipients need maximum latitude to recruit help. Practically, family members represent a large pool of helpers for people with disabilities.

Using public funds to pay family members for services to their relatives has provoked heated debate in the United States. Providing care to family members is generally seen as fulfilling a moral duty, and critics worry that public payment weakens the moral bonds that support family commitments. They also express concern about fraud and abuse by family members. Critics worry that costs will explode if the availability of public payment persuades large numbers of family members now providing services out of moral duty to demand payment instead. Moreover, some critics insist that family members should be the last choice in hiring, since familial ties complicate what should be an employer-employee relationship between consumer and workers (Simon-Rusinowitz, Mahoney, & Benjamin, 1998).

Relatively little research illuminates this debate. One study indicates that about one in five paid family providers had not previously provided unpaid services to the recipient prior to hiring, so that the pool of available help expanded as a result of payment to families. The same study found that with consumer-directed services, some service outcomes are more positive for consumers when the provider is a family member rather than a nonrelative (Benjamin et al., 2000). Recent findings from the Cash and Counseling Demonstration have indicated very little fraud and abuse in both family and nonfamily provider arrangements (Mahoney et al., 2000). As more states establish consumer-directed programs, pressures have grown to loosen prohibitions against using federal funds to pay close family members as home-care workers.

How Can Quality be Assured?

Quality assurance in home care traditionally begins with licensing and certification of home care agencies, which in turn agree to hire appropriate workers and provide training and supervision to them. If worker performance is unsatisfactory, the agency is expected to take action by sanctioning or replacing the worker. In consumer-directed approaches, judgments about worker performance are left to the consumer. States may establish registries of available workers and may arrange for intermediaries to train the consumer to self-direct (including how to fire a worker), but the public role involves providing these resources to the consumer, not resolving worker performance problems.

Critics of consumer direction worry that workers recruited and supervised by recipients will be unscreened, untrained, and unmonitored and thus more likely to neglect and abuse their clients. In addition, concerns are raised that without professional help, recipients will be unable to arrange for back-up assistance or manage service emergencies. Even for agency-based care, assessing the quality of home-based services is complex, because they involve delivery in relative isolation in literally millions of sites; service goals that are broad and diverse; and dimensions of quality that include both technical and interpersonal competence (Benjamin, 1999; Kane, 1999). Given the availability of professional approaches to quality assessment (Shaughnessy, Crisler, Schlenker, & Arnold, 1997), should we adopt models that rely on the consumer to judge the quality of care?

Advocates of consumer direction argue that uniform professional standards have only limited relevance to how people judge the quality of their supportive services and relationships with workers. In this view, professional oversight is unnecessary for services that are intimate and personal and only minimally medical or technical (Kapp, 1996; Sabatino & Litvak, 1992). For personal services in the home, values and preferences will vary about what are essentially quality of life issues like what is appropriate, adequate, comfortable, and secure. In this case, worker performance can reasonably be assessed by the person to whom services are provided (Geron, 2000; Kane, Kane, Illston, & Eustis, 1994).

Some studies suggest that the risks to consumers associated with self-direction seem no greater than those with agency-based services. A study of elderly Medicaid recipients in three states found a strong association between participation in a consumer choice program and recipient satisfaction with personal-assistance services (Doty et al., 1996). A small study of younger recipients of consumer-directed services in Virginia found that they reported higher satisfaction and greater work productivity than those receiving agency or informal services (Beatty, Richmond, Tepper, & DeJong, 1998). In a federally-funded program in California, service outcomes for the self-directing consumers were no different from those of agency recipients on measures of abuse and neglect and of unmet needs, and more positive on measures of service satisfaction and quality of life (Benjamin et al., 2000). This study also found that home-care agency workers received less service training than expected, while consumer-hired workers received more than predicted, although from diverse and unplanned sources (e.g., a family physician or home-health nurse).

As noted, a principal tenet of consumer direction holds that most personal assistance is not medical, but medically related procedures like assistance with medications, injections, catheters, and ventilators are part of daily life for many people with disabilities. Assuring the adequate oversight of medically related services delivered at home remains a challenge to policymakers. States in the United States have adopted nurse practice acts that define nursing tasks and prohibit nonlicensed personnel from undertaking them. Typically, family members are free of such restrictions.

Debate about quality is certain to persist. Due to accountability pressures on the government and demands from professional interests, policymakers seem to prefer erring on the side of too much rather than insufficient protection (U.S. GAO, 1999). The quality of the worker pool from which consumers hire is the primary target of state efforts, with initiatives to screen and do background checks, develop registries, and provide basic worker training. Most state programs have turned to contracted intermediaries to train consumers to be their own "watchdogs." We know very little about how these approaches work, but research is needed to assess the impact of providing advice and support to consumers to both self-direct and self-evaluate their services.

Is Consumer Direction Less Costly?

There is a paradox at the heart of recent growth in consumer-directed programs. Even as supporters invoke philosophical themes of independent living and empowerment, public officials seem drawn to consumer direction primarily because its services promise to be less costly than agency-based ones. In the United States, consumer direction is touted as more economical in the complete absence of research on this topic. In a home-care industry where workers make low wages, a substantial share of traditional home care costs involves agency overhead. When that overhead is minimized or eliminated because the self-directing consumer assumes the employer role, the hourly cost to public programs can drop sharply. However, total costs also depend on other program features, including the benefit level and caps, the generosity of support services for consumers needing assistance in making self-direction work, and the level of worker wages and benefits. In some states, consumer-hired workers average lower wages than do agency employees and receive far fewer benefits. On average, there is some consensus that for the same pool of dollars, more consumer-directed service hours can be purchased than agency hours. Recent analysis from the Cash and Counseling Evaluation is encouraging and will soon provide policymakers with the first careful assessment of the cost side of consumer direction (Dale, Brown, Phillips, Schore, & Carlson, 2003).

CONCLUSIONS

The appeal of consumer-direction in home care seems to lie in its potential to be less costly than agency-delivered services, to be more flexible in allowing recipients to meet their diverse needs, and thus to be more responsive to individual values and preferences in the delivery of personal-assistance services. The primary challenge to policy makers is determining how to design and implement consumer-directed programs so that they are cost-effective, flexible, and responsive, while also meeting public standards of accountability.

Recent federally supported research and evaluation is beginning to fill gaps in systematic analysis about the impact of different programs on people with disabilities and the public purse, but more research is clearly needed. Additional research is needed to understand what happens to consumers and families over time as they implement self-directed services, with attention paid to diverse disability groups like those over age 85, those with developmental disabilities, and children. We know little about the "careers" of people with disabilities generally and nothing about the relative impact of consumer direction over time. We also need evaluation of new initiatives, still to be designed, that are likely to introduce consumer-directed approaches into other settings, especially assisted-living facilities and nursing homes. Consumer direction also appeals to private insurers, who are experimenting with cash allocations in place of detailed service plans, and again more research on experience and impact is needed.

As consumer direction is disseminated more widely, there seem to be two primary threats to a fair test of its impact. Not surprisingly, the first is that in the name of cost-control, new programs may be inadequately funded. States face growing numbers of people with chronic care needs and continued pressure to provide community services for persons with disabilities. States will be pressed to provide more resources while also containing long-term care costs. Consumer direction is most likely to receive a fair test if public programs offer adequate benefits and supportive assistance to facilitate the shift to self-direction, and this will add to the unit costs of services.

The second threat is more pervasive and possibly more serious. There is considerable pressure to enrich consumer-directed models by including training for consumers as they start self-direction, along with training for workers and family members. Combined with pressures to introduce quality-assurance measures that satisfy professional and public concerns, there is some risk that consumer-directed services will become so layered with service providers, case managers, support teams, and quality assessors, that it will be transformed into another professional model of care. These pushes to reprofessionalize (and remedicalize) consumer-directed programs is an ongoing subject of concern for aging and disability advocates in the United States. For policymakers, the power of the agency model is enduring, since it permits delegation of responsibility to organized provider organizations with professionally conferred credentials.

Soon, nearly every American state is likely to offer people with disabilities an option for some version of consumer-directed home care under Medicaid or state-only programs. Soon, extending these approaches to the elderly and those with mild-to-moderate cognitive impairment will no longer seem experimental at the federal or state levels. Cash variants have been introduced in European nations with relatively little resistance and are being tested and disseminated in the United States. Consumer direction is becoming less an experiment than an established feature of the long-term-care policy menu in developed countries. Its appeal is the promise of empowering low-income people in need while avoiding the limitations and stigma associated with traditional welfare programs. In the United States, there is growing support for permitting older people and others to make their own choices about home-based services rather than conferring authority over public resources primarily to professionals.

REFERENCES

Batavia, A. I., DeJong, G., & McKnew, L. B. (1991). Toward a National Personal Assistance Program: The independent living model of long-term care for persons with disabilities. *Journal of Health Politics, Policy and Law*, *16*, 523-545.

Beatty, P. W., Richmond, G. W., Tepper, S., & DeJong, G. (1998). Personal assistance for people with physical disabilities: Consumer-direction and satisfaction with services. *Archives of Physical Medicine and Rehabilitation*, *79*, 674-677.

Benjamin, A. E. (1993). An historical perspective on home care policy. *The Milbank Quarterly*, *71*, 129-166.

Benjamin, A. E., Matthias, R. E., & Franke, T. M. (2000). Comparing consumer-directed and agency models for providing supportive services at home. *Health Services Research*, *35*, 351-366.

Benjamin, A. E., & Matthias, R. E. (2001). Age, consumer direction, and outcomes of supportive services at home. *The Gerontologist*, *41*, 632-642.

Benjamin, A. E., & Snyder, R. E. (2000). Consumer choice in long-term care. In S. L. Isaacs & J. R. Knickman (Eds.), *To improve health and health care, Vol.* 5. San Francisco, CA: Jossey-Bass.

Benjamin, A. E. (1999). A normative analysis of home care goals. *Journal of Ageing and Health, 11*, 445-468.

Brown, S. L., Lakin, K. C., & Burwell, B. O. (1997). Beneficiary centered care in services to persons with developmental disabilities. *Health Care Financing Review, 19*, 23-46.

Dale, S., Brown, R., Phillips, B., Schore, J., & Carlson, B. L. (2003). The effects of cash and counseling on personal care services and Medicaid costs in Arkansas. *Health Affairs*, Supplement Web Exclusives (W3), 566-575.

Damron-Rodriguez, J., & Lubben, J. E. (2001). *A framework for understanding community health care in ageing societies*. Kobe: WHO Kobe Center.

DeJong, G., Batavia, A. I., & McKnew, L. B. (1992). The independent living model of personal assistance in national long-term care policy. *Generations, 16*, 89-95.

Degenholtz, H. D., Kane, R. A., & Kivnik, H. Q. (1997). Care related preferences and values of elderly community-based long-term care consumers. *The Gerontologist, 37*, 767-776.

Doty, P., Kasper, J., & Litvak, S. (1996). Consumer-directed models of personal care: Lessons from Medicaid. *The Milbank Quarterly*, 377-409.

Doty, P. (2000). The federal role in the move toward consumer direction. *Generations, 24*, 22-27.

Eustis, N. N., & Fischer, L. R. (1992). Common needs different solutions? Younger and older home care clients. *Generations, 16*, 17-23.

Feder, J., Komisar, H. L., & Niefeld, M. (2000). Long-term care in the United States: An overview. *Health Affairs, 19*, 40-56.

Feinberg, L. F., & Whitlach, C. J. (2001). Are persons with cognitive impairment able to state consistent choices? *The Gerontologist, 41*, 374-382.

Foster, L., Brown, R., Phillips, B., Schore, J., & Carlson, B. L. (2003). Improving the quality of Medicaid personal assistance through consumer direction. *Health Affairs*, Supplement Web Exclusives (W3), 162-175.

Geron, S. M. (2000). The quality of consumer-directed long-term care. *Generations, 24*, 66-73.

Glover, J. J., & Hartman, A. (2000). The myth of home and the medicalization of the care of the elderly. *Journal of Clinical Ethics, 11*, 318-322.

Kane, R. A., Kane, R. L., Illston, L. H., & Eustis, N. N. (1994). Perspectives on home care quality. *Health Care Financing Review, 16*, 69-89.

Kane, R. A. (1999). Goals of home care: Therapeutic, compensatory, either, or both? *Journal of Ageing and Health, 11*, 299-321.

Kapp, M. B. (1996). Enhancing autonomy and choice in selecting and directing long-term care services. *Elder Law Journal, 4*, 55-97.

Lubitz, J., Greenberg, L. G., Gorina, Y., Wartzman, L., & Gibson, D. (2001). Three decades of health care use by the elderly, 1965-1998. *Health Affairs, 20*, 19-32.

Mahoney, K. J., Simone, K., & Simon-Rusinowitz, L. (2000). Early lessons from the Cash and Counseling Demonstration and Evaluation. *Generations, 24*, 41-46.

Rosenbaum, S. (2000). The Olmstead Decision: Implications for state health policy. *Health Affairs, 19*, 228-232.

Sabatino, C. P., & Litvak, S. (1992). Consumer-directed home care: What makes it possible? *Generations*, *16*, 53-59.

Shaughnessy, P. W., Crisler, K. S., Schlenker, R. E., & Arnold, A. G. (1997). Outcomes across the care continuum: Home health care. *Medical Care*, *35*, NS1155-NS123.

Simon-Rusinowitz, L., & Hofland, B. F. (1993). Adopting a disability approach to home care services for older adults. *The Gerontologist*, *33*,159-167.

Simon-Rusinowitz, L., Mahoney, K. J., Desmond, S. M., & Shoop, D. M. (1997). Determining consumer preferences for a cash option: Arkansas survey results. *Health Care Financing Review*, *19*, 73-96.

Simon-Rusinowitz, L., Mahoney, K. J., & Benjamin, A. E. (1998). Payments to families who provide care: An option that should be available. *Generations*, *22*, 69-75.

Stone, R. (2000). Opportunities, challenges, and limitations of consumer direction. *Generations 24*, 5-9.

Tilly, J., Wiener, J. M., & Cuellar, A. E. (2000). *Consumer-directed home and community services programs in five countries: Policy issues for older people and government.* Washington, DC: Urban Institute.

Tilly, J., Goldenson, S., & Kasten, J. (2001). *Long-term care: Consumers, providers, and financing—A chart book.* Washington, DC: Urban Institute.

U.S. General Accounting Office (U.S. GAO). (1999). *Adults with severe disabilities: Federal and state approaches for personal care and other services*. Washington, DC: Author.

Wiener, J., & Stevenson, D. G. (1998). State policy on long-term care for the elderly. *Health Affairs*, *17*, 81-100.

World Health Organization & Milbank Memorial Fund (WHO). (2000). *Towards an international consensus on policy for long-term care of the ageing*. Geneva: World Health Organization.

CHAPTER 3

Residential Care: Informed Choices

Cheryl Tilse, Jill Wilson, and Deborah Setterlund

Rose Daniels, an 85-year-old woman, was recently admitted to a 60-bed facility in the suburbs of a capital city. Until a recent admission to hospital, she was living in her own home with some support from community services. While in the hospital after another fall and a fractured femur, early-stage Alzheimer's disease was diagnosed. She cannot walk without considerable assistance and cannot manage personal care. Hospital staff strongly recommended that she not go home to live alone. Rose reports that staff told her: "you can't go home again": a view supported by her family who were concerned about her. While in the hospital, Rose was classified as having high-care needs by an Aged Care Assessment Team. Her daughter-in-law visited five aged-care facilities and selected one in an outer suburb that seemed well-run and had a vacancy at the time the hospital was seeking to discharge her. Mrs. D. was upset by the move, as she wished to go home. She reports, "I know I signed something" but is unsure of what agreements were made in relation to fees and entry. In the facility, she has a room of her own and some keepsakes from home. She would have liked to have brought her old sideboard with her mother's china and her wedding presents displayed but there was no room. Her son is now organizing to sell her home to finance the user charges. She is lonely when in her room by herself but is unwilling to ask staff to move her to other areas as "they all seem so busy." She also has trouble communicating if her hearing aids are not fitted properly.

Rose Daniels' experiences highlight many of the issues of informed choice in relation to entry and lifestyle choices in residential care. Informed choice is part of the discourse of consumer sovereignty, the customer and the market, as well as the rights and citizenship discourse. These discourses, which underpin current approaches to residential care in Australia, suggest that

1. There is a choice in the options available.
2. Individuals are well-informed as to the options available and the likely costs and impact of choices made.
3. Individuals are able to indicate their preferred choice and can exercise that choice.

As consumers and citizens, the choices available to older people in relation to residential care should include whether to enter a facility, which facility to enter, whether one can stay and "age in place" as care needs change and choices regarding daily living—resident choice over how to spend their day, use their time, who to socialize with, and how they present. A critical analysis of residential care in Australia highlights the issues that arise in implementing informed choice, a key value in theory, policy, and practice. Important dimensions of choice include access to an array of services to provide real choices, access to information on the choices available, and access to resources needed to exercise the choices made.

POLICY CONTEXT

The reform of Australian aged care over the past two decades is characterized by an increase in community services to support people in their own homes, assessment for entry into residential care linked to national eligibility criteria, rationing of residential places, an increase in user charges, a focus on resident-centered care, and regulation of quality of care linked to outcome standards. The notion of informed choice is central to many of the changes in policy and practice.

The structural reform package linked to the Aged Care Act (Australian Government, 1997), and its subordinate legislation the Aged Care Principles sought to enhance choice with relation to residential care in three main ways. First, the development of a wider range of community-care options that provide alternatives to residential care. Second, policies of aging in place that provide security of tenure by linking residential care provision to resident needs rather than facility characteristics. Finally, the development of outcome standards that include choice as a key aspect of residents' rights and responsibilities.

The policy changes have both restricted and enhanced choice over entry into residential facilities. Restrictions result from the capping of new residential facilities and the resultant reduction of residential places in the context of a growing aged population. Choice has been enhanced by the provision of alternatives to residential care through community-care packages, support for family carers to continue caring at home, and programs that deliver community care at home to older people with high care needs. These are rationed resources and are not currently available to all who require them.

Prior to the structural reform, the separation of high-care (nursing homes) and low-care (hostels) facilities was seen as a barrier to consumer choice. Residents had to move as their care needs changed, couples with differing care needs could not be accommodated in the same facility, and older people in rural areas generally had to move (Gray, 2001). The reform unified the two-tier system, allowing facilities to offer a full continuum of care. The restructure sought to facilitate aging in place by the removal of administrative and legislative barriers. The single funding tool linking funding to the care needs of residents allows for older people to receive an appropriate level of care regardless of facilities and to remain in place as their care needs change.

Research by the Australian Institute of Health and Welfare (2002) suggests there is strong evidence that aging in place has occurred with one in five residents of former hostels now classified at the high care end of the reimbursement scale. There has also been a dramatic reduction in the number of hostel residents transferred as a result of increasing dependency. A review of the aged-care reforms (Gray, 2001) based on consultations with providers and consumers suggests there is agreement in principle with aging in place but mixed reactions in practice. The review concluded that consumer capacity to enter and remain in their home of choice appears to have been enhanced (Gray, 2001). Providers, however, expressed concerns about the inappropriate physical layout of hostels and the lack of supportive staffing structures to offer a range of care within the one facility. Consumers reported difficulty in finding facilities that would admit couples with differing care needs.

Financial resources can influence choice. Older people with extensive financial resources can elect to privately fund home-care services and avoid residential entry. Although home-care services may be purchased, they may not be sufficient to keep an older person with high care needs at home. In Australia, entry to residential facilities is not generally dependent on the capacity of the older person or their family to pay. The cost of residential care is substantially subsidized by the Australian government and set at rates of no more than 88% of age pension income. During the 1980s and 1990s, a series of incremental steps required residents to pay more based on income and assets. The fees and charges differ according to the income source of the resident (pensioner/nonpensioner), their assets and whether they enter as a high-care or low-care resident. Facilities are required to offer a proportion of places to residents who do not pay the extra fees. In relation to high-care residents, there is no current evidence to suggest that these additional payments have resulted in those who are able to pay them having greater choice at entry or in choice of amenities (Tilse, 2002). An Extra Services Scheme does provide the option for residents with financial resources to pay more for accommodation options but not personal care. This provides choice in hotel-type amenities for those who are able to pay. The extra-service scheme remains a minor part of the residential program with 1.5% of all aged care facilities participating (Gray, 2001).

The reform and restructuring of residential care is driven by a changed philosophy of care reflecting a move from a medical model of care to policies promoting resident focused care. The changed approach is founded on an explicit recognition of the rights of residents and supported by philosophies that recognize adulthood and citizenship (Peace, Kellaher, & Willcocks, 1997). Initiatives include articulating residents' rights and responsibilities in charters, strategies to protect and enforce rights such as advocacy, and the development of resident participation in decision making through resident committees. A view of aged consumers as active participants in residential facilities is reflected in the Aged Care Act, 1997 and incorporated in national outcome standards that are regulated through accreditation and quality-assurance mechanisms.

Ideas about choice underpin notions of resident-focused care, rights, and participation in residential facilities. The Resident Charters of Rights and Responsibilities and the Outcome Standards (Australian Department of Health and Ageing, 2001) explicitly identify the right of residents or their representatives to participate in decision making about services and exercise choice and control over their lifestyle while not impinging on others. Resident's Agreements also form part of the strategy to enhance informed choice at the point of entry. These include a residential-care agreement in respect to a residential care facility, which provides the regulatory framework for a rights-based residency in a facility and arrangements about fees and charges, including extra-service agreements where appropriate.

Choice with relation to residential care has been enhanced by a changing philosophy of care, an increased array of care options for older people, and an improvement in the quality of residential care. Other outcomes that may limit choice include the impact on decision making of the higher levels of disability of those entering aged residential facilities (Gibson, 1995), complex systems of decision making around health and accommodation choices, and increased complexity of fees surrounding residential care of older people (Tilse, 2002). The case of Rose Daniels highlights the need to explore how the rights models and outcome standards are implemented in practice and the impact they have on consumer choice with regard to entry into and day to day living in residential environments.

A Commonwealth government evaluation (Braithwaite, Makkai, Braithwaite, & Gibson, 1993) of the initial reform concluded that for nursing-home (high care) residents, choice is limited by few alternatives and specialized needs and a target population characterized by relatively low expectations and little experience of consumer activism. This report also concluded that the capacity to exit is limited for highly dependent residents who are likely to have fewer resources to cope with a move, may be unwilling to disrupt established networks, or to move from a familiar location. Braithwaite and colleagues argued therefore that the point of entry becomes the critical stage for information and choice.

For many older people, "the institutional option casts a shadow of deep anxiety and uncertainty in later life" (Peace et al., 1997). Entry into residential care is generally rapid and involuntary and associated with a sudden deterioration in health status of the older person or their family carer (Gray, 2001). It is within this context that informed choice needs to be understood. Two decades of reform have increased choice regarding entry through the array of community-care options available. For many older people, however, a move to residential care is made with very little choice, with the outcome primarily determined by the absence of appropriate community support and the availability of a residential-care place rather than the suitability of the particular facility (Valentine, 2000). Preoccupation with finding a place, assessing its suitability, and pressure to make a quick decision due to perceptions of limited choice and pressures from others (e.g. hospitals, community services, or family carers), may all reduce capacity to focus on the rights aspects of facility living and to seek appropriate advice (Valentine, 2000). The demands on the physical and emotional reserves of all involved in decision making also affect perceptions of choice.

Whether older people and their family members are in a position to make informed choices at this time is open to challenge. Disability or illness can reduce the capacity of older people to actively participate in the decision to seek nursing-home care and to negotiate care agreements. The legal and financial complexity of entry into an aged-care facility has increased through the creation, in the Aged Care Act, of a number of agreements between resident and provider that need to be signed, depending on the type of care being provided (Wilson, Setterlund, & Tilse, 2003). The extent to which older people and their families are fully informed and thus empowered to make choices and to negotiate terms of residential life will often depend on receiving appropriate information, support and advice from informed intermediaries such as aged-care workers, Aged Care Assessment Team (ACAT) team members and legal practitioners. Surveys of informed intermediaries such as legal practitioners and aged-care workers suggest that knowledge of aged-care agreements is limited (Setterlund, Tilse, & Wilson, 2000).

In the Review of the Aged Care reforms, Gray (2001, p. 210) notes that awareness of care choices and details of the aged-care system remains low among residents, potential residents, and family members despite an information dissemination strategy.

This lack of knowledge has been linked to an unwillingness to engage in a rights discourse, the emotional stress associated with entry processes, and the reluctance to consider a move to residential care until there are few other options (Wilson et al., 2003). A fourth factor is that the information required to negotiate entry is complex, comprising personal-care preferences and legal and financial components, some of which require access to professional expertise (Tilse, 2002). Focus groups with families and older people (Wilson et al., 2003) suggest the majority of older people and family carers have little understanding of the legal aspects of entry to a facility and viewed agreements as a formality with little relevance to their ongoing care.

These factors reduce the ability of older people and their family members to appreciate and question the significance of the contractual agreements signed at entry and suggest the rights framework of the Act is not sufficient in and of itself to provide a useable framework that fits current resident populations and the complex environment of residential care (Valentine, 2000).

Within facilities, informed choice has been promoted by the rights framework linked to outcome standards and strategies seeking to enhance participation. Research suggests that it can be difficult to protect this individual approach in an organized environment (Peace et al., 1997, p. 44). There is evidence that "rights" talk (Gibson, 1995) played an important educative role in setting the context and changing expectations of staff, residents, and families (Tilse, Wilson, & Setterlund, 1997). Research and practice suggest, however, limitations in the capacity and willingness of residents and their representatives to exercise their rights and participate in decision making in the complex practice environments in which such strategies have been cited (Tilse, 1997; Tilse et al., 1997). The complexity of residential environments and the discretionary nature of care can reduce consumer willingness to voice concerns and exercise choice. Carney (1997) argues that the structures in place "do not correct for gross imbalances of negotiating power" with relation to getting care needs met.

THE PRACTICE CONTEXT

The application of policies that support consumer choice is not obviously controversial, but their implementation is problematic because the choice is often between competing, legitimate considerations (Kapp, 1990)—between, say, autonomy and safety or between individual and group interests. These competing considerations are also influenced by a range of personal, political, and attitudinal considerations about the nature of being old and of growing old "well."

Heumann, Boldy, and McCall (2001) offer a framework for exploring the impediments to empowering, choice-oriented models of care and support. The four areas of limitation are provider based, environment based, client based (examples are physical and mental capacity, family dynamics) and societal based. The following vignettes illustrate these impediments, which often overlap and interact with each other.

Provider-based issue: *Facility A allocates more staff to the morning shift, and it is at this time that activities for residents are organized. While this suits some residents, others are happier with a quieter morning and want to spend time with others in the afternoon. This is not possible because of staffing limitations. These limitations are imposed to meet budgetary requirements.*

Environment-based issue: *Facility B is relatively new, with spacious single rooms and a number of quiet, small gathering places. Frail residents spend up to*

90% of their time in their rooms, and a number are very lonely. When activities are organized they are in the large space that is poor acoustically. The small spaces are almost always empty.

Client-based issue: *Mr. V has aphasia, is frail, and spends much of his time in bed. He would enjoy a particular activity, but it takes place in the afternoon when his care plan says he should be resting. He relies on family members to let staff know his wishes, but staff are reluctant to take notice, viewing family suggestions as criticism.*

Societal-based issue: *Residents in facility B above are reluctant to ask staff for any extras, such as being taken to visit another resident, because they see the staff are busy and believe their needs are of little importance and that any shortness they experience from staff is only to be expected given they are so busy.*

They have applied their framework to frail and dependent people for whom independence and control in their own lives have real limits. They argue that change in existing, depowering forms of care needs to be driven by a change "in the attitudes and beliefs of care workers about the ability and worth of frail older persons" (p. 27). They argue that programs can promote choice by older people who receive care if they address the issues listed in all or some of these groups. While this framework provides an understanding of the barriers to informed choice within the residential-care environment, it is also important to develop an understanding of the dynamic, shifting, and complex interactions that surround the four areas identified.

Peace et al. (1997) note that residential care "is constituted through the actions and aspirations of several groups of interested parties" (p. 115). Consequently, any attempts to provide care that promotes resident choice must take into account the interests of and pressures on all stakeholders in the residential-care enterprise experience. These groups are made up centrally of residents and their relatives or friends, staff of all levels, the regulators, the owners of facilities, and society at large. While these authors note that there has been change in the experience of residential care, a number of factors impede the achievement of generally held goals for resident-focused, empowering care. These are noted as the practical, task-oriented nature of care, leaving little time to talk as noted by staff and residents (Worrall, Wilson, Tilse, Setterlund, & Hickson, 2002); the hierarchical nature of nursing home administration, leaving little authority with either residents or the frontline personal care workers; the challenging nature of the task of working with people with mental, emotional, and behavioral demands encourages staff to depersonalize these older people as sufferers or deviants (Peace et al., 1997, p. 118) rather than as adults who have rights; and the abiding negative attitude to aging in many societies.

Personal-care staff are frontline staff. They have some discretion to change policy by the way it is implemented; they also experience competing pressures and expectations that are characteristic of frontline work (Lipsky, 1980). Competing expectations in relation to implementing informed choice for residents arise from the various interest groups—co-workers, managers, family members, and residents—and from the nature of the environment as a workplace, a home for residents, and a business. Conflicts also arise from negotiating individual preferences in a communal environment.

Rose Daniels wishes to join an established group of women who play cards each morning. The group do not want her to join as her hearing impairment and early stage dementia disrupts the speed and enjoyment of the card game.

The resident's committee reports that one particular meal is disliked by the majority of residents. The management of the facility responds that the meals are centrally provided to several facilities, and that change is difficult because of economies of scale.

While it is appropriate to focus on achieving choice for residents of aged-care facilities, it is also the case that unless the staff with whom they have most to do—the personal care workers—feel valued and affirmed in their work, it will be difficult to implement policies around promoting resident choice (Boldy & Grenade, 2001; Worrall et al., 2002). Frontline staff are subject to a hierarchical structure that they tend to replicate in their dealings with residents.

The authors' current research on staff-staff communication reinforces earlier findings (Worrall et al., 2002). The parallel communication patterns within different levels of staff tend to be task rather than resident focused and hence there is little opportunity to know the resident as a person with interests and concerns. With these communication patterns, older people are subject to being managed rather than empowered to make choices.

THE ART OF ENHANCING CHOICE

The type of change required to bring about a choice-oriented, empowering environment requires a leadership style based on innovation and risk taking. The traditional "top down" management approach as described by Braithwaite (1993, p. 242), where managers control budgets, information, and power, will not be viable in this environment. What is needed is a more participative and empowering management style based on consensus, nursing, and non-nursing involvement, and effective communication, supported by improved work conditions and appropriate training programs for workers at all levels (Braithwaite, 1993, p. 242). Managers may choose to attempt to bring about the necessary change themselves with their existing staff group, or they may choose to support a staff member who has the job of facilitating "bottom up" change.

Harvey (2001, p. 156) describes a management-led "whole of environment" change process, which began with an analysis of the barriers to empowering, participatory and choice-based practices, and recognition of the need for a new philosophy of care: "the staff . . . felt the need to give the residents a central role, put them unequivocally at the heart of life in our nursing home, and, without reservation, acquaint them with their rights and ability to exercise them."

Continuity of change was addressed by the employment of a Living Environment Advisor who reported to the Director General of the Home and whose primary duties were to advocate and implement practices and mechanisms that ensured "the primacy of the rights of residents over those of the organization" (Harvey, 2001, p. 167). Human interactions are imbued with power, and while individuals' and groups' experiences of these power relationships will be both similar and different, it is residents who are most vulnerable and disempowered in the community. It is within this context that Harvey is proposing an advocacy process.

Power is conceptualized as the capacity of individuals to control or influence others and to exercise choice. The interactional nature of power means that "the outcome of any exchange is unpredictable: Individuals engage in multitudinous interactions, and a chance word or hasty intervention in any of them can transform the others for better or worse" (Harris, 1997, p. 30). Staff may constrain resident's capacity to make choices through disempowering language and practices. "Talking down" to residents for example, positions older people as childlike and, by implication, not adult enough to make choices, while practices such as imposing rigid physical-care routines positions the older resident as a "body to be managed" rather than as a self-determining adult. A staff-resident interaction observed in one research study noted that the staff response to a resident who asked for medication at a particular time of day was "Who runs this place, us or the residents? She'll get them when she gets them" (Worrall et al., 2002, p. 56). Residents of course can attempt to resist such practices by voicing their displeasure and preferred choices; however, the staff has the occupational and physical power to override resistance and to assert the dominant patterns of care (Davies, 2003).

In other interactional contexts, it may be residents who exercise power over staff, for example, a resident using racist language to refuse care from a minority group staff member: "She (resident) told me, 'go away—you're Black' . . . it really hurt (me) . . . but I turned the other cheek" (Worrall et al., 2002). The resident's comment devalued and constrained that staff person's choice to work as a personal carer capable of caring for all residents irrespective of race. Similarly, some staff members, in their interactions, may disempower other staff members. For example, in one study (Setterlund, 1995) dementia care workers commonly reported having their care work with residents with dementia trivialized by nursing staff: "They (nurses) really think you do nothing but sit on your rear end all day . . . they come into the room and say, 'there you are, sitting again.'" While advocacy is important when individuals are denied rights, it is perhaps of limited use when all players are feeling they have little power to change the situation. We would suggest that taking a community, rather than individual perspective is of value in enhancing informed choice.

A community perspective recognizes that residential settings are both a place of work for staff and a home to the residents who live there (Willcocks, Peace, & Kellaher, 1987) as well as a business. From this perspective, residential environments are envisioned as groups of people, residents, staff, and relatives of residents, who interact within the context of a physical environment and sets of policies, to produce outcomes of care, such as informed choice. This perspective also recognizes the power of relationships, the barriers to informed choice and hence provides a deep analysis of the dynamics involved as illustrated in the following vignette drawn from a research study on dementia care within large residential settings (Setterlund, 1995).

Mrs. P. has sight and hearing difficulties (client-based barrier), but is cognitively competent. Her clear lifestyle choice is to assist staff with cleaning duties, but she is in danger of being physically injured as she moves around the home (environment-based barrier) unsupervised due to staff shortages (program-based barrier) and her attempts to help domestic staff interferes with the smooth running of the home (program-based barrier). Although she attempts to exercise power (determining own lifestyle) by her stated choice not to participate in set activities, staff exercise their power (control over) to guide her to a closed room to take part in activities. Here she asks the time on a regular basis, to see if its time to leave, but once again the staff exercise their power to keep her there by "telling little white lies" so that it is "always 9 o'clock." Ultimately, it is another resident who continues the disempowerment process by telling Mrs. P. she is "naughty" and a "nuisance" when she gets up to try and leave. Eventually defeated, Mrs. P. attempts to put counters on the board of a card game, but has difficulty as she rightly reminds the others "I can't see." (Participant observation).

Within these shifting power relationships, it is clear that no one group, not staff, residents, or relatives, are all-powerful or all-powerless. Nevertheless, the devalued position of older people in society generally, the frailty and cognitive impairment experienced by the majority of older residents, and the impediments to implementing the empowering, choice-oriented models of care and support noted in the literature, all reduce the power of older people collectively comparative with other groups in the residential-care environment. Creating an environment that supports each resident's ability to exercise informed choice to their fullest capacity is both an art and a science. It requires a whole of community approach with change strategies directed at structural, interpersonal, and personal levels within the residential community.

A whole of community approach to change is likely to be perceived as a daunting venture by even the most committed participants. There are issues around starting points, for example, whether to first address values/philosophy or practice and regimes or the built environment. There are issues around engaging residents and some staff, especially those in low status positions, in processes such as voicing demands, which they may find threatening, given the disempowerment that many will have experienced. The very nature of residential care means that many residents, staff and relatives, have developed self-protective mechanisms that may constrain mutual trust, openness, ability to articulate preferences, and a level of comfort with conflict. Additionally many residents experience cognitive and sight, mobility and speech impairments that render their involvement in negotiation and change processes more difficult. The change process therefore may need to include individual and group-based strategies aimed at re-skilling individuals to participate in situations where they are encouraged to voice discontent and preferences.

Jackson, Mitchell, and Wright (1989, p. 68) provide a useful conceptualization of change within communities as a continuum which acknowledges the importance of preparing individuals to participate in change as well as the need to engage groups in collective action. This approach to community change was used by the authors in practice research in a residential setting (Worrall et al., 2002).

Work at the individual level included audiological assessments and interventions designed to reduce barriers to communication and hence, the ability to exercise choice. Work at the group level included residents, staff, and relatives. Residents were invited to participate in a number of communication and social skills groups. Staff participated in groups designed to assist them to identify their personal and professional models of care, their differences and common experiences as care workers, and to reflect upon and transform constraining uses of power embedded in taken-for-granted practices into choice enhancing practices. Staff also requested training in grief and loss to assist them to better cope with their own and residents' experiences of death and loss within the home. Groups were also held with relatives of residents, and once again the opportunity to meet, to voice concerns, to identify priorities for change, and to form networks of mutual support provided the groundwork for the development of change at a structural level. In this project, time and resource constraints precluded moving on to systematic structural change, although many suggestions raised by all three groups were implemented at the policy and program level.

At the whole of community change end of the continuum, there are three steps that need to occur: (1) separate meetings for staff, residents, and family members to identify their preferences with relation to key dimensions of residential life, (2) a forum for all three groups to articulate preferences, identify points of commonality and divergence, and develop a consensus regarding those aspects of care that could be changed to better meet the preferences of residents, and (3) discussion and implementation of change strategies aimed at enhancing residents' choices.

These steps were implemented in a residential setting in an earlier study (Setterlund & Wilson, 1989) where the groundwork of individual and group work had taken place over a period of two years. Resistance to increased choice within the community from staff and some residents had been raised, discussed, and to a large extent resolved within the small group context. The structural change outcomes included the establishment of a newspaper published by the residents themselves, and residents' meetings wherein residents controlled the agenda and difference of opinion was encouraged and viewed as a healthy prerequisite to creative problem-solving (Setterlund & Wilson, 1989).

Interestingly, one of the findings from this action research project was the need to use "art" as a catalyst for engaging the different groups in identifying needs and changes sought. A photo journalist was used in this setting to make photo portraits of residents and to randomly record interactions between different individuals in the home. The care interactions captured in the images were used for different purposes with each of the staff, residents, and relatives. Firstly, the touching and evocative resident portraits provided an "outsider" or different perspective of residents as people which enabled participants to "step outside" of their usual field of vision. Few residents had viewed themselves as subjects of artistic portraiture that seemed to capture the essence of their character and spirit; similarly staff that were more familiar with residents' bodily functions and deficits were amazed to see residents as whole people. Not surprisingly, relatives were most affected by the resident portraits, many moved to tears. One relative's response to seeing the portrait of her mother who had severe dementia was "I have never seen mum looking so beautiful."

The second use of the photojournalism images was to illustrate to all groups the contradictions and realities of everyday care practices, those that would be considered both excellent and poor by both lay and professional standards. For staff, for example, seeing such images was a powerful experience that enabled them to explore and confront their own practices. There could be no denying, for example, the indignity of residents seated on rows of chairs staring into space; nor conversely was it impossible not to celebrate joyful images of residents, staff, and relatives engaged in precious moments of conversation and laughter. Creative processes of this kind provided a starting point and a focus for the exploration of painful issues and the beginning of trust building so that relationships could later withstand the more challenging community development processes involving disagreement and the risk-taking associated with change.

Another creative approach to engaging participants in change processes identified in the literature is the use of poetry. This approach has been used successfully with residents with dementia, who have difficulty making their preferences known and often are excluded from meaningful involvement in change-oriented processes. One example is from an artist in residence at a Scottish residential-care home (Killick, 1994), who spent many hours with residents with dementia, recording their conversation, and working them into poems. This resulting collection is a powerful tribute to human understanding and empathy, attributes that may be tested in the day-to-day demands of care work and visits from relatives to residents with dementia. In one poem, Killick (1994) captures the depth of feeling seemingly associated with a resident's attempt to exercise choice by not accepting an approach from a staff member, an action that relatives and staff undoubtedly find frustrating:

GO AWAY!
You have hurt me,
You have hurt me deeply,
Because you will go away.
I want to be looking
for somewhere else.
I didn't choose this place.
I don't like this area.
And the noise!
I can't stand the noise!
What was that sound?
It really upset me.
I don't want to talk to you,
I don't want to see you again,
Because you will go away.

Once again, the creative use of words provides a means for staff, residents, and relatives to explore and challenge taken-for-granted practices as well as providing a different perspective into the inner life of residents. This helps create conditions for fresh understandings, for confidence to relinquish power, and for choice-enhancing practices to emerge.

CONCLUSIONS

Australian aged-care policy appropriately identifies procedures designed to assure older people and their families a choice with relation to life in a residential facility.

However, the way information on residential entry is disseminated, the financial base of these facilities and the regulatory mechanisms overseen by accreditation agencies do constrain choice for residents, staff, and families. Residential facilities have always been both a place to live and a place to work. They are now required to also be places that make a profit. These three functions intersect to constrain choice, and this constraint is amplified by the devalued status of frail older people (and those who work with them) in Australian society. Choice is not readily available to any of the players—staff, residents, family or friends—and in the environment of a residential facility, it needs to be actively encouraged.

Attempts to enhance resident choice must be based on a clear analysis of the barriers to choice-oriented models of care, the impact of power relations within the community that a facility forms, and care practices that may constrain or enhance choice. For change to occur, we have suggested that people need to know what change will look like; they need to have a belief that change is possible, even if it is difficult; and hence they are likely to need to identify some new ways of moving ahead. We have argued for a whole of community approach to choice-oriented change. This can be achieved through a process of changed leadership style and the use of an advocate or change agent within the facility. We have discussed some examples of these approaches that were successful in overcoming the structural and sometimes personal barriers to choice in residential aged care.

REFERENCES

Australian Government. (1997). *Age Care Act 1997*. Canberra, Australia: Author.

Australian Department of Health and Ageing, Ageing and Aged Care Division. (2001). *Residential care manual*. Retrieved July, 2004 from http://www.health.gov.au/manuals/rcm/rcmindx1.htm.

Australian Institute of Health and Welfare. (2002). *Ageing in place: Before and after the 1997 aged care reforms*. Catalogue No. AUS 26. Canberra, Australia: Author.

Braithwaite, J., Makkai, T., Braithwaite, V., & Gibson, D. (1993). *Raising the standard: Resident centered nursing home regulation in Australia*. Canberra, Australia: Department of Health, Housing, Local Government and Community Services.

Braithwaite, J. (1993). Identifying the elements in the Australian health service management revolution. *Australian Journal of Public Administration, 52*(4), 417-430.

Boldy, D., & Grenade, L. (2001). Promoting empowerment in residential aged care services: Seeking a consumer view. In L. Heumann, M. McCall, & D. Boldy (Eds.), *Empowering frail elderly people: Opportunities and impediments in housing, health and support service delivery*. Westport, CT: Praeger.

Carney, T. (1997). 'Righting' wrongs for the aged: A bill of rights? *Australian Journal on Ageing, 16*(2), 73-78.

Davies, S. (2003). Creating community: The basis for caring partnerships in nursing homes. In M. Nolan, U. Lundh, G. Grant, & J. Keady (Eds.), *Partnerships in family care*. United Kingdom: Open University Press.

Gray, L. (2001). *Two year review of aged care reforms*. Canberra, Australia: Department of Health and Aged Care.

Gibson, D. (1995). User rights and the frail aged. *Journal of Applied Philosophy, 12*(1), 1-11.

Harris, R. (1997). Power. In M. Davies (Ed.), *The Blackwell companion to social work*. Oxford, UK: Blackwell Publishers.

Harvey, G. (2001). The rights of elderly people in a nursing home—A little creativity, a lot of respect, a taste for adventure and an allergy to bureaucracy. In L. Heumann, M. McCall, & D. Boldy (Eds.), *Empowering frail elderly people: Opportunities and impediments in housing, health and support service delivery*. Westport, CT: Praeger.

Heumann, L., Boldy, D., & McCall, M. (2001). Opportunities and impediments in housing, health, and support service delivery. In L. Heumann, M. McCall, & D. Bold (Eds.), *Empowering frail elderly older people: Opportunities and impediments in housing, health, and support service delivery* (pp. 25-37). Westport, CT: Praeger.

Jackson, T., Mitchell, S., & Wright, M. (1989). The community development continuum. *Community Health Studies, X11*, 66-71.

Kapp, M. (1990). Home care client-centered systems: Consumer choice vs. protection. *Generations, (Supplement)*, 33-36.

Killick, J. (1994). *Please give me back my personality! Writing and dementia*. Stirling, UK: Dementia Services Development Centre, Department of Applied Social Science, School of Human Sciences, University of Stirling.

Lipsky, M. (1980). *Street-level bureaucracy*. New York: Russell Sage.

Peace, S., Kellaher, L., & Willcocks, D. (1997). *Re-evaluating residential care.* Buckingham: Open University Press.

Setterlund, D. (1995). *Care, work and contradictions: Experiences of dementia care in residential settings.* Unpublished Ph.D. thesis. Brisbane, Australia: The University of Queensland.

Setterlund, D., & Wilson, J. (1989). Social work with the elderly: Residential care as an example. *Australian Social Work, 42*(3), 31-39.

Setterlund, D., Tilse, C., & Wilson, J. (2000). *Legislative changes in aged care: Their implications for older people and their families, informed intermediaries and legal practitioners in Queensland.* Brisbane, Australia: University of Queensland.

Tilse, C. (1997). Family advocacy roles and highly dependent residents in nursing homes. *Australian Journal on Ageing, 16*(1), 20-23.

Tilse, C. (2002). Cash, customers and care: The experience and meaning of differential payment for high care places in aged care facilities. *Australian Journal of Social Issues*, 37(4), 381-394.

Tilse, C., Wilson, J., & Setterlund, D. (1997, September). Social work, social justice and residential care. *Proceedings of the Australian Association of Social Workers 25th National Conference* (pp. 634-641). Canberra, Australia.

Valentine, B. (2000). The Aged Care Act 1997: Improving the quality of residential aged care? *Australian Social Work, 53*(1), 15-19.

Wilson, J., Setterlund, D., & Tilse, C. (2003). I know I signed something: Older people, families and social workers understanding of the legal aspects of entry to residential care. *Australian Social Work, 56*(2), 155-165.

Worrall, L., Wilson, J., Tilse, C., Setterlund, D., & Hickson, L. (2002). *The effectiveness of the Participant Enablement Program in aged care facilities: A pilot study.* Brisbane, Australia: The University of Queensland.

Willcocks, D. M., Peace, S., & Kellaher, L. A. (1987). *Private lives in public places.* London, UK: Tavistock Publications.

CHAPTER 4

New Demands on Education and Training for the Care of Old People: The Case of Israel

David Galinsky

The second part of the twentieth century was characterized by a significant increase in elderly people. This worldwide biological and demographic phenomenon has many implications for a large number of different disciplines, such as politics, economics, social services, and others (Fries, 2002). Provision of services and training of personnel for elderly care have to be thoroughly reviewed and readapted to the new trends. It should be considered that, for historical reasons, the concept of care of the elderly was based on custodial models. This was the universal trend, and it is still prevalent in many countries. Thus, the training of personnel has traditionally taken place in old age homes, nursing homes, shelter houses, and in different centers in which groups of elderly people have been concentrated. Currently, the most rapidly growing group of elderly is of those aged 80 years and older. This segment of the population is living within the community, and only a small proportion live under custodial care. It should be noted that, for 50% of those people aged 80 or older, a combination of social and medical losses is manifested by the inability to perform basic activities of daily living, which leads to partial or total dependency (Guralnik & Ferrucci, 2003; Habib & Factor, 1993). As mentioned above, the vast majority of the elderly live in the community; therefore, the old-fashioned system of care and the education of personnel cannot cope efficiently with the problems of old people, particularly the disabled elderly, who demand a different and wider sort of care. The training of professional and nonprofessional personnel in the face of this new trend is of paramount importance.

THE CONCEPT OF CARE OF THE ELDERLY IN THE COMMUNITY

The care of old people in the community is based on three basic principles: multi/interdisciplinary teams, continuity of care, and prevention of the loss of autonomy (Galinsky, 1994).

The *Multidisciplinary Team* approach stems from the complexity of problems affecting the elderly, which indicates that problems should be addressed by the combined efforts of professionals from the social and medical disciplines. Moreover, a medical team should include not only doctors and nurses, but also experts in rehabilitation, thus taking into account the importance of the impact of functional dependency so prevalent in the aged. Social problems also have an influence on the health condition of elderly persons, and the complexity of the demands of this segment of the population requires special expertise on the part of social workers. Sophisticated scientific developments indicate that these professionals also need special education and training.

For many years, the efforts of these professionals were concentrated in old-age homes, shelter houses, and nursing homes. Studies conducted in those settings have contributed to the elevation of the level of care of elderly people living in these kinds of institutions. Today, attention to the comfort and well-being of the elderly, as well as advances in nursing care and understanding of physical activity for the elderly, have become priorities for personnel caring for old people in custodial settings (Medina-Walpole & Katz, 2003).

Continuity of Care is again based on the clinical impact of the loss of functional autonomy. Frailty is a cardinal problem in the care of the elderly: Whether reversible or irreversible, it demands special attention and expertise, the length of treatment can be very prolonged and requires different venues of care, which include both institutional and community services, such as general hospitals, home care (medical and social), and nursing homes.

The community services include community centers, meals on wheels, nursing assistance, and volunteers. All these different aspects of community services should be integrated and coordinated in order to make it easier to move elderly people to and from different venues according to their changing needs. Nursing homes function as the last resort when all the community services fail to maintain the elderly at home.

The concept of the well-being and fitness of the functional independent is also a new area that requires specific professional knowledge.

The *Concept of Prevention* in the third age group is embedded in all the above remarks. Avoidance of functional dependency is a main priority that should be kept in mind by all personnel when caring for the aged (Biderman & Galinsky, 2001).

The following example will illustrate the importance of the coordination of services necessary in offering adequate treatment to the elderly. Consider an aged woman living alone; if she should fall and break her hip, she would receive surgical intervention in a nearby hospital. She would then be transferred to the geriatric department for further medical care and rehabilitation. After two to three weeks, she could return to her home in the care of a nurse aid. At home, she could also receive meals on wheels. If everything goes smoothly and the patient is partially rehabilitated, she may require further rehabilitation and follow-up in an old-age care center in the community. During the time she is at home, she would receive medical care from a primary-care team.

If, however, the patient becomes totally functionally dependent due to the hip fracture, she would probably be referred to a nursing home. While she awaits admittance to a nursing home, the patient's condition may deteriorate, and she may come to require complex nursing care (such as gastric tubes or treatment for pressure sores). In this case, the patient would be transferred to a geriatric hospital.

Usually those different services are provided by different institutions, such as Health Insurance companies, the Ministry of Health, the Ministry of Labor and Welfare, local authorities, and voluntary organizations. All these institutions should be coordinated and working in an interlinked fashion; otherwise, patients can suffer delays, waiting lists, and errors, with the consequent deterioration of the person's condition of health. Obviously, the amount of knowledge and expertise of the professionals involved in these activities are of fundamental importance.

It is thought that 20% of elderly people living in the community suffer from different degrees of functional disability. At the age of 80, at least 50% are affected by some degree of disability (Vita, Terry, Hubert, & Fries, 1998).

Active and Dependent Life Expectancy is another important concept in terms of elderly care (Katz et al., 1983). Quality of life in geriatrics is defined as independence in the ability to perform activities of daily living (Katz, Ford, Moskowitz, Jackson, & Jaffe, 1963). At the age of 65, a person has a life expectancy of 18 years for women and 16 years for men. Studies indicate that at this age, a person will spend at least 7 to 8 years, in a condition called "disability life expectancy," which means that they experience different degrees of functional dependency. At the age of 80 to 85, life expectancy is 7, 8 years most of which will be in a state of disability. The period of time of dependent life expectancy is crucial. At this time, the demand for good care, both medical and social, increases, creating great effort and expense on the part of families, as well as on the part of social and medical services.

SPECIAL CHARACTERISTICS OF MANAGEMENT OF AGED PEOPLE IN THE COMMUNITY

The importance of loss of independence and autonomy within the elderly population has already been emphasized. For purposes of illustration, however, it would be worthwhile at this point to mention several conditions affecting the aged that highlight the importance of special knowledge required from all those involved in the care of the elderly in the community. Most of the following conditions are almost ignored by the classical education of the health professionals.

The Concept of Functional Dependency

The clinical presentation of disease in the elderly is unique. Lack of awareness of this characteristic can cause irreversible damage, therefore the knowledge of these processes and their prevention should be essential to geriatric practice. An understanding of the clinical manifestations of disease in the elderly is based on the interaction of biological changes of aging, multiple pathology, and social factors (Biderman & Galinsky, 2001; Guralnik & Ferrucci, 2003; Williamson, 1996).

The biological changes of aging affect every cell, organ, and body system and their ability to function. Multiple pathologies in the elderly are characterized by the presence of several diseases in one person at the same time. Studies have shown (Williamson, 1996) that people above the age of 65 have three to six diseases, on the average. In addition to the effect of biological and pathological conditions, social factors, such as loneliness, bereavement, retirement, and poverty, also play a major role in determining the health status of the elderly.

The biology of aging, with the multiple pathology and the social factors, is an ongoing, interacting process, which can lead to the loss of ability to perform activities of daily living (ADL) independently. The clinical consequences that emerge with this combination are often completely different from the symptomatology of similar diseases in younger patients.

The *Syndrome of Full Immobility* is a very common medical condition affecting the elderly as a consequence of many diseases interacting at the same time (Bravo, Jimenez-Rojas, Baztan, & Guillen-Llera, 1994). Such a syndrome can become chronic, starting with frailty, then partial dependency, and finally with the person becoming totally bedridden. Other conditions can take an acute course. In many cases, these conditions can be reversible; thus it is crucial that the professional caregivers be aware of the first manifestations of problems. If the first stage is missed by caregivers, the patient can very easily become severely dependent.

There are many causes of immobility. While discussing them in depth is beyond the scope of this chapter, several of the more common problems should be mentioned here. Stroke, hip fractures, or depression, for example, can lead to an elderly patient becoming totally bedridden; on the other hand, proper and timely treatment by well-trained personnel can reverse these conditions and restore the patients to functional independence.

Special consideration should thus be given to those elderly persons living in the community who are in a state of high risk of losing their independence and autonomy. This group includes those who are living in poverty, lonely, homebound, bedridden, recently bereaved, mentally frail, victims of abuse, or have had repeated falls or multiple hospitalizations (Biderman & Galinsky, 2001).

Efforts should be made to identify the people in this group and have them adequately treated by expert professionals using different community services as needed to avoid any further deterioration of health.

The Iceberg Phenomenon is also a very important issue in community care of the aged (Biderman & Galinsky, 2001; Williamson, 1996). Studies have shown that medical professionals in general are educated in the treatment of classical medical problems, such as cardiovascular, respiratory, metabolic (diabetes), or basic neurological problems. They tend, however, to ignore very common problems affecting the elderly, such as functional disturbances, dementia, depression, gait disturbances, postural instability, or polypharmacy. This aspect, known as The Iceberg Phenomenon emphasizes the need for special education in the care of the elderly.

All these examples indicate very clearly that a professional should have special knowledge and skills to properly manage all the needs of elderly people, either in the community, institution, or hospitals.

THE CASE OF ISRAEL: NEW DEMANDS IN THE TRAINING OF PERSONNEL

To illustrate the need for a new trend in the education of personnel to care for the elderly, we shall focus on the State of Israel, where 9.8% of the population are 65 years and older (about 630,000 people), and 4.4% (250,000) are above the age of 75. Life expectancy at birth is 80.61 years for women and 76.71 years for men. By the year 2025, the percentage of elderly in Israel will increase to 12% of the total population. The most relevant of these figures is the expectation of disability in old age, which is 8.3 years for women and 7.11 years for men. This group of elderly people comprises 120,000 persons (15% of the aged). They suffer from different kinds of disabilities that limit them in activities of daily living. The vast majority of these limited people are living in the community; only a small percentage (4%) are living in institutions (Brodsky, Habib, & Mizrahi, 2000; Galinsky, 2002). This group is eligible for services under the Community Long-Term Insurance Law (CLTIL). This is a law that provides comprehensive care to those elderly who are functionally limited and living in the community. This special group of disabled people is of paramount importance for the future planning of education of elder-care professionals.

Over the years, Israel has developed a wide network of services for the elderly that includes both medical and social services working in an interlinked system at the institutional and community levels (Galinsky, 2002). In terms of education and training of personnel, there is a formal track in gerontology, as well as informal courses for nonprofessionals. All Israeli universities have courses in gerontology included in the curricula of tracks leading to careers in social work and sociology, as well as a course on the biology of aging for students working toward careers offered by the Departments of Life Sciences. The universities of

Haifa and Beer-Sheva offer Masters programs in gerontology with possibilities for doctoral degrees. The Masters program of the Faculty of Health Sciences, Ben-Gurion University, has three different tracks of specialization; administrative, clinical, and research. There are also permanent courses for nonprofessionals in the field of gerontology and care of the elderly, which are oriented toward training nurses' aids and volunteers.

The same trend prevails in geriatrics. The four medical schools have mandatory clerkships in geriatric medicine at the undergraduate level. Of particular relevance is the curriculum in geriatrics of the Faculty of Health Sciences, Ben-Gurion University, in which the study of care for the elderly is spread over the entire 6 years of education (Galinsky, 1985). The program starts in the first year, in which observation and communication with older people is taught. Physical examination is taught in the fourth year of medical training. During the fifth year, within the clinical clerkship in primary care, students learn about primary care of the aged. Surgery and anesthesiology for aged patients are taught within the surgery clerkship. In the sixth year, students receive mandatory training in the diseases of old age. Geriatrics is now included in the curricula of nursing schools, as well as in schools of social work and physiotherapy.

Currently, there are sixteen certified geriatrics centers in Israel. The specialty of geriatrics in medicine was established almost twenty years ago. The basic requirements of this specialty are: A board examination in Internal Medicine, or a board in Family Medicine; 2-year fellowship training in a certified geriatric center; and a 2-phase final examination. The requirement for a certified geriatric center is an active department that includes acute, subacute, and rehabilitation care, as well as a long-term care facility. It should be noted that there is no formal requirement for rotation in the community. There are also formal and informal courses for nurses, mainly centralized in hospital and nursing homes. Community care is not considered a priority.

Research in Israel has been predominantly focused on gerontology, but lately, geriatric centers in universities have started different research projects, mainly on clinical and epidemiological issues. The research in nursing care has made a major contribution to the level of care in nursing homes (Globerson, 2001).

The development of gerontological research in Israel can be divided into 4 distinct periods, starting from the establishment of the State of Israel:

1949 to 1959: During the first decade, efforts were guided by the practical national need to establish proper health-care services. Landmark achievements of that period were the establishment of the National Insurance Institute and the introduction of the old age pensions.

1959 to 1969: In this decade, awareness of the need for well-planned research based on an academic approach and critical study design was growing, based upon the socioeconomic and epidemiological data that were collected.

1969 to 1979: The third decade was marked by continuity and expanding research in various disciplines of gerontology (i.e., biology, medicine, and sociobehavioral sciences), as well as applied social research in the care of older people. Israel's role hosting the 10th International Congress of Gerontology in Jerusalem in 1975, reflected the already well-established scientific community focusing on aging, and played an important part in furthering academic activities.

1980 to present: Since 1980, studies in gerontology have expanded in Israel. Numerous academic bodies, either independent or affiliated with universities and research institutes, have played an important role in promoting research and training of professionals. In general, research on aging receives no special priority in Israel.

Lessons from the Israeli Experience

The above description depicts the very thorough approach that Israel has developed for the care of the elderly. This approach includes services, education, and research. Studies indicate, however, that care of the elderly in Israel is characterized by fragmentation, lack of coordination of services, and severe budget restrictions. There is a major disjunction between acute and long-term care. Although these issues are beyond the scope of this chapter, they have an impact on the education and training of personnel. Aside from the bureaucratic obstacles that exist, there is a great discrepancy between the knowledge and skill of the medical professionals involved in the care of the aged in hospitals and nursing homes, and that of primary care teams. Different studies conducted in countries in the western world have reached the same conclusion (Clarfield, Bergman, & Kane, 2001; International Longevity Center, 1999).

There is an urgent need to extend geriatric training to professionals in primary care. The specialization in geriatric medicine does not require an obligation for rotation in the community. Furthermore, there is no mandatory rotation in geriatrics for family medicine trainees. Nurses working in the community are not required to have training in geriatric care; therefore older people living in the community are handled by professionals unskilled in geriatrics.

According to the National Insurance Institute, more than 15% of the elderly population in Israel are eligible for coverage under the Community Long-Term Insurance Law. The great majority of these people are still living in the community. By the year 2010, the number of persons over 80 years old is projected to increase by 48% (more than any other age group), and the projected number of beds in nursing homes will not meet their needs. This disjunction between acute and long-term care will increase the demands of the handicapped elderly in the community and the health system as well (Lubitz et al., 2003). The lack of basic geriatric knowledge on the part of the professionals involved in the care of old people in the community leads to further deterioration of the aged, who are at risk of functional incapacitation.

FINAL REMARKS AND CONCLUSIONS

The education of future professionals is essential to assure good care of elderly people. To cope with this challenge, medical schools should enhance their curricula in geriatric medicine. Postgraduate training in geriatrics should include a rotation in the community, and internships in family and internal medicine should include a rotation in geriatrics. Training of nurses and social workers should evolve in the same way. The last half of the twentieth century saw the development of an enormous body of knowledge about the care of older people. It is time to bring this knowledge to the aid of those who need it most: The aged in our communities.

Disability in later life is a period of expected incapacity to perform activities of daily living in an independent fashion. Thus, the care of elderly people in the community has particular characteristics that demand today's sophisticated knowledge and skills from the professionals who care for them.

In summary, the huge increase of older and elderly people living in the community has changed the old concept of custodial care for the aged—and in particular, for the segment of the population over the age of eighty. Current programs of formal education are not prepared to meet this challenge. Universities at a pregraduate level and postgraduate courses for physicians, nurses, and social workers should be carefully reviewed considering today's shifting attitudes toward the care for the elderly. To do otherwise will adversely affect the quality of life of the elderly in the future.

REFERENCES

Biderman, A., & Galinsky, D. (2001). Preventive geriatric medicine: Reality or fiction? *Israeli Medical Association Journal, 3*, 615-617.

Bravo, G. I., Jimenez-Rojas, C., Baztan, J. J., & Guillen-Llera, F. (1994). The syndrome of immobilization and pressure sores. In E. Anzola, D. Galinsky, F. Morales-Martinez, M. Sanchez-Ayendez, & A. Salas (Eds.), *Care of the aged: Challenge for the 90s* (pp. 159-172). Washington, DC: Pan American Health Organization (PAHO), C.P. 546, (Spanish).

Brodsky, J., Habib, J., & Mizrahi, I. (2000). *Long-term care laws in five developed countries: A review*. Jerusalem, Israel: JDC Brookdale Institute of Gerontology and Human Development.

Clarfield, A. M., Bergman, H., & Kane, R. (2001). Fragmentation of care for frail older people—An international problem; Experience of three countries: Israel, Canada and the United States. *JAGS, 49*, 1714-1721.

Fries, J. F. (2002). Successful ageing—An emerging paradigm of gerontology. *Clinical Geriatric Medicine, 18*, 371-382.

Galinsky, D. (1985). Ten years of experience teaching geriatric medicine. *Israel Journal of Medical Sciences, 21*, 349-353.

Galinsky, D. (1994). Progressive care. In E. Anzola, D. Galinsky, F. Morales-Martinez, M. Sanchez-Ayendez, & A. Salas (Eds.), *Care of the aged: Challenge for the 90s* (pp. 343-351). Washington, DC: Pan American Health Organization (PAHO), C.P. 546, (Spanish).

Galinsky, D. (2002). *Caring for the aged in Israel: Demography, services, manpower and long term care*. New York: The International Longevity Center (Special Report).

Globerson, A. (2001). Biogerontological research in Israel. *Experimental Gerontology, 36*, 3-19.

Guralnik, J. M., & Ferrucci, L. (2003). Demography and epidemiology. In W. R. Hazzard, J. P. Blass, J. B. Halter, J. G. Ouslander, & M. Tinetti (Eds.), *Principles of geriatric medicine and gerontology* (5th ed., pp. 53-75). New York: McGraw-Hill.

Habib, J., & Factor, H. (1993). Services for the elderly: Changing circumstances and strategies. In A. M. Kruger, D. Morley, & A. Shashar (Eds.), *Public services under stress: A Canadian-Israeli policy review* (pp. 154-175). Jerusalem, Israel: The Hebrew University, Magnes Press.

International Longevity Center. (1999). *The consequences of population ageing for society—Workshop report*. New York: Author.

Israel National Institute for Health Policy and Health Services Research. (1999). *Workshop on long term care for the elderly: Organizational and economic aspects*. Tel Aviv, Israel: Author.

Katz, S., Branch, L. G., Branson, M. H., Papsidero, J. A., Beck, J. C., & Greer, D. S. (1983). Active life expectancy. *New England Journal of Medicine, 309*, 1218-1224.

Katz, S., Ford, A. B., Moskowitz, R. W., Jackson, B. A., & Jaffe, M. W. (1963). The index of ADL: A standardized measure of biological and psychosocial function. *Journal of the American Medical Association, 185*, 914-919.

Lubitz, J., Cai, L., Kramarow, E., & Lentzner, H. (2003). Health, life expectancy, and health care expending among the elderly. *New England Journal of Medicine, 349*(11), 1048-1055.

Medina-Walpole, A., & Katz, P. A. (2003). Institutional nursing care. In W. R. Hazzard, J. P. Blass, J. B. Halter, J. G. Ouslander, & M. Tinetti (Eds.), *Principles of geriatric medicine and gerontology* (5th ed., pp. 197-211). New York: McGraw-Hill.

Vita, A. J., Terry, R. B., Hubert, H. B., & Fries, J. F. (1998). Ageing, health risk, and cumulative disability. *New England Journal of Medicine, 338*, 1035-1041.

Williamson, J. D. (1996). Characterization of older adults who attribute functional decrements to "old age." *Journal of the American Geriatric Society, 44*(12), 1429-1434.

SECTION 2

THE ART OF FAMILY CARE

Introduction

JoAnn Damron-Rodriguez

International aging is accompanied by multiple societal changes that influence the family's traditional role of providing care to its members. The chapters in this section on family care in aging societies provide national examples of the way in which these population transitions interact to create individual and policy dilemmas. The dramatic increase in the number of older persons has impacted the demand for family care and the following interrelated societal dynamics challenge the family's ability to perform its caregiving role. Yet it must be recognized that the family, in all its emerging forms, remains the major support system for elders. Research estimates that the family provides the majority, up to 85%, of the care to older persons in the United States (Damron-Rodriguez & Lubben, 2007).

One of the most defining characteristics of an aging society is the concurrent *drop in fertility* and the reduction in child/aged ratio societies, which increases the overall dependency ratio. Although the dependency ratio generally is used in economic calculations of the number of working persons in relationship to nonworking societal members, it is also related to caregiving roles. In aging societies, the relationship between the number of older persons who potentially require care and the number of family members who could care for them is specifically calculated as the parent/child ratio (PSR). The PSR divides those most likely to require assistance, persons over age 80, by those most likely to provide care, adult children age 50 to 64. Worldwide PSRs have been rising dramatically, growing from 8 in 1975 to a projected 41 in 2025(Lubben & Damron-Rodriguez, 2006). Thus, there has been *a rise in the dependent older-adult/child ratio.*

The fewer adult family members are also more likely to be engaged in the labor market. In particular, the traditional caregiving roles of women are challenged by their economic roles. In all developing countries, *women are working outside the home*. In the United States, the percentage of women from 16 years of age and older who are in the labor force has grown from 19% in 1900 to 59% in 2004 (U.S. Department of Labor, 2005). In Israel, labor force participation of women aged 15 and over has also increased from 43% in 1986 to 53% in 2002 (Israel Bureau of Statistics, 2003). Additionally, economic factors also relate to the *dispersion of families* with increasing numbers of younger persons moving to urban areas, leaving the older persons behind in rural areas.

Population ageing and other societal and demographic dynamics have profound impact on the *changing family structure* including:

- Up to four or five generations alive at a time
- Fewer members in each generation
- Increased divorce rate

Overall, families are smaller today but include more generations. For example, in the United States, only 21% of adults had a living grandparent in 1900, whereas 76% of adults currently do (Quadagno, 2005). Similarly, the chances of a 60-year-old adult having at least one parent still living has increased from 8% in 1900 to 44% currently (Quadagno, 2005). Though today's families may be smaller, many families have multiple elders, parents, parents-in-law, stepparents, aunts, and uncles, for whom they may have some level of responsibility.

The rise in the divorce rate in more developed countries has been dramatic and may change relationships of family members to each other. Iecovich (in Section 1) describes the rise in divorce in Israel, leaving women frequently as head of household and needing to be in the labor force. One of the results is being less available for elder care. In the United States, the divorce rate is currently 50% of all marriages as compared with 10% at the end of the nineteenth century. Thus, there is the emergence of step-families and blended families with varying degrees of commitment to elder in-laws.

The three countries written about in this volume have experienced large waves of *immigration resulting in very diverse populations*. This impacts family caregiving in two major ways; first, through the cultural and ethnic difference in filial responsibility and its demonstration and meaning. In Israel, elderly Jews may have been born in multiple countries throughout the world, which translates into a wide variety of values, norms, and roles related to family care. Iecovich (in Section 1) describes elderly Arabs, most of them Moslems, as living more predominantly in extended families than the majority of Israeli families. Household living in nuclear or extended families is one way in which cultural values are enacted, yet economic reasons may also govern living arrangements. Morse and Lau describe not only differences in cultural beliefs, but also myths about the cultural beliefs of non-English-speaking groups in Australia. One myth is that the culturally diverse groups in Australia "look after their own" and that their need for social services is low. Myths misinterpret filial values with the family's ability to enact those values in the face of current demands. Additionally, these myths misinterpret service use with service need.

Second, all societies have groups of persons who have *minority status* and who may be marginalized, having less access to services. U.S. ethnic minorities are at greater risk of economic insecurity, poorer health status, and social isolation in late life as described by Villa and Wallace (2007). Gender and race over the life course is a major reason that older minority women who live alone are the poorest group in the United States (Quadagno, 2005). Morse and Lau describe challenges in accessing needed services by aboriginal and Torres Strait Islanders.

In addition to cultural and ethnic diversity, there are major differences related to elder-care needs and responsibilities based on *gender*. Morse and Lau call attention to women's greater longevity and disability over time than their male counterparts. In the United States, Australia, and Israel, women provide the majority of unpaid elder care (Damron-Rodriguez & Lubben, 2007). Morse and Lau describe women's differential cost of care to their physical and emotional health as well as socioeconomic status. Raveis also describes the burden of care for the family, including financial costs. Family care is a gendered issue that has become increasingly burdensome for contemporary women, though not without costs to the men in the family.

The epidemiological transition of aging societies is a move *from acute to chronic illness* as the major cause of death and disability. Developed countries have experienced the tremendous progress of medicine in this century, including the introduction of antibiotics that allow persons to survive infectious diseases and other acute illnesses. Although persons have greater life expectation, they also are more apt to have more chronic illnesses as well as varying levels of disability. Thus, though age, chronic illness, and disability are not synonymous; they are associated, and they all relate to the demand for elder care by family members as well as the formal delivery system.

Two chapters in this section describe two major conditions that impact individuals over time and require ongoing family support and care. Raveis presents the stages and challenges of caring for older persons with various forms of cancer. Though not exclusively a disease of the old, Dr. Raveis reports that in the United States, 60% of the new cancers and 70% of the deaths are among persons aged 65 and over, and this figure will double in the next 20 years. Our success in medical diagnosis and treatment means that cancers are diagnosed earlier and treated more aggressively. Raveis describes the advancement of biomedical treatment for cancer as bringing with it complex care dilemmas, including a complex relationship between cancer and the aging process, co-morbidities, and iatrogenic responses to treatment. She notes that the use of technology such as infusion pumps and access technology in the home present additional care challenges. This means that older persons and their families are living with the effects of cancer and its treatment in combination with age for extended periods of time. Aberdeen describes caregiving for persons with dementia and its impact on family carers. For this disease, treatment is not aggressive, but the treatment of other illnesses may be complicated by the dementia.

In family care of both conditions, the trajectory of care for the family is emphasized. Raveis warns that the end of treatment is not the end of care. The time period of care for persons with cancer includes multiple waiting periods, which in itself is emotionally draining on families. Aberdeen also describes a series of transitions and emotional turning points in the trajectory of care for persons with dementia. Litwak (1985) has provided a useful conceptual framework for understanding the nature of family care as it relates to the medical regimen. Family care is a naturally occurring system that can be distinguished by continuity over time as well as strong emotional and symbolic ties. Family and other informal caregivers are generally not "on the clock" as are formal caregivers. Time commitment of family caregivers requires that they respond to unpredictable demands at all hours of the day or night.

Aberdeen relates the series of emotional losses that occur over time. She describes these as a process of letting go, including the final letting go unto death of the older person. Existential issues related to end of life are core aspects of family caregiving as described by Aberdeen. Raveis describes the psychological distress than family caregivers endure as well. However, all the authors acknowledge the value carers find in the meaning and spiritual aspects of this life task.

Raveis, Aberdeen, and Morse and Lau, all relate the personal challenges of family care to the need for societal responses. Raveis suggests that the increased emphasis on community-based care present a demand for the family to do more. Aberdeen targets the point where the family caregiver must transfer care to professionals through placement in a long-term-care facility. Morse and Lau describe the Australian experience with providing community-based care supports. The Hospital in the Home alternative has increased significantly in Australia and offers a viable option with its own set of challenges. Damron-Rodriguez and Lubben (2007) describe U.S. community-based health care and its fiscal and policy history. Given the issues of diversity, access remains a challenge for these services as Morse and Lau emphasize.

Around the world, a large majority of older persons have family, interact with them frequently, and receive their primary support from family. In the United States, only 7% of persons over 65 enter a nursing home from the community in any 2-year period (Lubben & Damron-Rodriguez, 2006). The availability of familial care remains the single most explanatory variable in differentiating persons who do not require extensive formal care arrangements from those that do. Morse and Lau report that in Australia one in three adults is a caregiver. Wives, daughters, and husbands who themselves are older persons are carers for most elders. The Australian government estimates that family carers provide over $16 billion worth of care annually. Medical advancements and the shift from the hospital to the community chronicled by Raveis mean that the family is being increasingly prevailed upon to attend to a majority of the health and personal needs of older persons. The multiple societal changes impacting the families' ability to care in an aging society require an equally strong societal response, or the emphasis on family responsibility will be societal irresponsibility.

REFERENCES

Damron-Rodriguez, J. A., & Lubben, J. (2007). Family and community health care for older persons. In S. Carmel, F. Torres-Gil, & C. Morse (Eds.), *Lessons on Aging from Three Nations: Vol. I. The Art of Aging Well.* New York: Baywood.

Israel Bureau of Statistics. (2003). *Yearbook of statistics in Israel* (p. 54). Jerusalem, Israel: Israel Bureau of Statistics (in Hebrew).

Lubben, J., & Damron-Rodriguez, J. A. (2006). World population ageing. In B. Berkman, & S. D'Ambruoso (Eds.), *Oxford handbook of social work in health and ageing.* Oxford, UK: Oxford University Press.

Litwak, E. (1985). *Helping the elderly.* New York: The Guilford Press.

Quadagno, J. (2005). *Ageing in the life course: An introduction to social gerontology* (3rd ed.). New York: McGraw Hill.

U.S. Department of Labor (2005). *Women in the labor force: A databook.* http://www.bls/data.booknews2005.pdf. Retrieved June 8, 2006.

Villa, V. M., & Wallace, S. P. (2007). Diversity and ageing: Implications for ageing policy. In S. Carmel, F. Torres-Gil, & C. Morse (Eds.), *Lessons on Aging from Three Nations: Vol. I. The Art of Aging Well.* New York: Baywood.

CHAPTER 5

In Care and On Call: The Endangered System of Australian Family-Based Caregiving

Carol A. Morse and Rosalind Lau

Family-based caregiving in Australia is provided by over 2.3 million people of all ages, marital/partner status, socioeconomic status, gender, those with and without children, in waged employment, or unemployed (Carers Australia, 2002). Of these, only about 11% *identify* themselves as a carer, while an additional 27.6% fit the definition but do not declare themselves as caregivers. In the Carers' Australia national survey (2002) carried out across six States, but excluding the two Territories, the prevalence of self-identified adult carers aged 18 and older ranged from a low of 3.4% to a high of 12.8%, but the prevalence of *undeclared* carers was from 22.3% in Queensland to 37.3% in Victoria. Taking into account both declared and undeclared caregivers reveals approximately one in three of the adult Australian population provides some sort of care or assistance to a family member or friend, whether that care is acknowledged or not.

Importantly, caregiving or receiving mainly involves an older person, as most caregivers at the present time are aged over 55 years, and most care recipients are over 65 years. In the *Survey of Disability, Ageing and Carers* carried out in 1998 (Australian Bureau of Statistics, 1999), 39% of the 2.1 million people canvassed required some occasional assistance of low intensity up to daily and profound in extent. Without the received support, many of these people would have been unable to remain in their home as community dwellers. Assistance tends to be sought for general property maintenance, transport, and housework at the minimal end of the continuum, while at the high demand end, daily personal care and assistance with communication needs dominate.

Formal care assistance is provided by three main sources: government agencies, private nonprofit organizations (which receive government funding) and for-profit organizations. Needs assessment is undertaken that categorizes the individual's core activity restrictions (CAR) in relation to the level of ability to provide self-care in dressing, personal hygiene, feeding, mobility and communication deficits, dependency evaluation, means testing, and consideration of the degree of help required, including an estimation of the required frequency. Activity restrictions that are also considered include the need for transport, general and specific health care, housework, meals preparation, paperwork, and property maintenance. Not infrequently, gaps occur between the care need expressed and the time taken and level to which the need is eventually met.

Of these core and other activity restrictions, the prevalence of people needing assistance with at least one activity rises with age from around 28% in the 65–69 years group to 43% in the 70–79 group to over 77% in the 80+ age group (Family & Community Development Committee, 1997). A key issue is that these increases over time directly reflect the rising numbers of aging women who need help and support, due to women's greater longevity and the evidence of their greater disability over time compared with men of the same age (Australian Institute of Health & Welfare, 2002). Thus, although caregiving is provided across a wide age range from teenagers to nonagenarians, the *dependency index*, defined as impairment and/or disability and activity restrictions, is most frequently reported by around 20% of the older population (i.e., by men and women aged over 65 years, a group increasingly dominated by women alone as age increases).

In recent years, in spite of some high profile reports emerging from the comprehensive *Victorian Carers Study* (Schofield, Herrman, & Bloch, 1997), many people when asked are unable to provide a clear consensus of from whom or where they can seek information or support for beginning or maintaining the caregiving role (Carers Australia, 2002). The only sources that are readily reported by more than one in five people are a doctor or General Practitioner (23%) or a family member or friend (20.4%). Only very few referred to expectations of approaching their Local Council or a Carers Association, and most of these respondents were already carers rather than noncarers. This chapter examines what is known from the Australian context about caregiving provided by co-resident family or friends to care recipients who are typically aged over 65. The burden of caregiving is identified as largely a gendered issue that is predominantly entrapping women—the daughters, mothers, or partners of people needing regular care across a wide spectrum of activities. The limitations of formal services are identified, and the underacknowledged or resourced provisions for minority segments of the population are discussed. Future policy directions are proposed that could alleviate the various burdens currently experienced by those who devote their lives to their dependents, who simultaneously relieve the government's duty of care for its less robust members of society.

THE PROMOTION OF FAMILY-BASED CAREGIVING AS "COMMUNITY CARE"

Community-based caregiving is not a new initiative, even though there is now greater public awareness of the need for individuals to remain in their own homes for as long as possible. There is also a stated preference by many older people not to enter an institution. These twin issues, home-based support and residential living with/without care supports, have been known in Australia for more than a century. "Indoor relief" referred to the large workhouse institutions where the frail and infirm with no independent means of support and care went to live out their days. "Outdoor relief" referred to support provided to maintain people in their own homes.

From the 1950s to the 1990s, government grants were provided initially as a modest subsidy for domiciliary nursing care, usually by the Royal District Nursing Services, to a gradual expansion that included the delivery of prepared meals for up to five days a week (Meals-on-Wheels), the provision of a few hours of home cleaning, and nursing care for personal needs, or specialist management of medications, wound care, and other forms of nursing practice for the chronically ill or disabled. In the 1990s, added to these provisions was the introduction of Hospital-in-the-Home (HITH) services for posthospital care following acute medical or surgical treatments, palliative care for the chronically or terminally ill, neonatal care for premature infants requiring tube feeding, and assistance to mothers following multiple births.

Since the late 1990s, the provision of HITH services has increased significantly with more than 42 programs operating in Victoria alone (Grindlay, Santamaria, & Kitt, 2000). The provision of expert nursing practices delivered in patients' homes has proven to be not just a unidirectional *benefit*, which patients report satisfaction with and preference for. There have also been difficulties experienced by nurses seeking to implement routine care that differed from the expectations of family members (Coffman, 1997); practice safety issues have received limited attention; procedural omissions have been identified in some programs (Grindlay et al., 2000); and cost effectiveness of this service has also been inadequately demonstrated. An aspect of paramount importance in HITH services is that families receive their relative back into the home at a stage in treatment that previously required recuperating within the hospital setting. Now, the patient is merely at an early stage of recovery, so even though at-home expert nursing is being provided, for brief periods only, the need for additional informal care is also required. Thus, the HITH program is another example of cost and burden shifting from the professional formal service to the informal care provider. As yet, a recent evaluation (Sheppard & Iliffe, 2004) of hospital care at home compared with inpatient care has not been able to identify which particular aspects of the programs shaped the patients' preference for, and satisfaction with, this formal service provided in the informal family setting.

In spite of the expansion in community care provisions, Fine and Thompson (1995) have remarked on the greater provisions by the Government to the residential nursing-home industry. Since the early 1990s, this industry has become dominated by private for-profit providers. Yet the Commonwealth government has claimed its strategies are to provide a "meld of balanced care" option (Department of Health, Housing & Community Services, 1991), so that people can remain in their own home and receive formal services that are matched to the care recipient's needs. The aspect that is overlooked and not spelled out clearly is the unavoidable requirement for someone in the home to be regularly available for the care recipient, who may be a frail aged person, a developmentally delayed child or adult, a person with a psychiatric or emotional disorder, or suffering a long-term chronic or terminal illness. Frequently, a care recipient has multiple conditions, or more than one family member or friend is in need of care simultaneously within the same family unit. Thus, although community-based care provisions have been framed in terms of *increased choices* for those in need, and different models of options are available, the popular perception and experience of those caught up in the system is frequently of dichotomous alternatives, rather than a series of blended provisions of differing proportions (Morse & Messimeri-Kianidis, 2002).

Feminist critiques (e.g., Moore, 1989) have referred to such community-care policies as regressive, patriarchal shifts of responsibility from the State to the family. In particular, the shifts are to the women of the family, as the burdens of home-based care fall largely to the daughters (of aging parents), mothers (of chronically sick or developmentally delayed offspring) and wives (of sick or frail partners).

While Fine and Thompson (1995) have commented on the fragmentation of many community support services, the low use of services is not due only to their insufficiency. Help-seeking behaviors appear to proceed in the form of *hierarchical compensation* (Cantor, 1989). This refers to the expressed and demonstrated preference for family or a friend caregiving source, where family and familiar ties exemplify the public normative consensus. Only when family or friend sources are absent, insufficient, or unable to respond is there a seeking out of formal care services to replace or supplement family-based caregiving. Alternatively, Kendig (1986) and Litwak (1985) have explained usage or avoidance of services according to the *complementarity hypothesis,* which explains help seeking as selective, where informal care is accepted for some unique provisions, and some formal services are sought to augment or extend family-based caregiving. These family values and normative behaviors are also shaped by cultural traditions and expectations of *intrafamilial reciprocity* (Feldman & Seedsman, 2003), which extends especially across generational boundaries and within marital and parental duties of care.

FAMILY-BASED CAREGIVING AS A GENDERED ISSUE

From research studies carried out in different societies, within dominant and minority cultures, the same profile of caregivers emerges. Women are the majority of the caregivers, providing informal and largely unpaid care, who are considerably affected by community care policies. The given figures of women as caregivers in several studies typically constitute 78–80% (Department of Human Services, 1997; Herrman & Schofield, 1993; Morse & Messimeri-Kianidis, 1996, 2002; Schofield et al., 1997). Men reportedly provide care predominantly for their elder spouse (Family and Community Development Committee, 1997), for psychiatrically ill sons rather than daughters (Morse & Messimeri-Kianidis, 2002) and for same sex partners suffering HIV/AIDS (Pakenham, Dadds, & Lennon, 2002).

In committing themselves to long-term caregiving, women and men experience different socioeconomic contexts, societal expectations, actual burdens, and care tasks undertaken. Women give many more hours per week to care tasks; they undertake more demanding forms of care; the range of tasks performed is broader therefore multiple; and they more often care simultaneously for more than one care recipient (Schofield et al., 1997; Morris, 2001). Inevitably, the caregiving roles and duties interfere with and skew the carer's lifestyle and impacts on all other members in the caregiver's immediate family, especially on children and partner. Although women are regarded as having larger social networks than men, carers report that when caregiving occupies daily hours, their extended family and friendship networks tend to shrink, leaving them to go it alone outside of their own family or, if single, to remain largely isolated (Family & Community Development Committee, 1997). Deterrents to the provision of regular assistance from others are usually attributed to geographic distance, paid work, and others' own family responsibilities.

Negative effects on the health of caregivers are apparent, especially where carers deny their own health needs, fail to make or keep appointments, to have regular preventive health checks, or to undergo minor and major treatments. This self-neglect is directly attributed to the inability to leave the care recipient unattended, even for short periods of time where no alternative attendant is available and also, due to the financial costs that are ill-afforded when the carer's income support is low. Many studies have reported that caregivers tend to report their physical health is no worse than others' of their age and sex without caregiving duties (e.g., Family & Community Development Committee, 1997; Herrman & Schofield, 1993; Lee, 2001; Morse & Messimeri-Kianidis, 2002). However, these same studies attest to the worse emotional health and well-being that directly emanates from the caregiving lifestyle that imposes pressured demands, unrelenting repetitive duties, feelings of entrapment, with no relief or rescue in sight until either the carer themselves or the care recipient is institutionalized or dies. Carers at many ages, especially those of young adulthood, perceive their own life as wasting away and their caregiving obstructs them from recreational pursuits, employment, and fulfilling personal relationships. Caregiving is not, however, an unremitting and profoundly negative experience for all (Family & Community Development Committee, 1997). A high proportion of men and women report their experiences provide particular spiritual meanings to their lives. Among these, the perceived severity of their caregiving duties is moderate in intensity and manageable, and they are more likely to be caring for someone able to assist to some extent in self-care, feeding, mobility, and communication.

Why do so many more women than men provide home-based care? Caregiving is generally perceived by society as the logical extension of a woman's traditional female gender roles—that caregiving is women's work. Women have always provided unpaid personal care for elderly parents, developmentally delayed or seriously ill children, and for those of all ages with short- or long-term illness and disability. In both the Victorian Carers Study (Schofield et al., 1997) and the Victorian Australian-Greek Study (Morse & Messimeri-Kianidis, 1996), around 20% of carers were men, providing care for a family member or friend who had a smaller range of disability, which also allowed for some competent abilities in self-care and self-help by the care recipient. Men's care contributions were more likely to involve providing home maintenance, gardening, instrumental tasks of chauffeuring, shopping, banking, that is, to perform activities that are of lesser frequency even though on a regular basis. By comparison, women more often provided daily and inflexible care duties, which were more extensive, complex, psychologically demanding, and physically heavy. Where little or no extended family assistance is available, women carers also attempt/are required to attend to home maintenance, transportation, shopping and financial management as well. What is different today from earlier decades of outdoor relief is the range of care duties needed to be provided at home emanating from government policies that discharge people earlier from formal services (e.g., hospitals).

ENHANCING ACCESSIBILITY AND ROLE ACCEPTABILITY

For the present and future, the provision of adequate funding for home-based and community-care support services is paramount. Over the past seven years, the Australian Federal and State governments have each provided extra funding to support family-based carers. For the years 1998 to 2001, the Federal government provided increased general funding of over $7 million and an additional $36.7 million to establish a National Respite for Carers Program.

At the State level from 1997, Carer Support Workers were introduced to provide regional support systems for caregiving families, information materials, access, and referral to coordinated services. Various forms of respite were made available providing for care recipients in out-of-home day centers, and adult day-activity support services for planned and emergency needs. In-home and flexible respite options are available for caregivers to have short term breaks during the day or evening, through volunteers providing assistance or allowing for care recipients to be taken shopping, for appointments or socializing.

In Victoria, the Carers Support Program and Carers Support Workers are now co-located, and $90 million per annum has been allocated to this Statewide initiative. The National Carers Australia organization, with central offices in every major capital city, is now funded to provide counseling programs for carers and to co-ordinate the National Carers Resource Centre. The Victorian Government is committed to interdepartmental carers policy establishment, but to date, and including the most recent budget in May 2004, has allocated no particular funds to effect this. Other States have sought to establish interdepartmental policy to varying levels of success and in different ways, but these various approaches do not provide opportunity for making meaningful comparisons.

Over the past decade, while increased recognition has been accorded to carers, society's attitudes are slow to show lasting change. In considering future caregiving in Australia, it is essential to recognize the particular needs of minority groups as well as mainstream communities. These minority groups include indigenous Aboriginal and Torres Strait Islanders (ATSI), migrants and refugees from non-English-speaking backgrounds (NESBs), and people with lifelong disabilities who are aging.

ABORIGINAL AND TORRES STRAIT ISLANDERS (ATSI)

The indigenous population of Australia comprises around 2.15% of the total 19.6 million and has a much younger age profile than the main group. Among ATSI people life expectancy at birth is up to 20 years shorter, so access to care of their older people occurs at a much younger actual age of around 45 years. Around 12% of indigenous people are defined as, or self-identify as carers and may be male or female, a parent, partner, sibling, grandparent, friend, neighbor, or young teenager or child of the care recipient. Care recipients are relatives or friends of the carers, with a disability, chronic physical or mental illness, or frail aged. Ninety percent of all caregiving is informal, and limited use is made of specific services. This low use of formal caregiving is attributed to problems of access and cultural inappropriateness of services perceived to reflect only dominant Australian values. ATSI carers experience the same range of physical and emotional burdens from their role as do white Australians, including social isolation and loneliness, changed family relations, and a profound sense of loss and grief (New South Wales Carers Association, 1998).

Following the International Year of Indigenous Peoples in 1993, an ATSI Carers Program, The Ngara Support Service, was established in 1995 in New South Wales, with an appointed Development Officer. Over time, other State Governments and the Federal Government gradually included ATSI-specific health- and community-care policies and services for this and other needy minorities.

In 1998, in South Australia, the North and West Metropolitan Adelaide Carer Respite Centre met with Aboriginal Health Workers to foster partnerships in order to improve access to services for Aboriginal carers (Lewis, 1999). A high level of unawareness of available respite services prevailed or, where known, a significant amount of disenchantment was apparent due to the perceived lack of cultural sensitivity and inappropriateness of those services. A series of workshops followed between the Respite Centre staff, Aboriginal Health Workers, Carers, and Aboriginal Elders resulting in consciousness raising that identified particular fears among ATSI and nonindigenous workers alike, which raised barriers to the use of care services. Fears emanated from not being understood or accepted, being taken over and disempowered, being exploited and labeled. From these group discussions, a shared vision emerged and a commitment to continue the dialogue and interactions and, with support from services from both sectors of the community, a Nunga Carers Support Group was formed.

In proposing a different model for ATSI communities, it is important that self-determination and *community* empowerment will be central themes that drive any service provision model. This must include the sensitive recognition that Aboriginal communities have a long, problematic, and dependent relationship with mainstream services. There is the legacy of past and recent experiences of "welfare" that was associated with the removal of children for "care" referred to as the "stolen generation," resulting in the widespread pain from community and individual dispossession dating back many decades. An accepted partnership between the Aboriginal and mainstream services is clearly essential and needs to be long-term to effect any meaningful changes (Rees & Brown, 1999).

Rees and Brown (1999) have outlined the distinct features of culturally empowering services that require the appropriate use of language, the establishment of trust by engaging an accepted intermediary or mentor, the development of indigenous-specific protocols for community networking, family controlled provisions, and culturally appropriate services that facilitate support from the community, not just from the recipient's family. These particular aspects are in addition to the usual carer's needs for a service to be outcomes focused, regular, reliable, appropriate to needs, and adaptive to changing needs over time. The clear preference for all ill, disabled, and frail aged people of any culture is for assistance to enable individuals to age in place, by remaining in their own homes for as long as is practicable. The Aboriginal and Torres Strait Islander care recipients and their carers are no exception.

NON-ENGLISH-SPEAKING MIGRANTS

For a considerable period, there have been several prevailing myths regarding the health-care needs of peoples from non-English speaking culturally diverse communities. One is that migrant groups are strongly cohesive and always ready to provide supportive roles and assistance through extended family networks and links, that they "look after their own" to a greater degree than do white Anglo cultures. A second myth refers to the belief that many migrants expect to return to their native countries in the future, so their commitment to a host country is short-term and circumscribed, and they make little financial provision for their later years. The frequently observed low use of formal services by migrant groups leads to a third myth that their need is low compared to that of the dominant host community. These notions have been firmly rejected through studies carried out over the past 15 years (e.g., Ebrahim, 1989; McCallum & Gelfand, 1990; Morse & Messimeri-Kianidis, 1996), which have revealed that migrant families are not more blessed by close family networks to take care of their needs; that their need for culturally sensitive services is as great as those of the mainstream community; that in many cases family-based caregiving is also an unremitting physical and emotional burden carried out alone by an immediate family member. These mythic ideas have been interpreted as the State's powerful means of ignoring the real needs of migrant people and especially of couples or single people (Ebrahim, 1989).

From the last Census in 2001 (Australian Bureau of Statistics, 2004) Australia has over 204 different ethnic groups, 26% of whom were born overseas, with over 80% of older people from non-English-speaking European countries, who represent 14% of all people of 70 years and older. The leading five birthplaces of people aged over 65 years are Greece, Italy, Poland, the Netherlands, and the former Yugoslavia, reflecting the large migration wave post-Second World War (Family & Community Development Committee, 1997). While studies have often presented findings that attest to the negative aspects of aging in migrant groups, many communities accord their older people with high status and respect. While within-group differences reveal the considerable heterogeneity of the people, some fundamental aspects transcend culture-specific differences. These are the need for secure income in later years, appropriate housing, affordable and accessible health services, and continued access to social support whether from family or community. Thus, it is impossible and not useful to make generalizations about the support needs of migrant people.

In terms of family-based care and support, it is particularly likely for people from Southeast Asian countries to live in co-resident establishments and more usual for Southern European families to co-reside across generations than it is for the dominant Anglo-Australian community. Even so, this family-establishment pattern does not preclude the need for formal services, although the indications are that such provisions are accessed to a considerably low level.

During the past decade, a range of studies has shown that people from migrant groups had little knowledge or understanding of Home and Community Care (HACC) services or how to reach these. When asked, the common reasons given attest to the perceived low cultural sensitivity and appropriateness of the mainstream services available. This picture has changed over the intervening years where older migrants aged over 65 are more likely to use *home*-based services, although less likely to use residential services unless these are culture specific. Even then, the uptake of residential-care services by the migrant aged is considerably below that used by Anglo-Australians (8.6% vs. 32%) as is home help (15% vs. 26%) and home delivered meals (6.5% vs. 14.5%), although this latter picture is changing as increasing numbers of Local Councils and community-support groups provide culturally appropriate foods.

Several models of residential support and care have emerged that include the provision of general facilities for multiple ethnicities, ethno-specific facilities, multicultural hostels and nursing homes, and three models based on partnership, co-location or clustering. In 1997 in Victoria, ethno-specific facilities were providing 557 residential beds and 1225 hostel beds, and these numbers have continued to grow. In these establishments, attention has also been given to appointing bilingual staff, culture-relevant foods, craft and leisure activities, and opportunities for relevant religious observance.

In family-based care, this role has typically been taken up by the most available person, generally women with limited levels of formal education and low income resources. While the physical health of these carers has been reported as robust as that of nonmigrants, it is their mental health and well-being that is more at risk, even before the caregiving role is commenced (Minas, Silove, & Kunst, 1997). This morbidity profile is attributed to the lack of bilingual health professionals and interpreters, poorer quality of mental services available to migrants in terms of high error rates in dementia diagnosis, inappropriate treatments involving drugs, and ECT with low provision of psychotherapies and occupational therapies.

Although it is difficult to generalize about migrant peoples from so many different cultures and their health needs as they age, there are as many similarities as differences when comparisons are made between migrants' experiences and those of the mainstream Anglo-Australian community. Over the past ten years, the situation has changed, especially for the longer-established migrant groups as their members become more accustomed to seeking help and services that are available and as services providers become more sensitive and responsive to particular needs and expectations of the cultural groups. With the advent of additional migrant groups into Australia, the lessons learned already can be adapted to provide the best fit with the newer cultures' needs and expectations. A key issue that will require consideration is that younger family members of migrant groups are enjoying higher levels of education and training, and the women of these cultures are not so willing or available to provide the long-term caregiving that earlier generations, who are now the older age groups, have done.

PEOPLE WITH LIFELONG DISABILITIES

As increased life expectancy is experienced by growing numbers of aging Australians through the demographic bulge of the baby-boomer generation, so too will the people with a lifelong intellectual or physical disability increase in numbers over the same time span. The number of older people with a lifelong disability is predicted to increase by 20% to the year 2010 (Ashman, Suttie, & Bramley, 1993), posing challenges to both the aged-care and disability sectors. Key issues refer to the older carers predeceasing their middle-aged and aging offspring with disabilities, uncertainty regarding what care services will be required, what might be the specific needs of this group, and which departmental sector should assume responsibility for them (Bigby, 2002).

There is a high correlation of a shorter lifespan in those people with developmental delay, the numbers reaching above 80 years are significantly fewer compared with the general population (7.6% vs. 20%) and nationally, they comprise just 0.7% of the total Australian population (Ashman et al., 1993). Many people with a lifelong intellectual disability will have had limited prior experience of independence, paid employment, or strong social networks and family life.

A pressing policy requirement is whether people with lifelong disabilities would have their needs met by the aged-care or disability sector and, if services are provided on an individualized basis, whether it matters which policy department responds. In reality, it is not uncommon for both divisions to fall short on services provision unless there is also a coordinating service bringing the two together. This is a role that could be provided by the Carers Support Service. However, aged care services are generally targeting the carer and the family as the beneficiaries, so as the older person with a disability may have outlived their carer, the service provision may not reach them.

Importantly, major differences exist between the provision of aged-care and disability services. The former is the responsibility of the Federal government, with shared funding between the central and State governments generally made available to people over 70. The disability services, policy, and directions are the responsibility of the States and applied to persons 55 and over. The aged-care system is primarily concerned with providing residential and community supports for the frail aged with increasingly higher dependency needs, including dementia sufferers. Also, many aged people have at least some personal finances and are less likely to be totally dependent on the public purse.

Conversely, aged people with disabilities are highly unlikely to have many financial assets, except for a minority who may inherit parental assets. Existing disability supports are more directed toward the development of usable skills in younger age groups and do not provide a primary focus on simple daily living support, social, or leisure opportunities. Supported accommodation for people with disabilities is created around the group home model primarily to cater to the younger middle-aged adult. When a crisis of care is triggered, swift reactive decisions are often made to move a resident to a more restricted level of accommodation, which often results in the provision of less than optimal conditions and surroundings. Whether these settings can adapt to the changing needs as people age and outlive any family member remains to be seen.

To make appropriate provisions for this minority group of Australia's population, the development and implementation of new services are required. Governments to date have given at most, lip service to cross-sectoral and interdepartmental initiatives while no dedicated monetary allocations have been made up to, and including, the most recent Budget. It is imperative for one sector to take the leading role in care provision for this minority group, and the most likely candidate could be the disability sector. The immediate tasks are to confirm government funding for new initiatives, seek ways to overcome obstacles to access, and ensure that usual retirement activities and aged-care services are also available to older disabled people (Bigby, 2002). It is apparent from the international literature that successful initiatives in this area have appeared in the United States (Janicki, Dalton, Henderson, & Davidson, 1999) directly due to benefits from mandatory cross-sectoral planning and policy developments. Similar mechanisms can be developed in Australia at regional and State levels, and these are needed now. Of note is the significant absence of any statement in the Victorian Government's large report *Inquiry into Planning for Positive Ageing* (Family & Community Development Committee, 1997) about the provisions for and future needs of the aging people with lifelong disabilities. Their total invisibility in this otherwise comprehensive document must be addressed now.

FUTURE PROVISIONS AND RECOMMENDATIONS

From the growing research literature on family-based caregiving that has emerged during the past 15 years, some general policy implications have been gradually established. These include the recognition of the need to improve and expand services, address negative societal attitudes toward caregivers, enhance the recognition of and value of the carer's role and contributions, transform the inequalities in caregiving (personal, social, financial), create better home and community care systems, and alleviate the immediate and long-term burdens of informal caregiving, where that is the main or sole form or the minor and additional source to formal services. While considerable ground has been covered, there is much still to be achieved. This is especially the case in responding to and providing for people from minority groups of Aboriginal and

Torres Strait Islanders, addressing the needs of Australia's multiple ethnicities, and preparing now for effective care and support provision for the emerging group of people with lifelong disabilities as this group ages and outlives their usual care providers.

All considerations for the future must embrace the gendered nature of family-based care that has maintained countless thousands of dependent care recipients long term in a range of unaided ways. As the baby boomers age and retire from paid employment, it is highly likely they will not be so ready to assume the emotional and physical labors of family-based care that other generations have provided. As more migrant younger women gain formal education and enter the paid workforce, they will not be so available to provide family-based care as was the case in earlier generations unless there is adequate funding for home and community care, support, and services. Of critical importance is the expressed demand for more affordable and flexible respite opportunities both for short-term and long-term periods and due recognition and acceptance from employers for workplace policies that allow for caregiving duties to be met.

The Australian Government has started to recognize and respond to the need for counseling services for caregivers and recipients. What is also needed is particular training for informal caregivers in the proper and effective management of necessary duties in order to minimize physical and psychological strains. There is still the need for many health professionals and the general public to learn to "see" and "hear" caregivers and their needs and to accord due respect for the tasks undertaken. Governments must also provide proper recognition of the load carried by informal carers and the contributions they make to the relief of the public purse. This recognition should be in the form of financial compensation through tax relief, income support, and indexed pension benefits to eliminate the near-poverty levels that are not uncommon among long-term carers unable to earn an income or lay down superannuation funds for the future. In Canada, Morris (2002) has called for a total gender-based analysis of all current and proposed policies, programs, and legislation in order that sound, evidence-based provisions can be made that will inform how women and men are affected. The situation for Australian home-based carers is very similar. Applied to these directions for policy is the simultaneous recognition of the remaining research gaps for the future. Data are needed on the experiences and perspectives of indigenous and migrant women and men carers, those with homosexual orientation as well as the heterosexual population, people with functional limitations across the lifespan who are caregivers and care recipients simultaneously, comparing the effects and strains of voluntary versus imposed caregiving, and the effects on carers from unexpected role reversal imposed through caregiving. Through these inquiries, many of the past and current inequalities that exist for women and men carers can certainly be improved and perhaps overcome.

REFERENCES

Australian Bureau of Statistics. (1999). *Disability, ageing and carers: Summary of findings, Australia, 1998*. Catalogue No. 4430.0. Canberra, Australia: Author.

Australian Bureau of Statistics. (2004). Demography, Australia, 2004, Final. Catalogue No. 3311.0.55.001. Canberra, Australia.

Ashman, A., Suttie, J., & Bramley, J. (1993). *Older Australians with an intellectual disability*. A report to the Department of Health, Housing and Community Services. Brisbane, Australia: Queensland University.

Australian Institute of Health & Welfare. (2002). *Older Australia at a glance, 2002* (3rd ed., pp. 40-45). Catalogue No. AGE 25. Canberra, Australia: Author.

Bigby, C. (2002). Ageing people with a lifelong disability: Challenges for the aged care and disability sectors. *Journal of Intellectual and Developmental Disabilities, 27*(4), 231-241.

Cantor, M. (1989). Social care: Family and community support systems. *Annals of the American Academy of Policy & Social Science, 503*, 99-112.

Carers Australia. (2002). *Final report on a research study on carers' and the public's attitudes to carers*. Sydney, Australia: Author.

Coffman, S. (1997). Home care nurses as strangers in the family. *Western Journal of Nursing Research, 19*, 82-96.

Department of Health, Housing & Community Services. (1991). *Aged care reform strategy: Mid term review*. Canberra, Australia: Australian Government Publishing Service.

Department of Human Services. (1997). *Victoria's mental health services: Tailoring services to meet the needs of women*. Australia: Aged Community and Mental Health Division.

Ebrahim, S. (1989). Health and ageing in ethnic minorities. In K. Morgan (Ed.), *Gerontology: Responding to an ageing society* (pp. 50-63). London, UK: Jessica Kingsley Publishing.

Family & Community Development Committee. (1997). *Inquiry into planning for positive ageing* (pp. 207-233). National Library of Australia: Victorian Government Printing.

Feldman, S., & Seedsman, T. (2004). Ageing within the family: Connections, contributions and identities of older Australians. In M. Poole (Ed), *Sociology of ageing*. Sydney, Australia: Allen and Unwin.

Fine, M., & Thompson, C. (1995). *Three years at home: The final report of the longitudinal study of Community Support Services and their users*. Sydney, Australia: The University of NSW Press.

Grindlay, A., Santamaria, N., & Kitt, S. (2000). Hospital in the home: Nurses safety-exposure to risk and evaluation of organizational policy. *Australian Journal of Advanced Nursing, 17*(3), 6-12.

Herrman, H., & Schofield, H. (1993). Characteristics of carers in Victoria. *Family Matters, 34*, 21-26.

Kendig, H. L. (1986). Towards integrated community care for the frail aged. *Australian Journal of Social Issues, 21*(2), 75-91.

Janicki, M., Dalton, A., Henderson, C., & Davidson, P. (1999). Mortality and morbidity among older adults with intellectual disability: Health services considerations. *Disability and Rehabilitation, 21*, 284-294.

Lee, C. (2001). Experiences of family care giving among older Australian women. *Journal of Health Psychology, 6*(4), 393-404.

Lewis, C. (1999). *Opening doors: Community, culture and the equation of care*. Paper presented to the International Home Care & Health and Community Care Conference, Brisbane, Australia.

Litwak, E. (1985). *Helping the elderly: The complementary roles of informal networks and formal systems*. New York: Guilford Press.

McCallum, J., & Gelfand, D. E. (1990). *Ethnic women in the middle: A focus group study of Australian daughters caring for migrant elderly*. Canberra, Australia: Department of Community Services & Health.

Minas, I. H., Silove, D., & Kunst, J. P. (1997). *Mental health for multicultural Australia: A national strategy*. Retrieved from http://ariel.its.unimelb.edu.au/~atmhn/www/poldev/mhma/current.html

Moore, S. (1989). Community care or carer's work? *Impact, 2*, 9-12.

Morris, M. (2001). *Gender sensitive home and community care and care giving research: A synthesis paper*. Ottawa, Canada: Women's Health Bureau, Health Canada.

Morse, C. A., & Messimeri-Kianidis, V. (2002). Keeping it in the family: Care giving in Australian-Greek families. *Social Work & Health Care, 35*(1-2), 299-314.

Morse, C. A., & Messimeri-Kianidis, V. (1996). Keeping it in the family: The health and social experiences of carers in Australian-Greek families. Canberra, Australia: Department of Immigration & Multicultural Affairs.

New South Wales Carers Association. (1998). *Aboriginal and Torres Strait Islanders carers*. NSW, Australia: Author.

Pakenham, K. I., Dadds, M. R., & Lennon, H. V. (2002). The efficacy of a psychosocial intervention for HIV/AIDS care giving dyads and individual care givers: A controlled treatment outcome study. *AIDS Care, 14*(6), 731-750.

Rees, T., & Brown, V. (1999). *Carers and community: Self-determination and empowerment*. Paper presented to the International Home Care and Health & Community Care Conference. Brisbane, Australia.

Schofield, H. L., Herrman, H. E., & Bloch, S. (1997). A profile of Australian family care givers: Diversity of roles and circumstances. *Australian & New Zealand Journal of Public Health, 21*(1), 59-66.

Sheppard, S., & Iliffe, S. (2004). Hospital at home versus in-patient hospital care (Cochrane Review). In *The Cochrane Library, 1* (pp. 1-135). Chichester: John Wiley and Sons.

CHAPTER 6

The Challenges and Issues Confronting Family Caregivers to Elderly Cancer Patients

Victoria H. Raveis

CANCER AND THE ELDERLY

Life expectancy has increased dramatically in recent decades, producing an equally dramatic expansion in the size of the elderly population. Cancer is a major cause of morbidity and mortality in older adults, its incidence rising appreciably with age. In the United States, almost 60% of new cancers and 70% of deaths from cancer occur in persons over 65 (National Cancer Institute, 2005a). As the population ages, the burden of cancer, already considerable in the elderly, will continue to grow. It is anticipated, based on cancer incidence rates and U.S. Census Department population projections, that the number of cancer patients 65 and older will double in the next 30 years. Perhaps even more significantly, the number of cancer patients aged 85 and older is expected to increase fourfold between 2000 and 2050 (Edwards et al., 2002).

Cancer is now more frequently screened for, detected earlier, and aggressively treated in older adults, as reflected in a policy shift by the National Institute of Health regarding the former exclusion of the elderly from most clinical trials. As a consequence, not only is the absolute number of elderly individuals with newly diagnosed cancer continuing to rise, but average age at diagnosis is increasing as well (Edwards et al., 2002). The current average age of cancer survivors is 68 for men and 64 for women (National Cancer Institute, 2002). About 60% of cancer survivors are 65 or older, with 32% of the survivors 75 and older (Edwards et al., 2002). Earlier cancer detection and more effective treatment options for the elderly have contributed to a greater number of older adults surviving for longer periods following a cancer diagnosis (Balducci & Yates, 2000). From a caregiving perspective, these developments mean that elderly patients and their families are living with the effects of cancer and its treatment for an extended time interval.

Treatment and Recovery Is More Complicated in the Elderly

Age-related physical infirmities can complicate cancer care and the management of symptoms in older cancer patients. Symptom control approaches that work well in younger adults may not readily translate for older adults. The physiological changes in organ function associated with aging place the older cancer patient at increased risk for treatment-related toxicities and may contribute to the emergence of late-treatment effects on normal tissues and vital organs, months and even years following treatment completion (National Institute on Aging & National Cancer Institute, 2001). Co-morbidities are common in older cancer patients, and this also increases the risk of adverse treatment-related side effects. For example, elderly patients may be on other medications that could interact with their chemotherapy, increasing its toxicity (Edwards et al., 2002). Co-morbidity can also contribute to the development of treatment-related functional impairment and the emergence of additional co-morbidities posttreatment (Yancik et al., 2001). Investigations have shown an increased incidence of pain and fatigue in cancer patients with co-morbid conditions, in some instances due to pre-existing, noncancerous conditions, such as arthritis (Balducci & Yates, 2000). Studies have found that older patients (60+) report experiencing significantly higher pain severity than younger patients, albeit with a trend for older patients to be more willing to tolerate pain (Yates et al., 2002).

Developments in Health Care Shift the Setting of Cancer Care to the Community

The trend in U.S. health care towards "de-hospitalization," in combination with advances in cancer treatment, is making it possible for many elderly cancer patients to be managed on an outpatient basis and remain in the community while in treatment. Diagnostic testing and treatments previously performed on an inpatient basis are increasingly administered in outpatient settings and in the home. In addition, complex chemotherapeutic routines and radiation treatments that in the past may have required an inpatient stay are routinely delivered in outpatient clinics and physicians' offices. Improved methods of medical management have increased cancer patients' tolerance of highly cytotoxic chemotherapeutic agents, making these treatments possible on an outpatient basis. The development of infusion pumps and vascular access devices have made it feasible for chemotherapy treatments to be delivered to patients at home. Similarly, radiation implants, which concentrate timed delivery of radiation over a sustained interval, reduce the need for multiple clinic visits and enable patients to remain at home. This shift from the hospital to community or home-based care means that family members, traditional sources of informal support and aid, are being increasingly prevailed upon to attend to a majority of the health-care and personal needs of elderly cancer patients.

Cancer Caregiving is More Complex with the Elderly

Age adds a layer of complexity to cancer caregiving not present in other cancer-care situations. The elderly are likely to have more extensive, complex, and long-term care giving needs, exacerbated by the shift from inpatient to outpatient care and shortened in-patient stays.

Older cancer patients may require a longer period of rehabilitation from treatment and experience more severe or longer-lasting treatment side effects (Balducci & Yates, 2000). The same physiological processes that slow down the progression of cancer in older adults may impede the recovery process. In addition, other age-related physical changes (e.g., decreased stamina and physical strength, frequent co-morbidity, and heightened disability) can also impede recovery and extend the rehabilitation period.

Families may not fully comprehend at the onset of their care provision that the completion of active treatment does not necessarily end the illness event, especially for older patients. Recovery from cancer and its treatment can be a lengthier process for older adults, and there may be occasional setbacks. Rehabilitation may be more difficult or complicated and restoration to pre-illness functioning may not be possible to achieve (Balducci & Yates, 2000). In addition, given that the number and severity of chronic health conditions increase with age, the cancer diagnosis may not initiate the family's caregiving role, but rather expand upon or add to an already existing set of care responsibilities (Kurtz, Given, Kurtz & Given, 1994).

Psychosocial Challenges Facing Familial Caregivers

Cancer is not a single disease. It is a collection of different types, all characterized by uncontrolled growth and spread of abnormal cells. The symptoms, treatment, illness course, life expectancy, and prognosis can vary with the type of cancer and its site (i.e., body location). The treatments for cancer (e.g., surgery, chemotherapy, radiation, hormone therapy) all have particular side effects, varying in controllability and duration. Thus, caregiving needs will differ, and families will not necessarily be dealing with the same set of treatment- or illness-related demands and stressors. Nonetheless, families face a shared set of psychosocial challenges imposed by their elderly relative's illness: coping with uncertainty, adapting to the losses and changes engendered by the illness, and dealing with care provision responsibilities. Caregivers are challenged in varying degrees in each of these areas at every phase of the illness.

Diagnosis and Treatment Period

The initial diagnosis period is a time of severe stress and crisis for cancer patients and their families, characterized by a series of unrelenting demands and intense activity. The diagnosis of cancer is an event of significant import to family functioning. As family members learn of their loved one's diagnosis and process its implications, they experience a period of crisis fraught with severe emotional distress and life/death concerns that parallels the existential plight patients encounter in the initial months following the diagnosis (Raveis & Pretter, 2005b). During this period, families are confronted with numerous difficult decisions that may necessitate the mastery of new and complex technical information in order to make an informed choice. Embedded within this decision process is the challenge of coming to terms with the uncertainty of whether a specific choice will achieve the desired health outcome.

Cancer treatment decisions necessitate weighing the risks and benefits of specific therapies (e.g., minimally invasive surgery, prophylactic therapy, etc.) in conjunction with quality-of-life considerations (e.g., the choice of potentially toxic, time-intensive interventions that might prolong life versus less aggressive measures that would improve short-term quality of life but not extend it). Even when a treatment may not entail any physical side effects, the emotional distress associated with the choice can still adversely impact patients' and families' psychological well-being. With elderly cancer patients, it is not uncommon for families to be faced with having to decide between palliative management of their relative's cancer symptoms or an aggressive treatment plan. Even when the former approach may be medically indicated, families are likely to experience extreme distress over needing to select between these options. For example, a common treatment approach to prostate cancer in the elderly is careful observation without immediate active treatment, "watchful waiting." Since more than 70% of all prostate cancer cases in the United States are diagnosed in men over 65 (American Cancer Society, 2004), many families are likely to be dealing with the challenge of living with this cancer management option. Research investigations have found that in those instances where prostate cancer was being managed with watchful waiting, patients and families have been found to experience emotional distress associated with knowing that although cancer is present, no clinical efforts are being made to slow down its growth process (Freeman, 1993).

Treatments for cancer create multiple demands for caregivers as they assist patients in dealing with the physical and psychological consequences of surgery, chemotherapy, and radiation, in addition to disease-related needs. Informal caregiving to elderly cancer patients can encompass emotional support, financial aid, and the provision of services ranging from instrumental aid and assistance with personal care, to health-care tasks and mediation with formal care providers (Raveis, Karus, & Siegel, 1998). The advances in the management and delivery of cancer treatments not only permit the portability of the treatment delivery (i.e., out of the hospital or clinic and into the home), but also require that families be involved in the delivery of technical and complicated care routines that previously could only be provided in an intensive care unit. As a consequence, the scope of families' cancer-care provision has broadened. Familial caregivers are now directly involved in health-care management, performing a broad range of specialized care routines, such as overseeing the delivery of complex drug regimes, being responsible for monitoring drug and treatment responses, adjusting dosages, maintaining the therapeutic delivery system, and ensuring adherence to symptom management routines (e.g., encouraging elderly relative to take the pain medication, providing reassurance of the appropriateness of attending to certain symptoms) (National Institute on Aging & National Cancer Institute, 2001).

With the advances in cancer treatment and the advent of managed care, families frequently need to function as their elderly relative's advocate, negotiating the health-care system and advocating for the best care. Elderly patients have been found to be more likely to disclose potentially serious health symptoms to family members than to their physician (Brody & Kleban, 1981). The elderly can have multiple illness conditions and be uncertain which symptoms merit presentation (Rost & Frankel, 1993). As family members are relied upon to act in their relative's best interest, elders may implicitly expect that caregiving relatives know when a health issue merits attention and follow-up. Thus, on their relative's behalf, they need to remain in close communication with health professionals and other service providers about their relative's care and symptom-management needs (Ferrell, Cohen, Rhiner, & Rozek, 1991).

Families are unlikely to have received extensive training in the various health-care and rehabilitation tasks to which cancer-care provision can expose them, and, at least initially, they may be ill-equipped to perform these duties. In a study of familial caregivers to advanced cancer patients, over two-thirds of the caregivers reported having to learn the skills that would enable them to manage patients' activities of daily living (e.g., assist with ambulation, handle personal-care needs, nutritional needs, and dietary requirements) and provide general comfort care (e.g., manage pain) (Grobe, Ilstrup, & Ahmann, 1981). Family caregivers, responsible for the operation and maintenance of any in-home medical devices, may also worry and feel anxious about the potential consequences to their ill relative should they inadvertently misuse this equipment.

Survivorship Period

Due to improvements in diagnosing cancers, treatment is more frequently being initiated earlier in the disease course than was formerly the case. As a consequence, there is a greater likelihood of effecting a cure or long-term survival. Thus, for an increasing number of elderly cancer patients and their families, the period of survival following medical intervention has lengthened. Once the initial crisis of the cancer diagnosis and the upheaval surrounding the implementation of the treatment plan begin to abate, a major challenge family's face is living with uncertainty centered on the treatment's efficacy and fears of recurrence (Lewis, Ellison, & Woods, 1985). Generally, cancer treatment outcomes cannot be fully assessed until a time interval has passed. This period of waiting can be an increasingly stressful experience for patients and family members, as the persistence of any symptoms, as well as the onset of new symptoms, raise concerns of a recurrence or spread of the cancer to other sites in the body.

During this survivorship period, elderly patients may be experiencing the sequels of the cancer therapy in addition to the persistence of symptoms of the disease itself. The clinical and research literature indicates that cancer patients can be free of disease, but still experience intense post-treatment symptoms. Indeed, there is a growing body of evidence to support that symptoms related to prior treatments can continue to emerge months to years following the completion of medical intervention (see review by National Institute on Aging & National Cancer Institute, 2001).

Even if a patient's prognosis for long-term survival is good, family members need to adjust to any permanent losses that may have been imposed by the illness, including changes in the patient's pre-illness roles and lifestyle. Also, given the persistence of treatment- and illness-related symptoms and impairments into the survivorship period noted above, family caregivers may be unable to fully relinquish their caregiving once treatment ends. New health conditions, precipitated by the cancer therapy, can also develop (National Institute on Aging & National Cancer Institute, 2001). Thus, surviving cancer does not necessarily mean that elderly patients are ultimately restored to their pre-illness level of functioning. From a care perspective, lengthened cancer survival for the elderly may translate into an extended period of caregiving.

Although advances have been made in cancer treatment, not all cancer conditions are amenable to treatment. When efforts to manage an elderly relative's cancer prove unsuccessful (i.e., the tumor continues to grow, the cancer has spread to another site in the body, or, following a period of remission, it has recurred), families face additional challenges. They need to deal with their distress and sense of desperation, while simultaneously continuing to be a source of emotional support and practical assistance to their ill relative (see review by Given, Given, & Kozachik, 2001). The intensity of families' emotional distress at this loss of hope is magnified by feeling powerless and ineffectual. Caregivers may also worry that a different treatment choice might have resulted in a better outcome. Knowledge of the range of suffering and pain that their relative has endured in futile treatments only adds to caregivers' regrets and despair. As an elderly spousal caregiver reflected, "My own fatigue is because I know where it is going; nowhere. He is going to die. So all of this is—nowhere" (Raveis, 2004b).

Disease progression and intensified treatment may render a patient more and more debilitated, intensifying families' care provision tasks and caregiver distress (see reviews by Pitceathly & Maquire, 2003). One consequence of cancer caregiving, particularly with advanced disease, is that it can expose the caregiver to situations where efforts to mitigate a relative's suffering and physical distress are limited and inadequate (Raveis & Pretter, 2005a). Pain is a common symptom that advanced cancer patients experience. It is one of the more difficult cancer symptoms with which family caregivers must cope. Research indicates that over 80% of elderly advanced cancer patients experience significant pain that their family caregivers feel helpless at being unable to adequately palliate (Ferrell et al., 1991). Family caregivers to cancer patients with pain have been found to experience more strain and depressive symptoms than caregivers to cancer patients without pain (Miaskowski, Kragness, Dibble, & Wallhagen, 1997).

Cancer-Caregiving Burden

The family is an integral component of an elderly patient's support system. The constant concern to meet their relative's needs for assistance and support can engender stress. While the practical and emotional benefits to elderly cancer patients of family support and assistance are readily acknowledged, the experience can be burdensome to the caregiver. Compelling evidence exists that the costs of providing support and assistance are far-reaching and diverse. Cancer caregiving can impact on all aspects of the caregiver's life, potentially resulting in restrictions on occupational, social, and leisure activities; a loss of privacy; financial burdens; conflicts with well family members; physical strain; and chronic fatigue (see reviews by Given et al., 2001; Kotkamp-Mothes, Slawinsky, Hindermann, & Strauss, 2005; Northouse, 2005). Because of the common prevalence of co-morbid conditions in older adults, families may have already been providing care to their elderly relative for other health conditions when the cancer was diagnosed (Kurtz et al., 1994), and this can further intensify the burdens families encounter. The cumulative effect of all these stresses and burdens over time may diminish caregivers' ability or willingness to continue this role.

Specifically, the demands of cancer caregiving compete with the day-to-day role responsibilities of the caregiver's own life, particularly when caregiving is long-lasting and intense, as can commonly occur with some types of cancers. Even though full time custodial care is usually not necessitated, as may be the situation with other common health conditions in the elderly (i.e., Alzheimer's disease), cancer care provision is still time intensive. Role overload is commonplace, as caregivers need to accommodate their other responsibilities and tasks with the demands of their care provision. Caregiving can also impose restrictions on social activities and disrupt carers' daily routines. Additional time burdens can emerge as a result of having to take on an ill relative's responsibilities. Care provision can compete with caregivers' employment, adversely impacting on their ability to engage in and perform work effectively.

The financial burden of cancer care is not inconsequential. In addition to the cost to family members of lost economic productivity, the hidden costs associated with caregiving encompass not only the out-of-pocket expenditures incurred in care provision, but also the cost of lifestyle changes necessitated by providing care, such as a change in residence or frequent travel for care-related visits. There are also the medical treatment costs that are not covered by the elderly patient's insurance plan that the caregiver may need to assume. As maintenance therapy can continue into the survivorship period for months and years, these additional out-of-pocket expenses can be substantial. For example, Medicare has not covered certain types of cancer therapies, such as the oral medications used for breast and prostate cancer, two common cancers in the elderly. Current estimates suggest that these expenses alone represent about 10% of the medical care costs for these cancers (National Cancer Institute, 2005b).

When caregiving is prolonged or lengthy, as may occur with cancer, the chronicity of care provision can be an added stressor. This situation is reflected in an elderly spousal caregiver's description of how she felt after two years of living with her husband's protracted cancer condition.

"This pattern of alive, not-alive, is very difficult to cope with. It's gone on for too long and it tires one out. It's like a slow leak. I'm completely exhausted" (Raveis, 2002).

Longitudinal studies substantiate that although burden may decline over time as care demands decrease, they do not completely subside (see review by Kotkamp-Mothes et al., 2005). Relative to the declines observed in other burden domains, investigations have found that even when the immediacy of hands-on care provision is reduced, the adverse social consequences associated with caregiving can endure (Raveis, Karus, & Pretter, 2004).

Psychological Impact of Caregiving on Family Carers

Perhaps the most significant consequences for the cancer caregiver are those in the psychological realm because of their implications for impaired social and role functioning. Studies have documented a variety of emotional sequels of caregiving for the familial cancer caregiver, including increased levels of depression, anxiety, helplessness, hopelessness, emotional exhaustion, low morale, distress, feelings of isolation, guilt, and anger (see reviews by Given et al., 2001; Kotkamp-Mothes et al., 2005; Pitceathly & Maguire, 2003). Diagnosable psychiatric disorders are also present for a notable proportion of caregivers (Raveis, Karus, & Siegel, 1998). Poorer psychological caregiver outcomes are associated with greater care needs, increases in patients' symptoms, declines in patient functioning, and disease progression (Kurtz et al., 1994), as well as greater caregiver burden (Raveis et al., 1998). The adverse impact of pain and other symptoms on older patients' quality of life and psychosocial functioning necessarily impacts the broader family system as well, and can contribute to heightened levels of depression, anxiety, and demoralization among family members of cancer survivors (Miaskowski et al., 1997).

Family Risk Status

For some cancers, such as breast or colon cancer, a family history of the disease is indicative of heightened susceptibility to the disease. Care provision may become more complex when at-risk family members are caring for a relative with cancer. As caregivers, they are afforded first-hand exposure to their relative's cancer experience. While this can serve to normalize or demystify the cancer experience for the caregiver, the opportunity to witness their relative's treatment and disease difficulties may intensify their own fears and dread of cancer. Any anxiety and concern these caregivers may be experiencing in regard to their personal risk status can be compounded by the distress and strain engendered through their care provision. These familial caregivers are further challenged in that they must integrate their reactions to their personal susceptibility while simultaneously dealing with their anxieties and concerns about their elderly relative's prognosis. They are also likely to be experiencing a high demand for emotional support for themselves, as they must live with the uncertainty of their relative's cancer outcome, while also having to cope with the uncertainty related to their own future (Raveis & Pretter, 2005a, 2005b).

FAMILY LIFE STAGE AND CANCER CAREGIVING

A full understanding and appreciation of the issues and demands facing family caregivers to older cancer patients necessitates consideration of the family's developmental stage. The demands of caregiving can compete with the day-to-day role responsibilities of the caregiver's own life, particularly when caregiving may be long-lasting and intense. Adult children, primarily daughters, are major providers of care and support to elderly relatives. The anxiety and concern that adult daughters may experience over their parent's cancer diagnosis can be compounded by the complex challenges they encounter as a caregiver. Adult daughters are likely to be at that stage in the life cycle where they are experiencing multiple role demands, due to marital obligations, child-rearing responsibilities, and work requirements.

Caregiving daughters have been described as the "sandwich generation" or "women in the middle" because of the pressures that many experience in trying to balance their responsibilities as a spouse, parent, and worker with the demands of caregiving (Brody, 1981). This can impair their ability to provide adequate care or maintain care over a lengthy time interval. Adult children may feel overburdened by their other responsibilities in their daily lives. With families of their own, they may find that their involvement in their parent's care adversely impacts their family life, as they have to reduce the time they spend with other family members, such as their spouse or children. Given the lengthier recovery period that elderly patients generally require and the greater likelihood that they will not fully return to their pre-illness level of functioning, adult children caregivers may be particularly challenged in maintaining their caregiving role over a long-term, protracted illness course.

Those adult children who are married or have children themselves may find that, although initially their spouse and children were sympathetic and supportive of their care provision, this support wanes over time. Their immediate family may become resentful of the alterations that care provision imposes on their family's life and may impatiently await a return to pre-illness normality. Caregivers may also experience guilt feelings about not being able to devote as much time to their family as they previously had done (Raveis, 2004a).

In the United States, extended families are often geographically dispersed. Consequently, when an elderly parent becomes ill, it may not be feasible for adult children in distant locales to provide long-term, hands-on care without major lifestyle changes. In these instances, adult children may be forced to engage in long-distance caregiving, while daily care responsibilities fall to nearby relatives. This type of care arrangement can contribute to strained extended family relationships.

Adult children caring for an aging parent are also confronted with the relationship changes associated with the role reversal inherent in providing care and assistance to an aging parent. Their parent's cancer diagnosis, coupled with their care provision experiences, can present caregiving children with an altered perception of their elderly parent as being vulnerable and susceptible to life's adversities. In those instances where a parent has previously been otherwise healthy, the cancer diagnosis can mark the beginnings of first-time caregiving. This marked role reversal can represent an unprecedented behavioral shift. As one caregiving daughter described this experience:

"It was really weird for me, like my mother's always taking care of *me*. . . . I felt the roles reversed. I had to be comforting her. . . . My instincts were to be the kid, but I couldn't. . . . I feel I have a kid to a certain extent, sometimes. Like my mother's my child" (Raveis & Pretter, 2005b).

For adult children caregivers, their parent's cancer diagnosis can be a significant life-cycle turning point that is challenging and emotionally distressing. Although significant progress has been made in reducing rates of cancer mortality, cancer can still be a fatal disease. The cancer diagnosis may force some caregivers to confront a life-cycle reality for which they feel ill-prepared (Raveis & Pretter, 2005b).

Spouses, primarily wives, are also very involved in the care provision of elderly cancer patients. Compared to other caregiving groups, across various illnesses, spouses generally provide the most extensive and comprehensive care, maintain the role longer, and tolerate greater levels of disability (Raveis, 1999). Age has an overarching impact on the challenges spousal caregivers face caring for a spouse diagnosed with cancer. Spousal caregivers are likely to be elderly themselves. As a consequence, they themselves may be physically frail or have a health-limiting condition that impacts their ability to provide ongoing care to their ill spouse. Even though serious illness and possible death may be more readily anticipated life events with the elderly, older caregiving spouses are also more vulnerable to the losses engendered by the serious illness of their spouse. Advanced cancer can require protracted and intensive care provision. Elderly spousal caregivers can experience severe lifestyle changes and financial burdens associated with their spouse's illness and care provision needs. Their own health may also be adversely impacted by their caregiving. They may also be mourning an altered future and be emotionally devastated at the prospect of impending widowhood and the loss of a lifelong companion. Indeed, older adults are at increased risk for mortality and morbidity following the death of their spouse. This risk can be exacerbated when the bereaved spouse has been involved in a protracted and intensive caregiving experience (Raveis, 1999).

IMPLICATIONS FOR PROGRAMS AND POLICIES ADDRESSING CANCER AND THE FAMILY

As the population ages, the number of individuals whose lives may be impacted by cancer will continue to grow. The diagnosis, treatment, and resolution of cancer not only affects the elderly patient, but also has profound and long-lasting ramifications for the entire family system. An understanding of the cancer experience needs to consider the psychosocial challenges cancer poses to the family. Elderly cancer patients and their families face lifelong health and psychosocial issues.

With the continuing shift to community-based care, there is a growing recognition on a national level of the importance of providing programs and services to assist families in their care-provision responsibilities. Legislative developments, such as the Older Americans Act, which established the National Family Caregivers Support Program, provide much needed resources and training to families in managing their caregiving responsibilities.

Less attention has been given to family caregivers' dual status. As providers of support and assistance to their elderly relative, family caregivers are considered part of the care team. However, they are also impacted by their relative's cancer experience (i.e., "second order patients") (see review by Kotkamp-Mothes et al., 2005) and may benefit from support and assistance tailored to their particular needs. Indeed, the National Cancer Institute defines cancer survivors as anyone touched by cancer and specifically includes family members in this definition.

Understanding of the complex ways in which cancer impacts upon the family is still evolving. There is a pressing need to focus more attention on the many different and connected issues and challenges that families encounter while caring for elderly relatives with cancer. Thus, in addition to the programs and services that attend to the challenges of cancer care provision to an aging population, consideration needs to be given to developing support and counseling efforts that address the psychosocial impact of cancer on family members.

REFERENCES

American Cancer Society. (2004). *Cancer facts and figures 2004*. Atlanta, GA: National Home Office American Cancer Society, Inc.

Balducci, L., & Yates, J. (2000). General guidelines for the management of older patients with cancer. *Oncology (Huntington), 14*, 221-227.

Brody, E. M. (1981). "Women in the middle" and family help to older people. *Gerontologist, 21*, 471-480.

Brody, E. M., & Kleban, M. H. (1981). Physical and mental health symptoms of older people: Who do they tell? *Journal of American Geriatric Society, 29*, 442-449.

Edwards, B. K., Howe, H. L., Ries, L. A. G., Thun, M. J., Rosenberg, H. M., Yancik, R., Wingo, P. A., Jemal, A., & Feigal, G. A. (2002). Annual report to the nation on the status of cancer, 1973-1999: Featuring implications of age and ageing on US cancer burden. *Cancer, 94*(10), 2766-2792.

Ferrell, B. R., Cohen, M. Z., Rhiner, M., & Rozek, A. (1991). Pain as a metaphor for illness. Part II: Family care giver's management of pain. *Oncology Nursing Forum, 18*, 1315-1321.

Freeman, H. P. (1993). The impact of clinical trial protocols on patient care systems in a large city hospital: Access for the socially disadvantaged. *Cancer, 73*, 2834-2838.

Given, B. A., Given, C., & Kozachik, S. (2001). Family support in advanced cancer. *CA: A Cancer Journal for Clinicians, 51*, 212-231.

Grobe, M. E., Ilstrup, D. M., & Ahmann, D. L. (1981). Skills needed by family members to maintain the care of an advanced cancer patient. *Cancer Nursing, 4*(5), 371-375.

Kotkamp-Mothes, N., Slawinsky, D., Hindermann, S., & Strauss, B. (in press). Coping and psychological well being in families of elderly cancer patients. *Critical Reviews in Oncology/Hematology*. Retrieved August, 11, 2005, from http://www.elsevier.com/locate/critrevonc.

Kurtz, M. F., Given, B., Kurtz, J. C., & Given, C. W. (1994). The interaction of age, symptoms, and survival status on physical and mental health of patients with cancer and their families. *Cancer, 74*, 2071-2078.

Lewis, F. M., Ellison, E. S., & Woods, N. F. (1985). The impact of breast cancer on the family. *Seminars in Oncology Nursing, 1*(3), 206-213.

Miaskowski, C., Kragness, L., Dibble, S., & Wallhagen, M. (1997). Differences in mood states, health status, and care giver strain between family care givers of oncology outpatients with and without cancer-related pain. *Journal of Pain & Symptom Management, 13*, 138-147.

National Institute on Aging & National Cancer Institute. (2001). *Exploring the role of cancer centers for integrating ageing and cancer research*. (Workshop report). Bethesda, MD: Author.

National Cancer Institute. (2002). *Cancer survivorship research*. Retrieved August, 2005 from http://dccps.nci.nih.gov.

National Cancer Institute. (2005a). *The nation's investment in cancer research: A plan and budget proposal for fiscal year 2006*. Washington, DC: Author.

National Cancer Institute. (2005b). *Cancer progress report—2003 update*. Retrieved August, 11, 2005, from http://progressreport.cancer.gov.

Northhouse, L. (2005). Helping families of patients with cancer. *Oncology Nursing Forum, 32*(4), 743-750.

Pitceathly, C., & Maguire, P. (2003). The psychological impact of cancer on patients' partners and other key relatives: A review. *European Journal of Cancer, 39*, 1517-1524.

Raveis, V. H. (1999). Facilitating older spouses adjustment to widowhood: A preventive intervention program. *Social Work in Health Care, 29*(4), 13-32.

Raveis, V. H. (2002). Bereavement and grief. In I. Higginson & D. Gass (Eds.), *Oxford textbook of primary medical care* (Vol. 2). Oxford, UK: Oxford University Press.

Raveis, V. H. (2004a). Psychosocial burdens experienced by adult daughters caring for elderly parents with cancer. *Annals of Behavioral Medicine, 27*(Supplement), S026.

Raveis, V. H. (2004b). Psychosocial impact of spousal care giving at the end of life: Challenges and consequences. *The Gerontologist, 44*(Special Issue 1), 191-120.

Raveis, V. H., & Pretter, S. (2005a). *Challenges of living with breast cancer in the family: Special issues confronting adult daughter care givers.* Era of Hope 2005 meeting for the Department of Defense (DOD) Breast Cancer Research Program. Retrieved August 2005, from http://mrmcweb4.detrick.army.mil/bcrp/era/abstracts2005/0010215_abs.pdf

Raveis, V. H., & Pretter, S. (2005b). Existential plight of adult daughters following their mother's breast cancer diagnosis. *Psycho-Oncology, 14*, 49-60.

Raveis, V. H., Karus, D. & Pretter, S. (2004). Impact of cancer care giving over the disease course: Depressive distress in adult daughters. *Psycho-Oncology, 13*, S47.

Raveis, V. H., Karus, D., & Siegel, K. (1998). Correlates of depressive symptomatology among adult daughter care givers to a parent with cancer. *Cancer, 83*(8), 1652-1663.

Rost, K., & Frankel, R. (1993). The introduction of the older patient's problems in the medical visit. *Journal of Ageing and Health, 5*, 387-401.

Yancik, R., Wesley, M. N., Riues, L. A. G., Havlik, R. J., Edwards, B. K., & Yates, J. W. (2001). Effect of age and co morbidity in postmenopausal breast cancer patients aged 55 years and older. *Journal of the American Medical Association, 285*(7), 885-892.

Yates, P., Edwards, H. E., Nash, R. E., Walsh, A. M., Fentiman, B. J., Skerman, H. M., McDowell, J. K., & Najman, J. M. (2002). Barriers to effective cancer pain management: A survey of hospitalized cancer patients in Australia. *Journal of Pain and Symptom Management, 23*(5), 393-405.

CHAPTER 7

Letting Go and Holding On: Support for the Carer and Dementia Care in the Final Stage

Suzanne Aberdeen

> Under the grateful façade, I suppressed the sick knot in my stomach and the tears I longed to let go "Oh Mum! How could we leave you here?" (Naughtin & Laidler, 1991)

For family and friends, providing unpaid care for people with dementia (carers), the pathway of care is a series of letting-goes: letting go of the person they know as they progress from diagnosis to death, letting go of their *own* identity as friend, wife, husband, child, or sibling and taking on the role of carer. Eventually the carer must also let go of part of his or her caring role because the person with dementia will require professional care. The final letting go is at the end of life, to an inevitable death.

Carers may be subjected continuously to grief for losses that began as many as 20 years earlier, at the time of the diagnosis of dementia. Health professionals have a duty of care to help, to identify these losses and stressors, and assist the carer in managing them in appropriate ways. It is essential that carers feel safe in transferring a significant part of their caring role to residential-care staff and perceive that they are supported and empowered to contribute, in a meaningful way, to the quality of life of the person with dementia. It is also important that informal carers, friends, and family are supported and have an opportunity to celebrate the life of the person with dementia, especially when letting go to death.

The challenge for health-service providers in residential care is to ensure the provision of appropriate physical, spiritual, and psychosocial care for both the person with dementia and the carer. The transitions in care from community-based to residential and then to end-of-life care are difficult for all concerned. Person-centered palliative care, which acknowledges the necessity of support for carers and the provision of holistic, client-led care, is a useful approach for people with end-stage dementia in residential aged care. However, professional leaders and practitioners should be critical and analytical in their evaluation of how well this approach to care is applied in residential aged care.

This chapter will identify the causes of stress and grief for the carers of people with dementia in the final stages. It will make recommendations for their care and that of people with dementia. The underlying aim is to include and support the carer through the process of end-of-life care of the person with dementia and, in so doing, improve the quality of care for that person and his or her carer.

DEFINING DEMENTIA

Dementia is a syndrome, a collection of signs and symptoms of cognitive deficits. The syndrome is progressive, has multiple causes collectively and commonly called dementing illnesses, and ends inevitably with death. The two major causative illnesses of dementia worldwide are Alzheimer's disease and vascular disease. The presentation and progression of dementia is dependant upon the causative illness. Alzheimer's disease progressively attacks and destroys cortical neurons, and people may live with it for 20 years or more. On the other hand, dementia caused by multiple strokes, as an outcome of cerebral vascular disease, can rapidly progress from diagnosis to death in just a few years (Access Economics, 2003).

The Alzheimer's Association Australia recently has funded and published a major report by Access Economics (2003) entitled *The Dementia Epidemic: Economic impact and positive solutions for Australia*. It defines dementia as

> . . . a progressive and disabling condition, primarily of older persons, that can bring turmoil and anguish to those involved. Different people may have different symptoms at various times, depending on the parts of the brain affected and the characteristics of each individual (p. 1).

The outcomes of dementing illnesses for clients are frequently described, or assessed, in terms of difficulties or deficits in abilities to manage activities of daily living. In the early stages of dementia, these can take the form of difficulties with shopping, driving, or handling money. In the later stages, more basic tasks are affected such as dressing, eating, and bathing. The person with dementia will need increasing supervision in order to remain as independent as possible. In the endstage, the person is totally reliant on the care of others and will be unable to weight-bear may develop contractions, convulsions, inability to swallow, and may appear to be unresponsive to most stimuli (Access Economics, 2003). The burden on the informal caregiver can be overwhelming, affecting his or her health, and can in some cases cause premature death. The carer may also require the intervention of the health-care team (Commonwealth Department of Health and Ageing, 2002).

Letting Go of Community Care and the Transition to Residential Care

Carers have been compared to the frog in an old Chinese proverb. The proverb suggests that if you put a frog into a pot of boiling water it will leap out. If you place the frog in a pot of cold water and bring it gently to the boil the frog will stay and be cooked. This rather gruesome analogy likens the response of those frogs to carers who suffer a gradual accumulation of life-threatening stressors. This is reflected in the fact that although caring impacts negatively on the health of the carer, Australian residential respite services are underutilized, and carers frequently complain that the effort of involving the person with dementia in respite services is so great that it is easier just to keep going (Access Economics, 2003). Carer health will improve after the person they are caring for is admitted to residential care, but the carer will continue to need specialized support during the transition, the period of residential care, and the death of the person with dementia (Grasel, 2002).

Reasons vary for carers wanting, or needing, to let go the full responsibility of care and seeking admission for the person with dementia into residential care. However, consistently at the top of the list is incontinence of bladder and bowel. The physical incontinence is only part of the problem, as this carer describes:

> Incontinence can be one of the straws that breaks the carer's back, especially when the person is urinating in all sorts of strange places, or hiding small parcels of feces around the house. It's a bit discomforting when these are handed with great gusto to an unsuspecting visitor or used for finger painting (Naughtin & Laidler, 1991, p. 27).

Other reasons for seeking a transition from community to residential care in Australia are the deteriorating health of the carer, insufficient support services, the health or behavioral problems of the person with dementia, unsuitable or risky home care environments, and family problems (Commonwealth Department of Health and Ageing, 2002).

Aging-in-place has been a philosophy of care in Australia since the implementation of policies under the Health and Community Care Act 1985 (Angus, 2003). This, in theory, enables people to be supported in their own homes until they die. Care is provided by State Government Home and Community Care (HACC)-funded organizations, but there is also heavy reliance on informal, or family care. Not every carer chooses that role; 54% of them state that they provide care because they had no choice or alternatives were too costly. Ninety percent of carers are 60 to 90 years of age and save the Australian Government $16 billion annually (Access Economics, 2003). The stress of caring can result in family conflict as well as situations of physical, emotional, or financial abuse or neglect of the person with dementia. The carer also may suffer from abuse by the person with dementia (Alzheimer's Association Victoria, 2000). According to an Australian study by Cahill and Shapiro (1993), 89% of carers will experience some form of aggression. What becomes evident is that caring, and letting go, may not be at the discretion of the carer, and choosing when to let go may not be a simple choice for a carer.

Isolation is a problem for carers. No matter how willing or loving, they will lose the companionship of the person they knew, lose friends and family as the behavioral outcomes of the dementia become embarrassing or offensive to those people, and lose their own social life as they give more of their time and energy to caring. As this carer says:

> On a personal level, I know that I gave Rob my best for ten years, and that I did achieve something worthwhile. I have been through my personal Gotterdammerung, and I'm still standing. I can understand why so many of my family turned away from the situation, but I often wonder if I shall ever really forgive them for leaving the help and support to our sixteen year old daughter (Naughtin & Laidler, 1991, p. 149).

When carers do let go, and the person with dementia is admitted to residential care for end-of-life care, it can trigger very strong and conflicting feelings (Commonwealth Department of Health and Ageing, 2002). A study in Queensland by Kellett (1999) of 14 families found that during a nursing-home placement, there were experiences in common by carers: feelings of loss of control, disempowerment, guilt, sadness and simultaneous relief, and a sense of failure at having made a forced and negative choice. Residential staff need to be aware of this on admission and plan to manage the carer's psychosocial and physical health.

A planned admission to residential care is less stressful, but in the United States (Nolan & Dellasega, 2000), and in Australia (Angus, 2003) such planning rarely happens. Nolan and Dellasega (2000) also state that a carer's unresolved grief or depression over an admission to a residential-care facility can result in anger. This is evidenced by an increasing number of lawsuits against those facilities in the United States. The road that carers have traveled to arrive at the residential-care option can continue to influence their relationship with the person with dementia, residential care staff, and their own quality of life and health. However, there is insufficient research internationally on the issues of how aged-care staff, some of whom have minimal formal education, can assist families to work through these feelings and to support them in remaining engaged as a member of the care team (Nolan & Dellasega, 1999).

RESIDENTIAL FINAL STAGE DEMENTIA CARE

The Access Economics (2003) report states that in Australia, 60% of high-care (nursing home) residents and 30% of low-care (hostel) residents have dementia and over 90%, and 54%, respectively have an obvious cognitive impairment that could be an incipient or undiagnosed dementia. Those residents will be unable to participate in their own care, or decisions about their own care, because of cognitive deficits such as inability to reason or make complex choices, poor judgment and insight, and inability to communicate caused by dementing illnesses. They will rely on the voice of the carer to represent them.

Palliative care is a holistic care option that residential aged-care staff can implement for both residents with dementia and their carers. This concept of palliative aged-care provision is theoretically sound, although in practice there is a shortage, especially in low-care facilities, of appropriately skilled staff able to deliver ongoing care including spiritual and psychosocial support to clients and their families, and staff able to evaluate the quality outcomes of that care 24 hours a day. A media release by Catholic Health Australia (2003) also makes the point that the current funding system does not allow for the extra cost of properly caring for dying clients in residential aged care.

A major issue for Australian residential-care facilities is the provision of culturally sensitive care. Both the numbers as a percentage of population and the multiplicity of culturally and linguistically diverse populations in residential care are increasing (The Healthy Ageing Task Force, 2000). The palliative model of care encourages cultural sensitivity, which is especially critical during transitions in care and the provision of end-stage dementia care. There are extensive cultural resources available to residential and community aged-care staff (Wositzky, 2004). However, resources are only useful if the client seeks out the service and staff access and use the information. In Australia, immigrants who are less proficient in English on arrival are less likely, statistically, to use community, or residential, aged-care services when required; they are more likely to use family assistance and co-residence with other family members. Little is known about reasons for these choices, how the resulting stressors are managed or the quality of life for all concerned (Benham, Gibson, Homes, & Rowland, 2000). What is probable is that this group, from diverse cultural and ethnic backgrounds, needs special care and support on admission to residential-care facilities if they are to willingly accept the facility and its staff's involvement in the care of their family member, relinquishing some of their caring role and re-establishing family relationships before a final letting go when death intervenes.

Of the resources available to Australian aged-care workers addressing cultural diversity in residential aged care, those dealing specifically with palliative care, or end-of-life care, are very few (Wositzky, 2004). *The Australian National Guidelines for a Palliative Approach to Residential Aged Care* (APAC) (Edith Cowan University, 2004) suggests that individuals not fluent in English are less likely to receive optimal palliative care. The needs of Aborigines and Torres Strait Islanders in particular have been underresearched, and the Australian Government is seeking to rectify this.

> In March 2002 the Commonwealth Department of Health and Ageing commissioned a study being led by Kate Sullivan into the palliative-approach needs of indigenous people across Australia. This study has identified significant issues in the delivery of a palliative approach to Aboriginal and Torres Strait Islander people (Australian Government Department of Health and Ageing, 2003, p. 132).

There are considerable barriers to palliative care in residential aged-care facilities, not the least of which is making the decision on when to commence the regime. Palliative care may begin at the stage when living with the dementing illness becomes dying with the dementing illness, the final stage. Thirty-five percent of clients in high or low residential care remain for less than a year, and the majority of clients live only six months after admission to a high-care facility (Access Economics, 2003). It would therefore make sense to commence palliative care as soon as possible after admission, especially since palliative care does not preclude active interventions such as surgery or antibiotics to ameliorate symptoms of physical, emotional, or spiritual distress. Palliative care will also ensure adequate pain relief in a group of clients for whom there is disturbing evidence of under- and mistreatment of pain (Kristjanson, Toye, & Dawson, 2003). The alternative, a curative approach to care, may result in prolonged and excessive suffering for both the person with dementia and the carer.

Two major U.S. research projects found that people with dementia are less likely to receive palliative care and more likely to experience burdensome interventions, since they are perceived as not having a terminal condition (Mitchell, Kiely, & Hamel, 2004; Van der Steen et al., 2004). Carers of people with dementia in residential care in the United States also report that residents with "problem behaviors" in the last year of life are less likely to have received appropriate end-of-life care (Bedford, Melzer, & Guralinik, 2001). Miriam, Moss, Braunschweig, and Rubinstein (2002), in a major survey of 400 nursing homes in the United States, noted that staff had problems managing palliative care for residents with dementia and felt that support during the process for families, other residents, and staff generally was poor. This would indicate that there is a common concern regarding the use of palliative care in aged care across the United States and Australia. There is an opportunity for international cooperation in researching this area of palliative care.

One way to encourage people with dementia and their families to discuss and make advanced decisions about care choices, and to consider palliative care, is to inform them and their families of their options in the early stages of dementia. In the early stages, the person with dementia may be able to discuss with their carer how they wish their care to be managed in the endstages. This can relieve a lot of the burden of the decisions the carer faces in the final stages. In most States of Australia an *Enduring Medical Power of Attorney* is recognized as giving a nominated person the power to speak for the person with dementia when he or she can no longer communicate. It is only possible to delegate this power in the early stages of dementia when the person suffering from the condition is still considered able to understand the consequences of their actions. In Queensland, South Australia and Northern Territory, *Advanced Directives* issued by the person when in sound mind, are also treated as legally binding (Doran, 2004).

Dr. Julie Mador (2001) of Lismore Base Hospital in New South Wales reported that initially only 2.5% of clients of that facility had knowledge of advanced directives or enduring powers of attorney. After education and information, and one month later, 77% of the 84% of clients who were successfully followed up, had taken action in this respect. It seems to suggest that the inability of service providers to inform, educate, and support people through the process of making decisions limits discussion and choice. Without this help in decision making, families can find themselves in the invidious position of having to resolve conflict about directions of care between health-service providers and individual family members, for example over issues such as end-of-life enteral and parenteral nutrition. When this is not possible, the Guardianship Board may need to be involved. Under these circumstances, the result may be a court-appointed guardian. Families, or individual family members, may lose the right to be involved in decision making, opportunities for a team approach with the family in the care of the client with dementia are lost, and support for the family can break down.

This quote from a carer after the death of her father illustrates what can happen when families are not encouraged to plan for the future as early as possible.

> Even though he once admitted he was not afraid to die, I did not want to hear about death. I did not let him tell me what he needed to say, what he wanted me to know. I thought there was time to discuss what I did not have the courage to face. I said to myself, "It's too early. We don't need to talk about death. Don't alarm him." I was wrong. It was not too early. I did not understand vascular dementia then, or how insidiously it claims its victims. I ran out of time (Henderson, 2001, p. 3).

Not all families want to be actively involved in care, and this should be respected. Lindgren and Murphy (2002) propose that with appropriate encouragement and care themselves, families can and will increase their contact with the person with dementia and their involvement in his or her residential care. Some of the significant barriers to family involvement are manageable; these are differing expectations of care, lack of understanding of the roles and responsibilities of staff, poor understanding of dementia, poor communication between staff and families, and lack of clear organizational policies covering the involvement and support of families (Lindgren & Murphy, 2002; Nolan & Dellasega, 1999). These barriers to family involvement are exacerbated by the fact that most Australian aged-care staff are unregistered workers, lacking the education and training needed to address the issues (Aberdeen, 2004). Managing the barriers to family involvement in care, and developing appropriate workplace directives and policies, is part of the role of health professionals. However, there is an unfortunate shortage of health professionals in residential aged care, and that needs to be addressed if we are to have successful palliative-care provision with appropriate family involvement (Access Economics, 2003).

One of the primary means professionals have of supporting carers and families at any stage of the dementing illness, but especially at the end stage, is to listen to them: listen actively and respond appropriately, give them the information they need to make decisions, grant their wishes where it is reasonable to do so, and inform and consult with them when it is not. The most obvious provider of this counseling and support for families of people with dementia in Australia is the Alzheimer's Association. The services that the Association provides can vary a little from State to State. Most of the Association's services are HACC funded. The Government rationale behind community-care funding is that if carers receive adequate support they will continue their cost-effective community care (Angus, 2003). However, the Alzheimer's Association's services are also needed by carers who have family members in residential care, and although the Association will endeavor to respond to carers' needs, it receives little funding for this. There is an argument for the support of the work of the Association in palliative residential aged care with increased Government funding.

It may also be argued that the Australian Government may have an undeclared economic reason for encouraging the use of palliative aged care in Australia, as it has for the promotion of aging-in-place. By reducing admission of aged-care residents into accident and emergency or acute care hospitals, and by not artificially prolonging the life and suffering of those residents, there will be a considerable cost saving. The risk is that a largely invisible residential-care population may be relegated to a backwater of inadequately resourced care. There is therefore an imperative for health professionals to apply professional ethics to concepts of equity in resourcing palliative residential aged care.

SPIRITUAL AND PSYCHOSOCIAL COMFORT FOR THE CARER AND THE DYING

Palliative care encourages us to treat the dying person as living until dead, and for some staff this is difficult. The person in end-stage dementia is often labeled as moribund, nonresponsive or vegetative, and their care is to be "managed," which implies the process is more important than the person. These terms are prejudicial and may be used by staff to excuse themselves from involvement in anything but basic physical care. The outcome can be a lack of equity for the person with dementia. Government aged-care funding is provided for holistic care, for psychosocial and spiritual care as well as physical care, but the former are easily overlooked and difficult to evaluate. Very little research has been done on evaluating aspects of psychosocial quality of life in end-stage dementia. There are, however, many anecdotal accounts of people who seem nonresponsive, yet are somehow able to respond to care and compassion in ways that carers and staff had thought lost to them. One considered thing staff can do for carers at this stage is to involve them in care planning for comfort, spiritual, and psychosocial support. Staff can demonstrate to families the positive benefits of the planned interventions for the person with dementia, for example in the reduction in symptoms like restlessness or calling out.

The stay in high care is likely to be less than 6 months (Access Economics, 2003), and so it would seem reasonable to ensure the family has had an opportunity to say their goodbyes and let go. As Henderson (2001) points out, even if the person with dementia is not responsive, families need to be able to say four things to the person they care about: *I forgive you, please forgive me, I love you, and goodbye* (p. 3).

What these four things have in common is a strong spiritual bias. Spiritual care for the person with dementia and his or her family is an important aspect of palliative care. Strengthening the spiritual aspects of a person can assist him or her to cope with distress. In most cases, nursing-home staff will ask about funeral arrangements on admission and file the information until time of death. In some circumstances, a referral will be made to a pastoral-care worker or a minister of religion, and staff will feel their duty is done. The key spiritual needs of people include the need for meaning and purpose in life, love and belonging, hope, forgiveness, a relationship with a god, and transcendence of human spirit (Van Loon, 2001). How this can be accomplished in a nursing-home setting is problematic, but it must be done and in an ongoing rather than haphazard manner, it must be part of the culture of the home, and reflected in its policies. It also needs to continue for the carer after the death of the person with dementia; avenues of communication should be kept open. Many carers find comfort in continuing to come back to the nursing home on a volunteer basis, but others can suffer an increase in grief for months after the death and badly need support at that time. All carers should feel comfortable about calling the staff at residential-care facilities about their concerns, guilt, or need for comfort and for forgiveness of the person with dementia.

Spiritual well-being allows us to experience the feelings of love, joy, hope, trust, forgiveness, inner peace, meaning, and purpose in life, and these are, in a sense, an antidote for carer stress over death, dying, and bereavement (Van Loon, 2001). They are also critical for carers when they have to be involved in difficult care decisions about medical interventions such as intubations, possible admission to acute care, or antibiotic use. There is little research into this aspect of residential aged care, and more needs to be pursued.

To treat the person with dementia who is dying as living until they die can mean appealing to their remaining senses. Some approaches, or complementary therapies, used to comfort the dying person need expert therapists, but there are many that families can use under the supervision of staff. Hearing can be engaged by familiar family voices, the rhythms of music to sedate or enliven is popular (Opie, Rosewarn, & O'Connor, 1999; Remington, 2002). The rhythms of voice in poetry readings or song, recollections of youth from seaside, farmyard and bush sounds, or the sounds and smells associated with religious or spiritual ceremonies can bring comfort, not just for the client but also for the family. Lack of sound can also be therapeutic, and a calm environment is imperative. Aroma can trigger pleasant reminiscence: favorite perfumes on a swab beside the pillow or worn by staff, smells of favorite foods such as mandarin oranges, scents of Christmas-like pine trees. Traditional aromatherapies can be used at this stage and can add value to the impact of touch when essential oils are used to scent massage oil. Aromatherapy has been demonstrated to reduce restlessness and agitation in clients with dementia (Burns, Byrne, Ballard, & Holmes, 2002).

Touch is important, and the value of therapeutic massage in improving mood, relaxation and in providing relief from pain is well evidenced (Opie et al., 1999; Remington, 2002; Roberson, 2003). Touch techniques can be taught to families. It does not have to use formal massage methods; it can be simple stroking of hands, feet, or back. Touch is a wonderful way of celebrating the personhood of the individual with dementia. The long soothing strokes of such touch have been shown to have a beneficial outcome for those who are giving it as well as those receiving it.

Few expressions of sexuality remain to a person in the end-stages of dementia, but an expression of sexuality may be important for the carer, especially if he or she is a spouse. The bedside environment of the person with dementia should reflect their maleness or femaleness, and this can be a way of celebrating their sexuality. The spouse may be able to meet his or her own need for intimacy with the gentle touch of massage. Little is known or acknowledged of the special needs of people with younger-onset dementia and their spouses in this respect. What is acknowledged is that many partners welcome the opportunity to discuss these issues when these are raised by health professionals (Beattie, Daker-White, Gilliard, & Means, 2002).

A textured patchwork blanket can provide a kinesthetic experience; patches of rough and smooth, furry and silky surfaces can provide a sensory experience for hands that grope, as can pet or doll therapies. Ways of appealing to the body's senses at the end-stages of dementia are only limited by imagination. Snoezelen, or multi-sensory environmental stimulation, is also an option. This approach requires a carefully constructed environment and constant supervision of the client (Chitsey, Haight, & Jones, 2002). The ways in which the stimulation is provided can vary between low-technology taste sensations and scented oils, and high-technology lighting effects. However, more research is required into the effectiveness of Snoezelen programs (Chitsey et al., 2002).

There is a growing body of evidence of the positive effects of light therapy for people with dementia (Opie et al., 1999). When we consider that those in the end stage of the condition may be deprived of natural sunlight, it makes sense to address that need. Traditionally, light therapy is the use of natural or artificial light to treat altered circadian rhythms thereby reducing sleep problems and treating seasonal affective disorder (SAD), also known as the "winter blues." Practitioners usually recommend sitting for 15 to 20 minutes in front of a light box with a 1000 lux capacity. Average nursing home lighting has been measured at a dim 54 lux, compared to a bright sunny day of approximately 500 lux (Patrick, 2003). More recently, light therapy has been used to treat sleeplessness, anxiety, evening restlessness and agitation in people with dementia with some positive results, although more valid research is needed (Kim, Song, & Yoo, 2003; Opie et al., 1999).

Being person-centered requires that we understand that person and view the world through their eyes. One way for staff to assist families to celebrate the life of the person with dementia and to say goodbye is to create a life book (Clarke, Hanson, & Ross, 2003). A life book, ideally, should be commenced by the person with dementia as early as possible so that they can tell their own story. A life book is more than just a written record or a photograph album; it presents a personal view of life events, the knowledge of both the strengths and weaknesses of the person, their skills, their likes and dislikes, and the significance of other people in their lives. It can be used by families as an aid to reminiscence and conversation, especially at end of life when families question whether their visits are beneficial. It can teach a younger generation about the person and allow a peer generation to celebrate the life of the person before letting go. It enables staff to value the person and understand the context of their life and its relationships. It is also a source of ideas for distraction, leisure, and pleasure for the person in their care. A life book does not literally need to be a book; it may be a collage in a picture frame, a poster, or even a calendar. The latter is particularly useful in the earlier stages of dementia since it can be an orientation tool as well as one for reminiscence. Creating a life book is within the scope of anyone with a computer and scanner, or more simply with scissors and glue.

CONCLUSION

It is apparent that the majority of people in residential care in Australia will die of, or with, dementia, and there are opportunities to improve their care and the care and support of their family and carers. It is the responsibility of health professionals and professional leaders in aged care to advocate on behalf of clients, to lobby for and obtain sufficient resources to enable the provision of quality carer support and palliative care in residential aged care. Without this proactive stance, there is the probability that poor or mediocre care practices will be developed and perpetuated. Staff currently have inadequate palliative-care skills, and there is little available education to develop those skills. Further research regarding the spiritual and psychosocial support needs of carers needs to be undertaken.

Some aspects of care that can be improved are the early preparation of people with dementia and their families for decisions about end-of-life care. This will require the early involvement and sensitive intervention of health professionals. Better processes and policies for involving families and carers in residential care and care planning need to be established and standardized across aged-care facilities.

In particular, there is a strong need for

- an assessment of the psychosocial, spiritual, and physical health needs of the primary carer and/or referral to a pastoral worker, social worker, and medical practitioner
- establishing family dynamics and the expectations of family about staff, the facility, and the family's/carer's goals for the health and well-being of the person with dementia
- information and education for carers about the roles and responsibilities of the facility and staff in relation to carer support and palliative-care provision
- establishing a process for, and encouraging, ongoing communication between carer, family, staff, and management
- counseling and support group access if necessary

Further, the special experiences and needs of diverse cultural and linguistic groups in Australia in relation to death and dying in residential care need to be better understood in order to establish appropriate responses.

REFERENCES

Aberdeen, S. (2004). PCs in aged care: Problems and possibilities. *Australian Nursing Journal, 12*(1), 15-17.

Access Economics. (2003). *The dementia epidemic: Economic impact and positive solutions for Australia.* The Alzheimer's Association, Australia. Retrieved August, 2004, from www.alzheimers.org.au.

Alzheimer's Association Victoria. (2000). *Overcoming abuse of older people with dementia and their carers.* Retrieved August, 2004, from http://www.alzheimers.org.au/upload/Overcoming_abuse_Report.pdf.

Angus, J. (2003). Community care: Challenging the assumption of gratuitous care. *ACCNS Journal for Community Nurses, 8*(2), 13-15.

Australian Government Department of Health and Ageing. (2003). *Draft guidelines for a palliative approach in residential aged care.* Retrieved August, 2004, from apacproject.org/files/Draft%20Guidelines.pdf.

Beattie, A., Daker-White, G., Gilliard, J., & Means, R. (2002). Younger people in dementia care: A review of service needs, service provision and models of good practice. *Ageing and Mental Health, 6*(3), 205-212.

Bedford, S., Melzer, D., & Guralinik, J. (2001). Problem behavior in the last year of life: Prevalence, risk, and care receipt in older Americans. *Journal of the American Geriatric Society, 49*(5), 590-595.

Benham, C., Gibson, D., Homes, B., & Rowland, D. (2000). *Independence in ageing: The social and financial circumstances of older overseas-born Australians*. Canberra, Australia: Department of Immigration and Multicultural Affairs and the Australian Institute of Health and Welfare.

Burns, A., Byrne, J., Ballard, C., & Holmes, C. (2002). Sensory stimulation in dementia: An effective option for managing behavioral problems. *British Medical Journal, 325*, 1312-1313.

Cahill, S., & Shapiro, M. (1993). 'I think he might have hit me once': Aggression towards care givers in dementia care. *Australian Journal on Ageing, 12*(4), 10–15.

Catholic Health Australia. (2003, March 3). Palliative Care and Dementia Left Waiting in Aged Care. [Press Release] Retrieved: August 2004, from www.cha.org.au/chinfo/docs/303cha.html.

Chitsey, A., Haight, B., & Jones, M. (2002). Snoezelen: A multisensory environmental intervention. *Journal of Gerontological Nursing, 28*(3), 41-49.

Clarke, A., Hanson, E., & Ross, H. (2003). Seeing the person behind the patient: Enhancing the care of older people using a biographical approach. *Journal of Clinical Nursing, 12*, 697-706.

Commonwealth Department of Health and Ageing. (2002). *The carer experience: Essential guide for carers of people with dementia*. Canberra: Commonwealth of Australia.

Doran, J. (2004). *Palliative care and advanced directives*. Retrieved December, 2004, from www.medicineau.net.au.

Edith Cowan University. (2004). *Guidelines for a palliative approach in residential aged care*. Canberra, Australia: Department of Health and Ageing.

Grasel, E. (2002). When home care ends—Changes in the physical health of informal care givers caring for dementia patients: A longitudinal study. *Journal of the American Geriatrics Society, 50*(5), 843-849.

Henderson, K. (2001). End-of-life gifts: A daughter's tribute to her father. *Alzheimer's Care Quarterly, 2*(1), 1-4.

Kellett, U. (1999). Transition in care: Family carer's experience of nursing home placement. *Journal of Advanced Nursing, 29*(6), 1474-1481.

Kim, S., Song, H., & Yoo, S. (2004). The effect of bright light on sleep and behavior in dementia: An analytic review. *Geriatric Nursing, 24*(4), 239-243.

Kristjanson, C., Toye, C., & Dawson, S. (2003). New dimensions in palliative care: A palliative approach to neurodegenerative diseases and final illness in older people. *Medical Journal of Australia, 179*(6 Supplement), S41-S43.

Lindgren, C., & Murphy, A. (2002). Nurses' and family members' perception of nursing home residents' needs. *Journal of Gerontological Nursing, 28*(8), 43-45.

Mador, J. (2001). Advanced care planning: Should we be discussing it with our patients? *Australasian Journal on Ageing, 20*(2), 89-91.

Miriam, S., Moss, M., Braunschweig, M., & Rubinstein, R. (2002). Terminal care for nursing home residents with dementia. *Alzheimer's Care Quarterly*, Summer.

Mitchell, S., Kiely, D., & Hamel, M. (2004). Dying with advanced dementias in the nursing home. *Archives of Internal Medicine, 164*(3), 321-326.

Naughtin, G., & Laidler, T. (1991). *When I grow too old to dream: Coping with Alzheimer's disease*. Australia: Collins Dove.

Nolan, M., & Dellasega, C. (1999). "It's not the dame as him being at home": Creating caring partnerships following nursing home placement. *Journal of Clinical Nursing, 8,* 723-730.

Nolan, M., & Dellasega, C. (2000). "I really feel I've let him down": Supporting family carers during long-term care placement for elders. *Journal of Advanced Nursing, 31*(4), 759-767.

Opie, J., Rosewarn, R., & O'Connor, D. (1999). The efficacy of psychosocial approaches to the behavior disorders in dementia: A systematic review. *Australian and New Zealand Journal of Psychiatry, 33*, 789-799.

Patrick, R. (2003). Bright light therapy: Hope for dementia. *Journal for Respiratory Care and Sleep Medicine,* Spring, 16-17

Remington, R. (2002). Calming music and hand massage with agitated elderly. *Nursing Research, 51*(5), 317-323.

Roberson, L. (2003). The importance of touch for the patient with dementia. *Home Health Care Nurse, 21*(1), 16-25.

The Healthy Ageing Task Force. (2000). *Commonwealth, state and territory strategy on healthy ageing.* Canberra, Australia: Commonwealth Department of Health and Aged Care.

Van der Steen, J., Kruse, R., Ooms, M., Ribbe, M., Vander Wal, G., Heintz, L., & Mehr, D. (2004). Treatment of nursing home residents with dementia and lower respiratory tract infection in the United States and in the Netherlands: Oceans apart. *Journal of the American Geriatrics Society, 52*(5), 691-670.

Van Loon, A. (2002). Assessing spiritual needs. In S. Koch & S. Garratt (Eds.), *Assessing older people: A practical guide for health professionals.* Sydney, Australia: Maclennan & Petty.

Wositzky, K. (2004). *Cultural diversity resource kit for aged care residential and community based services*. Retrieved December, 2004, from http://www.ageing.health.gov.au/specneed/picac.htm.

SECTION 3

THE ART OF LETTING GO

Introduction

Sara Carmel

A time to be born and a time to die (Ecclesiastes 3:2).

At the dawn of the third millennium, industrial countries can be praised for outstanding social achievements. Today, we are privileged with higher than ever standards of living and levels of education, improved environmental and working conditions, and unprecedented advances in technology and medicine. However, as honey sometimes comes with the sting, progress often breeds unexpected social problems.

During the second half of the twentieth century, industrialized societies witnessed liberation from the hazards of most infectious diseases, and chronic diseases have become the focus of modern medicine. Developments in medical research and technology have provided physicians with the tools to prolong the lives of severely ill and disabled people. All these advancements have significantly empowered physicians and health-care institutions. Doctors, who in the past had mainly provided sympathy and compassion, have gained the skills to save the lives of people with failing organs and chronic diseases. Hospitals, which, in the beginning of the century, functioned mainly as hospices, have become institutions providing a variety of healing treatments. However, while the steady rise in life expectancy and increase in the percent of elderly persons in the population are beneficial outcomes of these societal accomplishments, the concomitant increase in the average number of years that people live with disabilities and in the absolute numbers of people with severe disabilities and chronic diseases is becoming a burden upon society (Lentzner, Pamuk, Rhodenhiser, Rosenberg, & Powell-Griner, 1992; Pifer & Bronte, 1986; United States Department of Commerce, 1983; World Health Organization, 2004). Furthermore, despite the changes in the image of hospitals, most of the deaths in developed nations occur within general hospitals. People who die in these facilities often end their lives in alienated surroundings while attached to plastic tubes and electronic machines. This occurs because the advances in medicine and medical technology have become a double-edged sword. On the one hand, physicians are more potent than ever in fighting diseases, extending life, and improving the quality of life, but on the other hand, the same practices too often only prolong the suffering and misery of severely ill and dying patients. Since solutions are difficult to find and implement, due to the ethical, medical, economic, political, and legal dilemmas involved, the use of life-sustaining treatments at the end of life has become a major social problem in all developed nations.

The source for this social problem is what sociologists call a cultural lag. Culture can be defined simply as all the things learned and shared by members of a society. It is a social creation composed of three different components: ideological, normative, and materialistic. The ideological component refers to an accepted system of values and beliefs such as the sanctity of life and the physician's mission to heal and preserve life. The normative component refers to the accepted directives for social behavior including guidelines, rites, and rules. The materialistic component comprises the artifacts and technology used by members of the society. When these three components complement each other, the culture provides its members with a comprehensive framework of beliefs and norms that regulate daily behavior. Due to the interwoven relationships among these three dimensions in all cultures, archeologists can make conclusions about behavior and lifestyle in ancient societies—the normative and ideological components—from the excavated materialistic component, such as buildings, dishes, pieces of art, etc. For example, in the absence of written documents, sarcophagi can tell us not only about the burial customs, but also about people's beliefs in afterlife.

Every society strives to have a harmonious cultural system since it enables smooth societal functioning. When one component in this system changes rapidly, the other components have to adapt by undergoing concomitant changes in order to maintain a comprehensive and coherent structure of social organization and regulation. If the other components do not change accordingly, a cultural lag occurs, causing confusion in daily behavior (Parsons, 1951). Frequent disagreement and conflict, as well as personal stress, are consequences of such a situation, which can thus be defined as a social problem. In comparison to changes in the materialistic component, which can be implemented relatively rapidly, changes in ideas, beliefs, and values are usually very slow (Ogburn, 1957), especially when basic social values are at stake. Only social revolutions can bring about swift changes in a society's value system, and even then, the changes often remain superficial for a long period of time.

One of the expressions of the cultural lag in end-of-life care (EOLC) is the lack of appropriate social guidance in this specific area of life. As a result, patients and their family members are facing a crisis, caused by a critical illness, in a milieu of social disorientation and confusion, while being deprived of the basic and significant collective coping resources of formal social support and regulation. People in these situations lack essential social knowledge as to what to expect from physicians, from their families, and even from themselves, struggling with questions such as whether to accept the physician's decision and recommendations for further treatment or to oppose them, and whether to dare asking the physician's help to end life, knowing that it is an illegal act.

The current situation in EOLC also causes emotional difficulties for the formal caregivers of the dying patients. Physicians and nurses prejudiced by negative stereotypes of elderly persons tend to minimize contact with elderly patients (Carmel, Galinsky, & Cwikel, 1990), and often misdiagnose and undertreat them (Boyd, Teres, Rapoport, & Lemeshow, 1996; Meier & Monias, 2003; Weiss, 1981). Medical personnel also have the tendency to subconsciously avoid dying patients. This phenomenon, which has been recognized by researchers since the seventies, was interpreted as emotionally self-protective coping behavior (Gow & Williams, 1977; Kübler-Ross, 1969; Todd & Still, 1984; Whitfield, 1998). Furthermore, these distancing behaviors often cause medical personnel to experience uncomfortable feelings of guilt about avoiding their dying patients. The documented lack of EOLC-related communication between doctors and their elderly patients also puts the doctor in the position of the sole decision maker, which increases his emotional burden and interpersonal conflicts. Such hidden emotional difficulties and overt behaviors augment the stress of the dying patients, who feel even more abandoned in the last stages of their lives.

The scope of this social problem is spreading as more and more people are becoming involved in these painful and problematic situations. The tragic cases of patients or families asking for withdrawal of life support treatments that reach the courts and the mass media are just the tip of the iceberg of these painful social situations that affect many families today, not to mention professional caregivers. Some aspects of this social confusion, including hidden agreements and disagreements among the involved parties about the preferred EOLC, are presented in Carmel's chapter.

The price paid by society in the physical and psychological agony of patients and their families, and in the high economic cost for individuals and society, raises confusion and uneasiness also among policymakers, legal and religious authorities, and politicians. These authorities have to deal with the dilemmas that arise not only from the implications of these problems, but also from the initiatives directed to address them, and find the appropriate solutions for the benefit of individuals as well as society at large. Wenger and Davis present in their chapter this unsolved dilemma of distributive justice related to EOLC.

Awareness of these EOLC-related problems has increased in recent decades and produced various solutions on two parallel tracks—legal and medical. On the legal track, some societies have resolved the conflict between the values of sanctity of life and the right for self-determination in EOLC by increasing patients' autonomy. Legalization processes in some Western countries, such as the United States, the Netherlands, England, and Australia, as described in Tulloch's chapter, have acknowledged patients' right to control their medical treatment at the end of life and even stretched their autonomy to the condition of being mentally incompetent by the use of various means such as, power-of-attorney, living wills, and other forms of advance directives. Yet, the application of these new laws and regulations is encountered by significant difficulties in all the countries dealing with these issues, especially when old people are involved (Cherniack, 2002; Taylor, Ugoni, Cameron, & McNeil, 2003). Cohen-Mansfield as well as Wenger and Davis describe and illustrate in their chapters such difficulties, as well as other unexpected developments, following the use of advance directives in the United States.

On the medical track, palliative care has been developed as a new specialty, which focuses on comprehensive treatments intended to ease the physical and psychological suffering of severely ill and dying patients and those of their families. However, the problematic professional orientation toward treating elderly people and the dying, which deters physicians from specializing in this field, as well as the resources needed to implement palliative care in educational institutions and in the current health-care system, form barriers to this promising initiative. Some of the problems faced when trying to promote such initiatives, especially among elderly and demented people, are presented through the relatively long Australian experience, by Kristjanson, Walton, and Toye. All the authors in this section emphasize the importance of providing palliative care to dying patients. However, the lack of accessibility to palliative care is still a worldwide problem.

Difficulties in the application of both kinds of solutions derive mainly from deeply rooted beliefs and behaviors, requiring concomitant change. These include the embedded denial of death and dying in Western societies, the ever-prevalent paternalistic model of doctor/patient relations, and what stems from both of these factors—the lack of open communication about death and the dying process between doctors and patients, as well as patients and their families. Another barrier to a rapid application of these initiatives is the overpowering approach in medical education, that perceives the doctor's role as that of a life savior. One of the results of this orientation is the lack of educational programs in medical schools about how to communicate with and treat elderly people and those who can no longer be cured or saved. Furthermore, because of lacking such skills and trying to deny death, medical personnel tend to alienate themselves from their dying patients when they need them most. The traditional medical orientation has also influenced our health-care systems, which are designed to manage emergencies and injuries, to diagnose diseases, and treat patients with prognoses of survival, but not to address the various needs of dying patients (Lynn, Schuster, & Kabcenell, 2000). Thus, the guiding orientation and structure of the current health-care systems form a further barrier to implementing changes for the benefit of the dying. Additional, more specified barriers and recommendations for overcoming them and promoting both initiatives are presented in all the chapters of this section.

Currently, the application of a combination of solutions from both tracks, including advanced care planning, comfort care, psychological support, and spiritual guidance, what is called the "Mixed Management Model," seems to be the best method to address the needs of the dying and their families.

Although all developed nations try to close the cultural lag in EOLC by adopting both solutions, the pace of adopting them varies according to the differences in the relative dominance of the basic values of sanctity of life and personal autonomy and in the other related beliefs, which have become social barriers to the implementation of these solutions. For example, the focus in the United States on the right for self-determination, on individualism and consumerism is significantly stronger than in Israel. It is, therefore, not surprising that public pressure directed the United States toward legalizing advance directives years before this jurisdiction will be implemented in Israel. Furthermore, multicultural societies, which constantly absorb new immigrants of diverse cultural and ethnic backgrounds, such as Australia, Israel, and the United States, often face resistance to social change by some of their cultural subgroups.

However, since modern media have torn down the barriers of communication, information about common problems and the ways in which they are dealt with spreads among societies, influencing their public's opinion directly, and indirectly, through their own societies' mass media and courts. Furthermore, lacking the ability to conduct laboratory experiments on social life, the experiences of other countries in the implementation of new social initiatives are the best sources of knowledge for enhancing social adaptation and closing cultural lags. Often, societies that prolong their adaptation processes benefit from observing the long-term social outcomes of initiatives implemented in other countries. Such experiences, however, have to be carefully evaluated and the changes cautiously adapted, while considering the cultural differences among societies and the cultural diversities within them. Steinberg's chapter is an example of the delicate process of finding the golden path to interweaving significant changes in EOLC, such as the withdrawal of life support treatments from dying patients and advance directives, into the Israeli multicultural society.

Changes toward increased patient autonomy and open communication about life-threatening diseases, which are necessary conditions for planning EOLC, are occurring in many Eastern and Western nations, including those where intentional legalization solutions are still lacking. These changes, which are actually accelerated by the EOLC-related problems and legalization of advance directives, will, in the long run, not only close the cultural lag in EOLC matters, but also influence many other areas of social life.

The pace of change in basic values, beliefs, and behaviors is, however, very slow. In most countries, the legalization of new norms of behavior is the last step of a slow change in public perceptions and beliefs, expressed in debates in the media and in precedent court rulings. Moses waited forty years before letting the children of Israel, whom he liberated from slavery, enter the Promised Land as a nation of free people. Considering EOLC-related problems, we are the desert generation that is living during this transitional stage of social adaptation to the technological and medical advances of our societies.

In this and the previous sections, through the experiences of Israel, Australia, and the United States, we present manifestations of various aspects of the EOLC social problem and the encountered difficulties in the application of both kinds of solutions—palliative care and legalization of advance directives. We hope that the experiences of these three countries and the authors' recommendations for further changes in orientations, policies, and practices will enlighten some aspects of this global problem and take us out of the desert by enhancing the application of effective initiatives for promoting "the art of letting go" and achieving the ultimate goal of easing the burden of dying worldwide.

REFERENCES

Boyd, K., Teres, D., Rapoport, J., & Lemeshow, S. (1996). The relationship between age and the use of DNR orders in critical care patients. Evidence for age discrimination. *Archives of Internal Medicine, 156*(16), 1821-1826.

Carmel, S., Galinsky, D., & Cwikel, J. (1990). Knowledge, attitudes and work preferences regarding the elderly among medical students and practicing physicians. *Behavior, Health and Ageing, 1*, 99-104.

Cherniack, E. P. (2002). Increasing use of DNR orders in the elderly worldwide: Whose choice is it? *Journal of Medical Ethics, 28*, 303-307.

Gow, C. M., & Williams, J. I. (1977). Nurses' attitudes toward death and dying: A causal interpretation. *Social Science & Medicine, 11*, 191-198.

Kübler-Ross, E. (1969). *On death and dying*. New York: Macmillan.

Lentzner, H. R., Pamuk, E. R., Rhodenhiser, E. P., Rosenberg, R., & Powell-Griner, E. (1992). The quality of life in the year before death. *American Journal of Public Health, 82*, 1093-1098.

Lynn, J., Schuster, J. L., & Kabcenell, A. (2000). *Improving care for the end of life: A source book for health care managers and clinicians* (pp. 3-9). New York: Oxford University Press.

Meier, D. E., & Monias, A. (2003). Palliative medicine and care of the elderly. In D. Doyle, G. Hanks, N. Cherny, & K. Calman (Eds.), *Oxford textbook of palliative medicine* (3rd ed., pp. 945-944). Oxford: Oxford University Press.

Ogburn, W. F. (1957). Cultural lag as theory. *Sociology and Social Research, 41*, 167-174.

Parsons, T. (1951). *The social system*. New York: Free Press.

Pifer, A., & Bronte, D. L. (1986). Introduction: Squaring the pyramid. *DAEDALUS—The Ageing Society, 115*, 1-11.

Taylor, D. M., Ugoni, A. M., Cameron, P. A., & McNeil, J. J. (2003). Advance directives and emergency department patients: Ownership rates and perceptions of use. *Internal Medicine Journal, 33,* 586-592.

Todd, C. J., & Still, A. W. (1984). Communication between general practitioners and patients dying at home. *Social Science & Medicine, 18,* 667-672.

United States Department of Commerce, Bureau of the Census. (1983). *America in transition: An ageing society*. Series P-23, No. 128. Washington, DC: U.S. Government Printing Office.

Weiss, H. J. (1981). Problems in the care of the aged. In M. R. Haug (Ed.), *Elderly patients and their doctors* (pp. 79-90). New York: Springer Publishing Company.

Whitfield, B. H. (1998). *Final passage: Sharing the journey as this life ends.* Deerfield Beach, FL: Health Communication Inc.

World Health Organization. (2004). *World Health Report: Changing the history.* Geneva: Author.

CHAPTER 8

Bioethics and End-of-Life Issues

Gail Tulloch

End-of-life issues include the treatment and care of the dying patient, refusal of treatment, euthanasia, and palliative care, advanced directives and end of life decision making. The focus of this chapter is on the specific issues of euthanasia and physician-assisted suicide considered from the standpoint of bioethics.

BIOETHICS

Bioethics is a branch of ethics that deals with the ethical and social implications of biotechnology and the revolutionary developments in the biological sciences. It is at the interface of law, medicine, and ethics and is concerned with the whole of human life from the moment of conception to the point of death. In fact its concern begins at the point before human life has commenced, with the use and limits of reproductive and genetic technologies—in vitro fertilization, surplus embryos, stem cell research, somatic cell nuclear transfer techniques, organ transplantation, and xenotransplantation, where cross-species techniques are involved.

Bioethics really began as a field more than 30 years ago in the United States, when the Hastings Center was set up to consider the human meaning of medical developments. Death and dying was one of the four original areas of interest with behavior control; genetic screening, counseling, and engineering; population policy and family planning. Early concerns in this area first manifested over issues concerning termination of treatment and letting die—issues around choice and death.

It was the United States that was the source of the influential brain death criterion that became the international standard definition of death (with the exception of Japan). This definition emerged from the 1968 Harvard Ad Hoc Committee, established within the context of the ethics of experimentation, which asked for "further consideration of the definition of death" in kidney transplantation, following the groundbreaking heart transplant in South Africa in 1967 by Dr. Christiaan Barnard. The Harvard Committee's primary purpose was to define irreversible coma, where absence of heartbeat and breathing had long been taken as the defining criteria that determined death. In 1968 the Committee made the revolutionary recommendation that *irreversible coma*, or brain death, be the new criterion for death. A comatose patient with a permanently nonfunctioning brain with no brain waves, who was nonresponsive to external stimuli, showed no spontaneous respiration, muscular movements or cephalic reflexes should be regarded as dead if the condition had persisted for more than 24 hours. This was a momentous change, brought about by the presence of patients in a persistent vegetative state and, after Barnard's breakthrough, the mounting pressures for organ donation. Kidney transplants had become almost commonplace and involved no problems about death as kidneys can be taken from a patient whose heart has stopped. With a heart transplant, however, the heart must be removed as soon as possible after the donor has died. Permanently unconscious patients thus became potential donors for other patients, but to remove the heart of a still-living patient was murder under the current understanding of death. So the Harvard definition of death was a great leap forward in terms of both policy and practice.

In 1974, the U.S. Congress established the National Commission for the Protection of Human Subjects in Research, with a brief to identify basic principles to apply to biomedical and medical research. In 1978, the Commission issued the Belmont Report, which identified three basic principles—*autonomy, beneficence,* and *justice,* reflected in one of the early classic bioethics texts *Contemporary Issues in Bioethics* (Beauchamp & Walters, 1978). Later, a fourth principle was added, *non-maleficence*, or "do no harm," and together these four became known as "the Georgetown mantra," and principlism emerged, as an approach to bioethics. In this early phase of contemporary bioethics, the parameters of concern included life, death and personhood, the patient/doctor relationship (including medical paternalism, informed consent, truthfulness and the right to know, and medical confidentiality), biomedical research and technology, and issues of allocation and health policy. This approach was criticized for proposing principles as having meaning without needing to be applied within specific contexts, whereas the details of the situation were crucial in determining whether a given action was in fact murder or manslaughter.

As a corollary to the rise of feminist ethics, a critique was also mounted by active feminists of the day as a reaction to, and critique of, the Cartesian model of the moral self (derived from Descartes): a disembodied, separate, autonomous, unified self—a rational being essentially similar to all other moral selves and implicitly, male. Feminist views highlighted the ways western ethics had excluded women, or rationalized their subordination, and criticized the gender blindness and bias in much traditional ethical theory. Though many different approaches flowed from this common starting point, in common was an insistence on the need for contextualization in ethical theory and social policy and the need to recognize particularity and difference.

Feminist ethicists pointed out that masculine attributes are valued more highly than feminine ones, and that men have more access to whatever society esteems, allowing them a position of privilege and moral superiority. Carol Gilligan (1982) challenged Lawrence Kohlberg's (1981) hierarchical, analytical, and rationalist model of moral development, which was based on his studies solely of teenaged boys. Gilligan asserted the "different voice" of women and the validity of their concern with feelings and relationships in making moral judgments. In the sphere of bioethics, this approach led to recognition of the importance of seeing the broad implications of developments, rather than simply as single issues. Who are mainly the primary caregivers in society? Why are nursing, teaching, and social work such female-dominated professions? What power imbalances are at work there?

Yet feminist ethics itself did not represent a single approach, rather feminist bioethicists consider not only the standard moral questions regarding autonomy, paternalism, and justice, but how the issue in question relates to the oppression of women and what the implications of a proposed policy would be for the political status of women. They also tend to look at each issue in relation to other practices and assess its structural and systemic implications. Feminist bioethicists are therefore likely to be extremely cautious about any developments in relation to physician-assisted suicide, euthanasia, and end-of-life decision making that place the doctor in the potentially paternalistic position of gatekeeper. They are also likely to be particularly sensitive to safeguards that protect the patient's autonomy, especially in situations of extreme vulnerability. It may therefore be ironic, even problematic, for feminists, that reliance on the doctor's discretion in physician-assisted suicide or voluntary euthanasia has the potential to elevate the male doctor again to the paternalistic position of godlike gatekeeper that was first critiqued by feminists within the context of medical paternalism in the 1970s.

Bioethics in an Era of Expanding Longevity

As advances in medicine and technology continue, novel possibilities have continued to challenge society. These include keeping people alive from diseases that once would have been fatal, and hence contributing to the aging of the population. Women are overrepresented among the elderly because of the dual impact of women outliving men and women marrying up; that is, usually choosing a partner older than they themselves. These two factors are a recipe for at least a decade of widowhood. In the context of resource allocation, this can produce age discrimination. For example, in the United Kingdom (Charlesworth, 1993), renal dialysis was only available to those aged under 45, and women would figure disproportionately among those to whom it was denied.

Women also figure prominently in euthanasia cases, although not exclusively, (see the landmark U.K. case of Tony Bland, 1989, and Bob Dent in the Northern Territory of Australia, 1997). Is this simply because women are living longer? Is it because women are more deferential to doctors in seeking "expert" assistance? Are they more self-sacrificing, and is this too seen as appropriate? Are they more likely to be treated less favorably by the medical system? Are they under more financial pressure? All of these possibilities are embraced as the legitimate concerns of feminist bioethicists.

What is abundantly clear is that such debate revolves around the very issues feminists have long highlighted: rights of self-determination and autonomy; physicians' duties of beneficence and caring; the importance of context; and differences of power and resources. The priority of care, context, and relationships highlighted by Gilligan (1982) remain prominent themes in bioethics, as does the importance of autonomy. Autonomy, similarly a prominent value in Aristotle, Kant, and Mill, can also be expressed as *respect for persons*, with an emphasis on human dignity.

END OF LIFE ISSUES

United States

It is appropriate to start with the United States, for after the adoption of the Harvard brain death criterion, the test case was Karen Quinlan, the first celebrated "right to die" case, whose parents wanted cessation of treatment for their daughter, as she was in a persistent vegetative state, maintained on a respirator. The Quinlans did not support the use of "extraordinary means"—a respirator and artificial nutrition via a nasogastric tube—to save her life. The hospital initially resisted due to lack of a precedent, but in 1976, the U.S. Supreme Court found in the Quinlans' favor and her respirator was turned off. However, Karen lived for a further eight years. The case received extensive media coverage and changed public opinion. In the same year, California passed its Natural Death Act (1976), which gave legal status to living wills and protected doctors from being sued for failing to treat incurable illness.

The Quinlan case involved withdrawal of *treatment* that was clearly medical and settled the issue as far as the withholding of life support was concerned. It was the Cruzan case that extended the scope of the permissible to allow the *removal of artificial nutrition and hydration*. In 1989, the Nancy Cruzan case went to the Supreme Court—for the first time for such cases, as what was being sought was the more problematic issue of removal of a feeding tube. The Supreme Court recognized that competent adults had a constitutionally protected liberty interest that included the right to refuse medical treatment, but upheld the state of Missouri's insistence on clear evidence that Cruzan would have exercised this right if she could. After hearing friends' testimony to this effect, the Missouri

Court relented. This landmark case was referred to in Casey (1993) and in Washington v. Glucksberg and Vacco v. Quill (McStay, 1993), two New York cases where the Supreme Court returned the issue to the states. In 2005, during the recent and prolonged Terri Schiavo case, the Supreme Court again declined to override the state—in this case Florida—despite the earlier active intervention of Governor Jeb Bush. His action was censored as unconstitutional by the Florida Supreme Court, and the issue was taken up by Congress, which referred the matter to the Federal Supreme Court.

All these decisions were extremely close and, given the recent resignation of Justice Sandra Day O'Connor and the nomination by President Bush of John Roberts (now Chief Justice), it is possible that a differently constituted bench would rule differently should a similar case arise in the future. That future may not be long in coming, as during the next term, the court is scheduled to hear the Bush administration's challenge to Oregon's law. This is discussed below.

Bills to legalize assisted suicide or euthanasia have been introduced unsuccessfully since 1992 in states including Alaska, Arizona, Colorado, Connecticut, Hawaii, Iowa, Maine, Maryland, Massachusetts, Michigan, Nebraska, New Hampshire, New Mexico, Rhode Island, and Vermont. In 1964, Oregon's Death with Dignity Act, permitting assisted suicide, was approved by voters, but due to an injunction from the District Court did not go into effect until 1997. The Act defined *physician-assisted* suicide as a death caused by ingesting a lethal dose of medication obtained by prescription from a physician for the purpose of ending one's life. By contrast, *euthanasia* refers to death that occurs as a result of more direct intervention.

The Oregon Death with Dignity Act (1964) was detailed and set four strict preconditions. A patient had to be aged eighteen or over; a resident of the state; capable of making and communicating a clear decision; and terminally ill, with a prognosis of under six months to live. Importantly, as in the Netherlands but unlike Switzerland, Oregon has a "residents only" provision. The patient then has to go through the following rigorous steps:

> Make two verbal requests to the physician, at least fifteen days apart; make a written request to the physician; the patient's physician should call in a second physician to confirm the diagnosis and progress, and assess the competence of the patient to make the request (any sign of depression means the patient must be referred for counseling); the patient's physician should inform the patient of alternatives, such as pain management and palliative care; the physician should request that the patient notify his or her next of kin of the request.

The permission was thus stringently circumscribed and could in no way justify "slippery slope" alarmism. Nevertheless, in 2001 John Ashcroft, the U.S. Attorney General and a member of the Pentecostal church, attempted to overturn the Oregon Act, arguing that physician-assisted suicide is "not a legitimate medical purpose"—so begging the very question at issue and overriding the decision of his predecessor, Janet Reno. The Oregon District Court judge blocked the maneuver, which argued for the right of states to make their own decisions on matters of medical ethics, on the grounds that the attempt was a perversion of a federal law that had previously been created to deal essentially with drug abuse and trafficking. Unsurprisingly, the attempt was seen as partisan political adventurism, particularly given recent related federal attempts to encroach into areas of reproductive rights. Nevertheless, at the time of writing, Oregon is the current touchstone for the legal status of physician-assisted suicide in the United States.

England

The landmark "letting die" case in England was that of Tony Bland, a young man caught in a crush of spectators at Hillsborough Football Stadium in 1989. He was in a persistent vegetative state after his lungs were crushed and his brain deprived of oxygen, maintained by artificial hydration and nutrition via a nasogastric tube. In 1992, the Airedale Hospital petitioned the High Court for permission to withdraw his artificial feeding and hydration. The case was appealed up to the House of Lords, which significantly found that artificial hydration and feeding were *medical treatments,* and that a doctor had no duty to continue medical treatment where it would be of no benefit, particularly where it was invasive and consent had not been given. On February 22, antibiotics and feeding were discontinued and Bland died nine days later. What was significant in the Bland case was that he was not dying in the accepted sense, and that food and drink were deemed to constitute medical *treatment* and not normal care. This action contrasts with the lack of action of the U.S. Supreme Court in the similar case of Cruzan, where life-saving treatment could initially not be terminated because she was not competent to refuse treatment herself.

In the Bland case, British law formally abandoned the idea that life itself is a benefit irrespective of its quality, and affirmed that for life to be of benefit to the person living it, the person must, as a minimum, have some capacity for awareness or consciousness (Singer, 1994). Nine judges each made it clear that they did not value human life when that life is only in a biological sense. Moreover, it was obvious that the proposal to discontinue the tube feeding and hydration was *intended* to bring about Tony Bland's death. This viewpoint is at loggerheads with Lord Devlin's 1957 judgment in the case of Adams, that it is the *intention* to end life that marks the boundary between murder and sound medical practice, and that it is hence always wrong to intentionally end a human life. This doctrine survives in the "double effect" or "foreseen but unintended consequences" doctrine that is still the position of the American Medical Association and the Australian Medical Association. So long as the doctor's professed primary intention is to relieve pain or suffering rather than to end life, treatment by the provision of escalating doses of morphine that lead to death is permissible. Physician-assisted suicide remains illegal.

In 1994, the House of Lords, U.K., issued a three-volume report on euthanasia, which recognized the prohibition of intentional killing and closed the matter of voluntary euthanasia in England. Pressure to reconsider came from the Diane Pretty case (Diamond, 2002), where, diagnosed with motor neuron disease, Pretty petitioned the Director of Public Prosecutions for an assurance her husband would not be charged if he helped her to die. She was unable to act herself, and while the Suicide Act 1961 decriminalized suicide, it was a crime for anyone to assist, punishable by up to 14 years in prison. The Director upheld the law, as did the High Court and the House of Lords. In a precedent-setting move, the Prettys then appealed to the European Court of Human Rights, as the European Convention on Human Rights had been subsumed into U.K. law with the Human Rights Act 1988. They appeared in Strasbourg in March 2000, but she was again unsuccessful, and as feared, she died of suffocation in May 2000. The case attracted extensive media coverage and considerable public sympathy, and her widower presented the British Prime Minister with a petition signed by 50,000 people, calling for the legislation of voluntary euthanasia and assisted suicide. At the time of writing, Committee on the Assisted Dying for the Terminally Ill Bill (House of Lords, 2005) is at the reading stage, having been introduced by Lord Joffe. It proposes that those who are terminally ill, in sight of death and suffering severely, but are of sound mind and have expressed a wish to die before their condition becomes even more unbearable, may be assisted to die, without the risk that those who assist them—doctor, friend, or family member—will be charged with murder. Not only is the proposed legislation limited in extent, but it provides that more than one doctor would have to agree that all conditions were satisfied. It is therefore likely that the situation in England will soon change.

The Netherlands

Long regarded as the change driver in relation to voluntary euthanasia and physician-assisted suicide, the Netherlands was the only country that legalized euthanasia until joined by Belgium in 2001 (Hendin, 2003). Of significance, the Dutch legislation in 2001 had been preceded by nearly three decades of practice where euthanasia was in effect, legal, in the sense that doctors were assured they would not be prosecuted provided they followed appropriate guidelines. This experience makes it the only country that can provide long-term empirical data that can confirm or deny trends alleged by both advocates and opponents of euthanasia.

Just as in other countries, the move to voluntary euthanasia and physician-assisted suicide began in the Netherlands with a troublesome case. In 1971, Dr. Geertruida Postmaa was charged with murder under Article 293 of the penal code, after she injected her suffering mother with a dose of morphine. Dr. Postmaa was found guilty, but given only a one-week suspended sentence and probation for a year, though the maximum penalty was twelve years in jail. This suggests considerable public acceptance of what she had done. Letters poured in to the Ministry of Justice, including an open letter signed by other doctors, acknowledging that they had committed the same crime. Opinion polls found a substantial majority of the public supported voluntary euthanasia. People in Dr. Postmaa's village formed a Society for Voluntary Euthanasia, which in a decade had 25,000 members and now has 90,000—bigger than any political party. In 1976, the Royal Dutch Medical Association (KNMG) issued a statement advocating the retention of Article 293 of the penal code, but urging that doctors be permitted to administer pain-relieving drugs and withhold or withdraw futile, life-prolonging treatment, even if death resulted. This applies to a patient who is ill and in the process of dying. A court should then decide whether there is a conflict of duties that justified the doctor's action.

This defense was used in the Alkmaar case in 1984, where a doctor was charged with the mercy killing of a 95-year-old patient who had pleaded with her doctor to end her suffering. The doctor was convicted without punishment. Both the lower court and the Court of Appeals rejected his argument that he had faced an emergency situation of conflict between his legal duty not to kill and his duty to relieve suffering. The case was sent to the Rotterdam Court for rehearing, which produced the "Rotterdam criteria" to guide doctors facing decisions on ending life.

The government and the KNMG published a list of conditions under which it was appropriate for doctors to administer voluntary euthanasia that would not result in prosecution. The patient has to make a voluntary request and the request must be well considered; the wish for death must be enduring; the patient must be suffering unacceptably; the doctor shall have consulted a second doctor, who agrees with the proposed course of action.

These procedures have been in place since 1990 and became law in 1994. It is important to note that the Dutch definition of euthanasia is a narrow one, restricted to active voluntary euthanasia.

In 1990, after more than a decade of de facto legalization of euthanasia, the Remmelink Commission, chaired by the Attorney General, was set up to investigate euthanasia practice. Some 4,600 physicians were surveyed, and the results reported in 1991. In 1995, a second Remmelink survey evaluated the adequacy of the notification procedures introduced in 1990 and legalized in 1994. Importantly, it did not show any increase in the rate of nonvoluntary euthanasia, thus empirically dispelling fears that the country was sliding down a slippery slope. A third Remmelink report in 2003 confirmed that the rate of voluntary euthanasia, assisted suicide, and the practice of medical decision making relating to the end of life in the Netherlands appeared to have stabilized. The Dutch legislation passed in April 2002 with the support of an astonishing 92% of the population and 92% of the media. Five regional committees have been established since the end of 1998 to decide whether doctors carrying out euthanasia have complied with the 1993 guidelines. Now, only obvious breaches of the guidelines are reported to the prosecutor's office.

Three characteristics of Dutch society are important to acknowledge: its openness, the long-term relationship people have with their GP; and the fact that nursing care is free, so there is no economic pressure to end life. There is a recognized need for training in pain management and palliative care, and a special unit, a network of 20 GPs acting as consultants to physicians, who are required to be consulted before euthanasia is proceeded with. In terms of scrutiny and a staged response, the Dutch experience seems close to exemplary and has managed to progress carefully and in stages, without polarizing the country—unlike the other three countries currently being discussed.

Australia

Australia was for a brief period in 1996–1997 the site of the only jurisdiction in the world that permitted euthanasia—the Northern Territory, one of two territories (the other being the Australian Capital Territory) that are not fully self-governing and can hence have their legislation overruled by the Commonwealth of Australia. This happened in 1997 with the passage of the Euthanasia Laws Act, which overruled the Rights of the Terminally Ill Act of 1996 passed nine months earlier in the Northern Territory. This Act was preceded by a review of the Natural Death Act 1987, which did not protect a patient's right to refuse unwanted medical treatment, or protect doctors by permitting a defense of "double effect" if they gave pain relief that hastened death.

The Act stated that a terminally ill patient, experiencing pain, suffering, and distress to an extent deemed unacceptable, could request a medical practitioner for assistance to end his or her life. The doctor had to be satisfied on reasonable grounds that the illness was terminal and would result in the patient's death in the normal course and without application of extraordinary measures. A further requirement was that there were no medical measures acceptable to the patient that could reasonably be taken to affect a cure and that any treatment was only palliative in nature. The procedures were comprehensive and rigorous. A doctor needed to certify that the patient was of sound mind and making the decision freely, voluntarily, and after due consideration. A second medical practitioner, a resident of the Northern Territory, was required to examine the patient and confirm the prognosis, to be recorded under the schedule used for certifications under the Act. The coroner was subsequently required to report to Parliament the number of patients using that Act. So the procedures were comprehensive and rigorous.

The legislation was not implemented until July 1, 1997. There was a very short window of operation, with only four cases. Bob Dent was the first, a sufferer of metastatic prostate cancer, who sought the help of activist doctor Philip Nitschke as soon as the legislation was enacted. He died on September 22, 1997 in the presence of his wife and Dr. Nitschke. However, the Euthanasia Laws Act was introduced into federal Parliament a month after Dent's death and passed both Houses after a conscience vote. This made the Northern Territory legislation inoperable.

In 2002, the case of 64-year-old pensioner Nancy Crick again raised the issue of voluntary euthanasia (Tulloch, 2005). Unlike Diane Pretty, she was a conscious and competent patient who underwent three operations for bowel cancer, had a colostomy bag, and was constantly ill. She wanted to end her life but also wanted to die surrounded by family and friends. As in the Diane Pretty case, while suicide is not a criminal offence in Queensland, aiding, abetting, and assisting is, and she wished to spare from the risk of prosecution both her friends and Dr. Nitschke, whom she had consulted. She had multiple keys to her house made and invited 21 friends to be present (Dr. Nitschke was not one of them), having obtained a lethal medication over the internet. She died on May 22, 2002.

Reflecting the unsatisfactory ambivalence over the issue in Australia, it was not until March 8, 2004 that Dr. Nitschke, whose medical records had been seized the next morning, was cleared by police and only on June 18, 2004 was he and the 21 witnesses informed that there would be no prosecutions. At the Australian Medical Association conference that took place the weekend after Nancy Crick's death, Dr. Nitschke moved a motion to adopt a neutral position on euthanasia. It was defeated, but by a narrower margin than before. The "double effect" doctrine was convincingly endorsed; supporting doctors whose "primary intent is to relieve suffering and distress in terminally ill patients in accordance with their wishes and interest, even though a foreseen secondary consequence is the hastening of death." This principle and the practice of terminal sedation that it endorses, in fact allow de facto euthanasia.

Terminal sedation is another strategy also used in palliative care. Seen a decade ago as an alternative, even a rival, to euthanasia, palliative care grew out of the cancer experience embraced by the hospice movement of the 1960s, founded by Dame Cicely Saunders in the United Kingdom. When oncology treatment could do no more for the patient, palliative care came into its own. Reflecting the religious hospices of the Middle Ages, palliative care today is best understood as a kind of service rather than a specific place, holistic in extent, able to be delivered in hospital, residential nursing homes or a patient's own home.

In The Netherlands, there are six centers for palliative care in teaching hospitals, and palliative-care teams are attached to regional hospitals. In Australia, an example is the La Trobe University Palliative Care Unit in Melbourne, directed by Professor Alan Kellehear (Kellehear, 2000), which has received bipartisan political support from the last two Victorian governments, with recurrent funding as a demonstration project. The mainstreaming and growth of palliative care seems certain.

A prominent recent case invoking the removal of life support is that of Maria Korp ("The Age," 2005), a 50-year-old woman strangled by her husband's lover and left in her own car trunk for four days in the summer of February 2005. When found, she did not regain consciousness, remaining in a permanent vegetative state, her limbs so badly contracted that they had to be forced apart for routine nursing care. On July 1, 2005, her husband's lover was sentenced to 12 years in jail for attempted murder, a charge also faced by her husband. Upon Maria's death, the charge was likely to be upgraded to murder.

The case was referred to the Public Advocate, Julian Gardner, when doctors feared conflict of interest between Korp's daughter, who supported the hospital's application to remove life support, and her husband who, by invoking Maria's religious beliefs, not surprisingly, did not. On July 26, 2005, the Public Advocate announced that her life support would be removed on the grounds that the treatment was futile, unsustaining, and unduly burdensome. The treatment is regarded as futile in the dual sense that in the first place, nothing can be done to reverse the dying process, and that this is merely slowing her dying, not prolonging her living. In the second place, the treatment is futile in the sense that there is no patient left to care for—no person; Maria Korp no longer exists.

The decision provoked public furor and the expected criticism from churches and Right to Life advocates, as well as certain members of the public—particularly as it was expected to take up to two weeks for her to die. Maria Korp died on August 5, 2005. Her husband committed suicide on August 12, the day of her funeral. In contrast to Terri Schiavo's case in the United States, where Mr. Gardner said her condition was stable, Maria Korp's condition was unstable, terminal, and deteriorating.

In 2003, Julian Gardner was involved in a similar case, "BWV," where the Supreme Court in the State of Victoria granted him the right to order doctors to remove the feeding tube of a woman who had been in a persistent vegetative state in a nursing home for three years. She had told her family she would not want to be kept alive, but had not given medical power of attorney to her husband. Right to Life Australia and the Catholic Church opposed the move. In a landmark ruling, Justice Stuart Morris decreed that artificially feeding a terminally ill person was *medical* rather than palliative care and could therefore legally be withdrawn. Mr. Gardner said of this case that the patient had no signs of trauma or physical injury, and her condition was relatively stable.

There the issues rest in Australia. The risk is that different state laws are played off against one another or against Commonwealth legislation. Activists in Australia seem to be trying to work via legislation as well as through the courts. The passionate polarization in the community over the Korp case—represented by Letters to the Editor in leading newspapers, media, and public comment—shows how unlikely it is that these issues arising in the different cases could be resolved by legislation in the near future.

CONCLUSION

Two fundamental points are amply shown. The first is how these issues will continue to tragically recur—with patients who are conscious and competent, conscious and incompetent, and unconscious and incompetent, in Dworkin's (1998) felicitous classification. This last group is composed of cases that may end up in the courts due to family conflict, or with the Public Advocate. Less controversially, these are the cases that involve those with dementia, or Alzheimer's disease, or any of the other conditions that lead to progressive mental disability, especially among older people.

The second fundamental point is that appeal has been made to quality of life in so many cases in all four countries. Quality of life has become a fast-growing field of professional concern in nursing literature over the last decade. Within an ethical context, quality of life has been a paramount consideration in deciding whether we are dealing with a person—whether in fact we are dealing with a human life, from Tony Bland to Maria Korp.

In such cases, involving those who may no longer be who they were—and may indeed no longer be a person at all from the autonomy view, as Dworkin (1998) has pointed out in discussing life beyond reason—we must consider that person in the light of the whole of their life and their past competent self. Even if they are no longer a person in the fully fledged sense, as a human being they should still be treated in a way that accords them human dignity. It is for our sake as a society, as well as theirs. As society ages, it is not only the common good but our own possible future, as well as considerations of compassion, that urges us to careful consideration of what we as a society endorse in this most troubling area of end of life issues.

REFERENCES

Beauchamp, T. L., & Walters, L. (1978). *Contemporary issues in bioethics.* California: Wadsworth, Inc.

Callahan, D. (1997). Reply to commentaries: Facts, values, ideologies and ageing, *Ageing and Society, 17*(1), 89-92.

Charlesworth, M. (1989). *Life, death, genes and ethics.* Crows Nest, NSW: ABC Enterprises for the Australian Broadcasting Corp.

Committee on the Assisted Dying for the Terminally Ill Bill, House of Lords. (2005, April). *House of Lords Report.* London, UK: Author.

Deliens, L., & Van der Waal, G. (2003). The euthanasia laws in Belgium and the Netherlands. *The Lancet, 362*, 1234.

Diamond, B. (2002). Should Diane Pretty's husband be allowed to help her die? *British Journal of Nursing, 11*(9), 598.

Doyal, L., & Doyal, L. (2001). Why active euthanasia and physician-assisted suicide should be legalized. *British Medical Journal, 323*(10), 1079-1080.

Dworkin, R. (1998). *Life's dominion.* New York: HarperCollins.

Dworkin, G., Frey, R. G., & Bok, S. (1998). *Euthanasia and physician-assisted suicide.* Cambridge, UK: Cambridge University Press.

Gilligan, C. (1982). *In a different voice, mass.* Boston, MA: Harvard University Press.

Hendin, H. (2002). The Dutch experience. *Issues in Law and Medicine, 17*(3), 223-224.

Jaggar, A. (1989). Feminist ethics: Some issues for the nineties. *Journal of Social Philosophy, 20,* 91-107.

Kass, L. (2002). *Life, liberty and the defense of dignity.* San Francisco, CA: Encounter Books.

Kellehear, A. (Ed.). (2000). *Death and dying in Australia,* Melbourne, Australia: Oxford University Press.

Kohlberg, L. (1981). *The philosophy of moral development.* New York: Harper and Row.

Kuhse, H. (1994). *Willing to listen, wanting to die.* Harmondsworth, Australia: Penguin.

McStay, R. (2003). Terminal sedation: Palliative care for intractable pain, post Glucksberg and Quill. *American Journal of Law and Medicine, 29*(1), 45-76.

Quill, T. (1991). Death and dignity: A case of individualized decision. *New England Journal of Medicine, 324,* 691-694.

Rawls, J., Thomson, J. J., Nagel, R., Dworkin, R., Scanlan, T. M., & Nagel, T. (1997). Assisted suicide: The philosophers' brief. *The New York Review of Books,* March 27.

Rowland, R. (1992). *Living laboratories.* Santa Fe, NM: Sun Books.

Sanderson, M. A. (2002). European convention on human rights—Assisted suicide: Pretty vs. U.K. *American Journal of International Law, 4,* 943-949.

Singer, P. (1994). *Rethinking life and death.* New York: St. Martin's Press.

Singer, P. (2001). Voluntary euthanasia: A utilitarian perspective. *Bioethics, 17*(5/6), 526.

The Age, Newspaper, Melbourne, July 27, 2005, p. 12.

Tulloch, G. (2005). *Euthanasia—Choice and death.* Edinburgh, UK: Edinburgh University Press.

Tulloch, G. (2005). A feminist utilitarian perspective on euthanasia: From Nancy Crick to Terri Schiavo. *Nursing Inquiry, 12*(2), 155-160.

Tulloch, G. (1995). Avoiding the slippery slope in ethics and bioethics. *Nursing Inquiry, 3*(1), 59.

Tulloch, G. (1989). *Mill and sexual equality.* New York: Harvester Wheatsheaf.

Tulloch, G. (1996). Why Euthanasia? A reflective response. *Nursing Inquiry, 2,* 225-230.

Tulloch, G., & Hart, G. (1996). Ethical issues. In M. Clinton & S. Nelson (Eds.), *Mental health and nursing practice.* Upper Saddle River, NJ: Prentice Hall.

Veatch, R. M. (2003). *The basics of bioethics.* Upper Saddle River, NJ: Prentice Hall.

Wolf, S. (1996). *Feminism and bioethics.* Oxford, UK: Oxford University Press.

CHAPTER 9

End-of-Life Care in Israel

Sara Carmel

In 1988, for the first time, an Israeli court directly addressed the question of a patient's right to forego medical treatment at the end of life. Mr. Eyal was a mentally competent adult who suffered from a terminal degenerative muscular disease. Aware of his condition, he requested not to be connected to a respirator when his lungs stop functioning. The District Court of Tel-Aviv granted his request, pointing out that the principle of sanctity of life, although important, is relevant in conditions where medical treatment can save and improve life, but is not as sacred in reference to a terminal patient. The court also stressed that this ruling does not oblige any doctor to commit it.

In June 2004, the District Court of Tel-Aviv complied with a family's request to disconnect a patient from the life-supporting instruments. The patient was a 71-year-old man who suffered from significant and irreversible brain damage and had been unconscious and paralyzed for 7 months. Judge Goren noted that the verdict was given to that specific case only.

These two court verdicts reflect the changes that have occurred in Israeli society during the 16-year lapse between them. While the first Israeli court case on end-of-life care (EOLC) addressed an appeal for withholding medical treatment from terminally ill patients, the latter dealt with withdrawing life-saving treatments. Furthermore, while the first court appeal was made by a mentally competent patient, the second was made by family members of an incompetent patient, based on his undocumented wishes that were presented solely to his family. These developments in Israeli court rulings indicate the need to change beliefs and EOLC-related behaviors in Israel. However, until December 2005, rules regarding EOLC were not stated in the Israeli Law. The withdrawal of life-sustaining treatments (LST), and advance directives were not legalized. Needless to say, homicide and assisted suicide are considered criminal felonies, although committing suicide is no longer considered a felony. The punishment for assisted suicide is up to twenty years in jail.

The fact that the 2004 verdict was given in Israel 28 years after the 1976 Supreme Court of New Jersey ruling in favor of ceasing life-support treatments from an unconscious young woman, Karen Ann Quinlan, illustrates the similarities among different countries in terms of needs, and in moving toward similar solutions, as well as differences in the pace of addressing these problematic issues.

Similar to other developed nations, Israel enjoys the fruits of using the most advanced technological and scientific developments, and has to face the new problems and challenges that follow. The unique cultural and structural characteristics of Israeli society, however, influence its adaptation to changes in general, including the process of finding solutions to the problematic issues related to end-of-life care.

This chapter presents some of the sociocultural features of the Israeli society and how they have influenced the limited responses that Israel has provided to EOLC-related problems. EOLC-related problems are illustrated by research results, indicating significant discrepancies between the wishes of elderly persons and the actual practice of physicians. The chapter concludes with recommendations for substantial changes in approaches, policies, and medical practice.

SOCIOCULTURAL CHARACTERISTICS OF THE ISRAELI SOCIETY

The State of Israel was established after the holocaust in 1948 as a Jewish and democratic state. Israel's commitment to the Jewish and democratic systems of values appears in the Declaration of Independence. Since then, these two value systems have been the ethical sources for social guidance in daily life. The sanctity of life, quality of life, and personal autonomy are the basic principles in these value systems, as well as in those of many other societies. However, in comparison to Western countries, the value of personal autonomy in Israel is limited, in favor of preserving life (Glick, 1997).

An additional, quite dominant set of values that influenced the leaders, who established Israel and shaped many of its institutions, was a strong socialistic ideology. Thus, social solidarity, a principle deeply rooted in both the Jewish and socialistic orientations, was one of the cornerstones of the new nation, the influence of which was apparent in all areas of life. Israel's health care system is one of the institutions that have been based on this orientation and on the principle that unlimited health services should be provided according to one's needs, and paid for according to one's ability. Therefore, since the establishment of the state, the Israeli health-care system has been largely public, financed through a system of payroll progressive taxes and general taxation.

Under the 1995 national New Health Care Law (NHCL), every Israeli citizen is insured and eligible to a basket of basic health services, including hospitalization, ambulatory services, and medications. This basket, however, is limited. On the national level, the achievements of the NHCL are mainly noticed in the reduction of national expenditures on health. Israelis strongly criticize this reform, because, although personal expenses on health-care services have increased, the introduction of the health-care basket actually limits the availability of and accessibility to health services, mainly for the poor. Furthermore, before the NHCL, the cost of medical care had no influence on treatment decisions made by physicians or patients. Currently, although in the daily provision of health services, neither physicians nor patients actually see a medical bill, they often have to deal with monetary problems regarding aspects of care that are not included in the health basket. All of these changes, which contradict Israelis' basic beliefs and their principles about the delivery of health-care services, have caused significant frustration to the public and have become constant sources of political debates in the Knesset (the Israeli parliament).

These repeated debates can be better understood against the background of the centrality of health in Israeli society, which can be noticed in the relative resources allocated for health on both the national and personal levels. Israel is considered one of the countries with the largest share of nonmilitary resources spent on health (Rosen, 1987), and in which the ratio of physicians per population is among the highest in the world. On the personal level, sociological studies repeatedly show that Jews, significantly more than other ethnic groups, tend to be immersed in health worries and in illness behavior (Zborowsky, 1952). This tendency is expressed in the overuse of health services by both Jews in the United States, and in Israel (Anderson & Antebi, 1991; Mechanic, 1972).

The health profile of the Israeli population is probably an outcome of all of these orientations toward health and health behaviors, as well as the relatively high standard of living and the well-developed national health and social services. The average life expectancy at birth in Israel is 77.3 years for men, ranking sixth in the world, and 81.4 years for women. Life expectancy in Israel is higher than in other developed nations such as the United States, Belgium, and Germany (World Health Organization, 2004). Israel is also a rapidly aging society. The percentage of elderly people aged 65 and above in the Israeli population has more than doubled since the establishment of the state, from 3.8% in 1948 to 9.9% in 2002. The percentage of the old-old aged 75 and above grew even faster, to 45% of all the elderly in 2002 (Mashav, 2004). However, in comparison with other developed nations, Israel is still considered a young society.

All of these factors—the significant increase in the number of elderly people in Israel, the dominant perception that there are no limitations when prolonging life because it is sacred, the use of the most advanced medical technology, and a paternalistic approach in the provision of heath care—have expanded the scope of EOLC-related problems in recent decades. However, public awareness of these problems is relatively recent and has reached the stage of legalization only in December 2005. This law will be enacted in December 2006. In the meantime, court rulings take the leading role of expressing and shaping the Israeli society's approach to EOLC.

LEGAL DEVELOPMENTS

In a period of just over a decade, two laws applicable to the right to forego medical treatments were passed in Israel. In 1992, the Basic Law: Human Dignity and Liberty was enacted. One of the specified purposes of this law was to anchor in a Basic Law the values of the state of Israel as a Jewish and democratic state. Personal autonomy, the rights to human dignity, to bodily integrity, and to privacy evolve from this basic law (Shalev, 2000).

The Patient's Rights Law of 1996 was an outcome of recent changes in public opinion, including an increasing resistance to the paternalistic orientation prevailing in the delivery of medical care and the erosion of trust in doctors, which started with the long physicians' strike of 1983. This law formally regulates doctor/patient relationship and ensures patients' rights for self-determination and openness in doctor/patient communication. Medical treatment that is given to the patient without his or her explicit consent can be considered a criminal assault according to this law.

The original bill of Patient's Rights Law included a provision regarding the right of patients to die with dignity in accordance with his or her belief, requiring doctors and medical institutions to assist their patients in realizing these rights—item 10. This item was, however, removed from the last vote in the Knesset due to pressures from some of the religious parties. Two other personal attempts to legalize EOLC took place in 2000 but failed. In the same year, the Israeli Ministry of Health asked Professor Steinberg to establish the first professional committee for the preparation of a legislation proposal on EOLC. The proposed law was completed in 2002 and was accepted by parliament only in the end of 2005, but has not yet been enacted. A description of this committee's work is presented in Steinberg's chapter in this section.

Due to lack of clear and specific laws, over the years Israeli courts have dealt with numerous appeals regarding EOLC, all of which included requests for limiting or discontinuing treatments of severely ill patients. No physician was ever sued for assisting a patient in committing suicide or for intentionally hastening the death of a patient—active euthanasia. Although all the courts were guided by the Jewish and democratic values and the new laws, inconsistency can be noticed among the different rulings, especially with regard to the difference between withholding and withdrawing LST. The inconsistencies in rulings are explained by the different interpretations given to the guiding values and laws, which are influenced by the personal and religious view points of the judges. Nevertheless, an analysis of the verdicts of Israeli courts on EOLC issues indicates a number of points of agreement (Shalev, 2000): (A) Direct active euthanasia and physician-assisted suicide are not acceptable under any circumstances; (B) Futile treatment may be withheld from dying patients; (C) Patients have a right to refuse treatment corollary to the right to informed consent; (D) Doctors are not obliged to act contrary to their conscience; (E) In the case of an adult competent patient, the principle of autonomy and liberty is favored over the principle of sanctity of life. In the case of minors, the Supreme Court gives advantage to the principle of sanctity of life. In general, as presented in the introduction to the chapter, a clear trend has been noticed toward increased permissiveness for withholding and withdrawing medical treatments at the end of life.

The formal position of the Israeli authorities within the health-care system has been expressed in guidelines for health-care professionals. In 1996, the Israeli Ministry of Health issued some basic guidelines for Treatment of the Dying Patient. According to these guidelines, any intervention intended to hasten death is prohibited. However, treatments considered medically futile, that may only prolong the patient's natural dying process, such as a cardiopulmonary resuscitation performed on a terminally ill patient, may be withheld. This is also the formal position of the Israeli Medical Association. The withdrawal of LST is unacceptable according to these statements.

Court appeals and new guidelines often represent only the tip of the iceberg. Little is known in Israel about the iceberg of EOLC-related problems, including the needs, preferences, and behaviors of the public and physicians.

SOCIAL TRENDS IN ATTITUDES AND PRACTICE

One of the justifications for not advancing legislation on EOLC can be a silent agreement that exists between patients, families, and their doctors. The court appeals on EOLC, all of which were about limiting care, have indicated, however, that EOLC problems are not always silently solved. In a democratic country, preferences and behaviors of the most involved parties, in this case the public and physicians, have to be considered when trying to address social problems. Yet, very little was known in the early 1990s, about what people in Israel wanted and what actually happened in this area of social life. In view of the lack of open social debate on EOLC problems, scarcity of studies on these issues and shortage of any legalization initiatives, my group has begun a series of qualitative and quantitative studies about attitudes, preferences, and behaviors of the most involved parties, including elderly people, the public, and patients on the one hand, and physicians as well as paramedical professionals, on the other hand.

The first quantitative longitudinal study on a population group was conducted in 1994 on a national sample of 1138 Jewish elderly persons aged 70 and over (Carmel & Mutran, 1997a, 1997b). Another relatively large scale study on physicians was conducted in two stages, in the years 1997 (Carmel, 1999a) and 1999 (Carmel, 1999b), with similar results. A total of 443 doctors, working in four medical centers, in wards where terminally ill patients were treated, participated in this study.

The main issues investigated in both of these studies were what are often called passive euthanasia, including withholding and withdrawing LST, and active euthanasia, meaning intentional acts taken to end the life of another person. Active euthanasia encompasses two types of actions: A direct act of giving or injecting a lethal dose of a medication to a patient in order to end his life, and physician-assisted suicide, which is an indirect act of assisting a person to commit suicide.

A comparison between the two studies of elderly persons and physicians has shed some light on the degrees of agreement and disagreement between Israeli doctors and their potential patients regarding medical treatment at the end of life.

Passive Euthanasia: Preferences and Practices

Three scenarios were presented to the elderly participants of the study: terminal cancer, severe dementia, and physical disability, where they are bed-ridden and incontinent. After each scenario, the participants were asked about their wishes regarding the use of tube feeding, respirators, and cardio-pulmonary resuscitation (CPR) if they themselves were in this grave condition. The physicians received the same scenarios and were asked whether they would provide the same three treatments to an 80-year-old patient in these identical situations. Three major discrepancies were discovered between the desires of the elderly participants and the doctors' treatment (see Figure 1).

(A) Differences in the Extent of Desired and Provided Treatment

In general, physicians provide more treatment than desired by elderly people, with the exception of mechanical ventilation and CPR in the cancer condition, where physicians were willing to provide less than the elderly desired. The most noticeable differences were those in regard to tube feeding. The percentage of elderly who expressed a positive response ranged from 22% to 28%, in comparison to 54% to 90% among the physicians. This finding is in accordance with studies from other countries such as the United States, Germany, and Japan, showing that physicians tend to treat dying patients more aggressively than the patients would wish, even when patients leave advance directives with requests to withhold life-support treatments (Asch, Hansen-Flaschen, & Lanken, 1995; Sehgal, Weisheit, Miura, Butzlaff, Kielstein, & Taguchi, 1996).

(B) Gaps in Perceptions of Different Illness Conditions

The elderly participants did not differentiate among the three illness conditions described above. In all the conditions, 21% to 31% expressed the wish to receive one of the three treatments, with a minor preference to be treated more intensively in the cancer condition, while physicians would treat significantly different patients in the three illness conditions: They would provide the most treatment

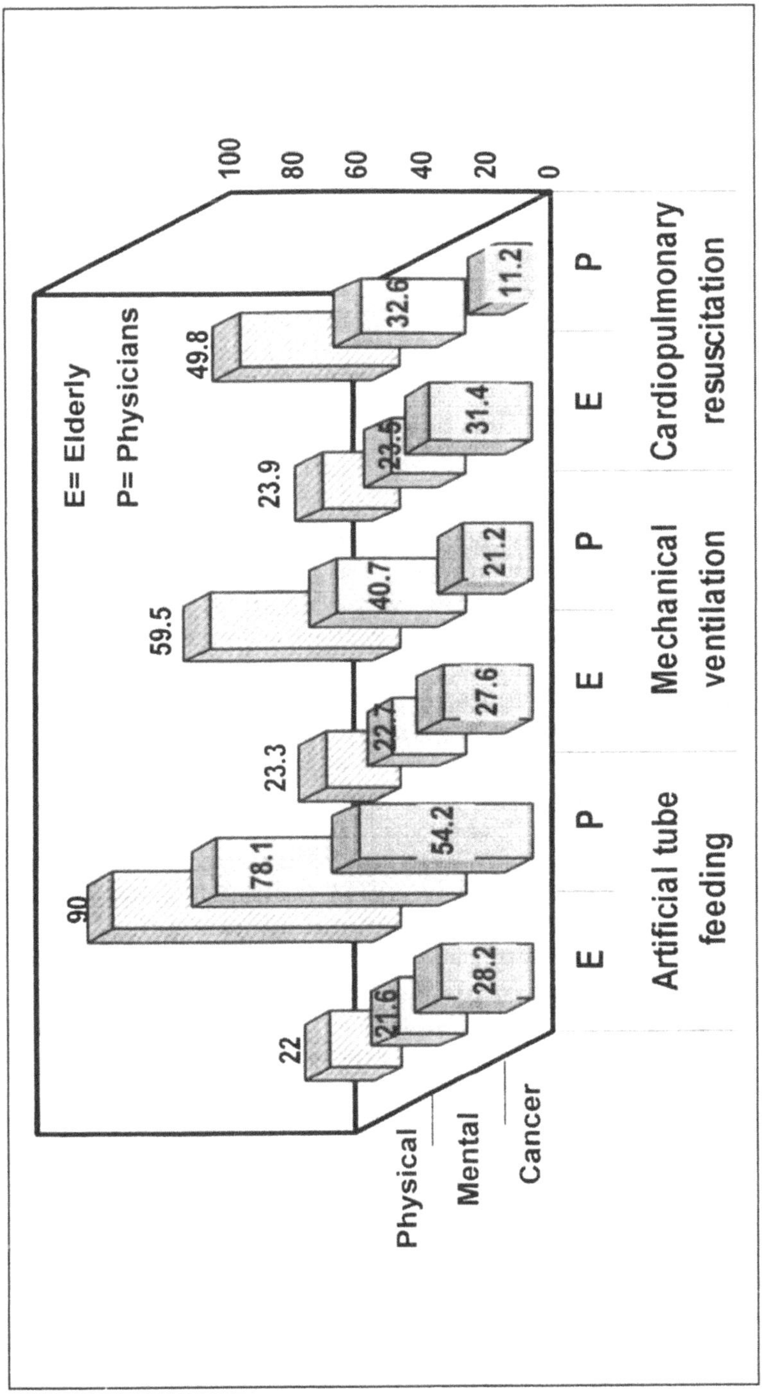

Figure 1. Physicians' practice and elderly patients' wishes regarding the use of different life-sustaining treatments in three illness conditions (in percent).

to bed-ridden patients (50% to 90%), less treatment to those with dementia (33% to 78%), and the least to cancer patients (11% to 54%). These findings indicate that physicians are mainly guided by their orientation and training, which direct them to focus on the chances of prolonging life, while potential patients concentrate on the quality of life.

(C) Differences in Preference for the Use of Different LST

Patients did not significantly discriminate between the three types of treatments that were described to them, although a preference for CPR over artificial tube feeding and respirators was noticed. This preference was significantly stronger when patients were asked about two other less-severe illness conditions (Carmel & Mutran, 1997a). Physicians, however, showed clear preferences. They were most likely to provide tube feeding (54% to 90%), less respirators (21% to 60%), and least resuscitation (11% to 50%) (Carmel, 1999b).

The most marked differences between the physicians and the elderly related to their perceptions of artificial feeding and CPR. Physicians' hypothetical behaviors represent the symbolic and emotional significance of giving food and drink—the essence of care (Lynn & Childress, 1986). This perception, which has also been observed in other countries, is a forcing factor in providing hydration and nutrition, even to patients for whom it is contraindicated (Micetich, Steinecker, & Thomasama, 1986), while the elderly persons seem to be influenced less by the symbolic meaning of tube feeding and view it as an artificial, invasive, and inconvenient procedure. They also prefer CPR over tube feeding and to a higher degree than the physicians would provide to terminal cancer patients. This tendency, recorded also in the United States, indicates that the public wrongly views CPR as a noninvasive intervention that either succeeds or fails, as it is demonstrated on TV and in the movies (Carmel & Mutran, 1997a; Murphy et al., 1994). Physicians view CPR differently because they are aware of the poor prognosis of this intervention, particularly for elderly patients. Similar responses to the same questions were received from Israeli nurses and social workers (Werner, Carmel, & Zeidenberg, 2004), indicating that professional caregivers in Israel share similar attitudes with regard to withholding medical treatments from the severely ill in different illness conditions.

In general, this tendency of medical personnel to address the basic physiological needs of patients, through hydration and nutrition, and the lesser use of heroic interventions, such as CPR, is not only in accordance with basic Israeli social values and law, but also with the leading Jewish religious authorities, who advocate that the dying process should not be prolonged, but the basic needs should be provided, including fluids, food, and oxygen (see Steinberg's chapter in this section).

Similar results from two parallel studies conducted in the Ukraine, which included 107 adults aged 50 and over and 107 physicians (Carmel & German, unpublished), and those of a large scale Japanese study of 5,000 adults and 3,104 physicians (Miyashita, Hashmoto, Kawa, & Kojima, 1999), indicate that the discrepancies found in our studies between physicians' practices and the public's preferences are also common in other countries.

An interesting question that arises in view of such disparities between doctors and patients is how the doctors would want to be treated when becoming severely ill themselves.

PHYSICIANS' PREFERENCES FOR MEDICAL TREATMENT FOR THEMSELVES VERSUS THEIR PRACTICE FOR ELDERLY PATIENTS

Our results, as presented in Figure 2, indicate that physicians want significantly less use of all four treatments for themselves should they be in the metastatic cancer condition, than they would order for elderly patients. In contrast to this statistically significant discrepancy, it is interesting to note that their preferences for the different LST are consistent with their practices for patients, indicating a clear preference for the use of artificial hydration and nutrition versus artificial ventilation and CPR. This finding supports the thesis presented earlier that the variances between physicians and the public regarding the use of the different LST derive from basic differences in knowledge and perceptions of these treatments by the two parties (Carmel, 1999a). This argument is also supported by studies conducted in the United States, demonstrating that after an informative intervention about the low chances for survival following CPR, a significant increase in the patients' Do-Not-Resuscitate orders is noticed (Murphy et al., 1994), which indicates that transmitting information and open communication can reduce underlying disagreements.

The finding that physicians want the use of LST less for themselves, should they be in a severe cancer condition, than they would order for their elderly patients in the same condition, supports those of previous and later studies conducted on Japanese and Japanese-American physicians (Asai, Fukuhara, & Lo, 1995), and on physicians in Russia and the Ukraine (Carmel, unpublished).

Further examination of the Israeli physicians' responses showed that the majority of Israeli physicians have positive attitudes toward withdrawing treatment in hopeless cases (82%) and providing "double effect" medications to lessen suffering, even if they shorten life (79% responded "always," and another 12% agreed with some reservations). Our findings, however, indicate that the physicians are much more conservative in their realistic practices than their expressed attitudes (Carmel, 1999b).

In practice, although Israeli physicians very rarely discuss the use of LST with their patients, many of them withhold and withdraw LST from their severely ill patients (Carmel, 1996, 1999b; Sonnenblick, Gratch, Raveh, Steinberg, & Yinnon, 2003). However, physicians clearly distinguish between withholding

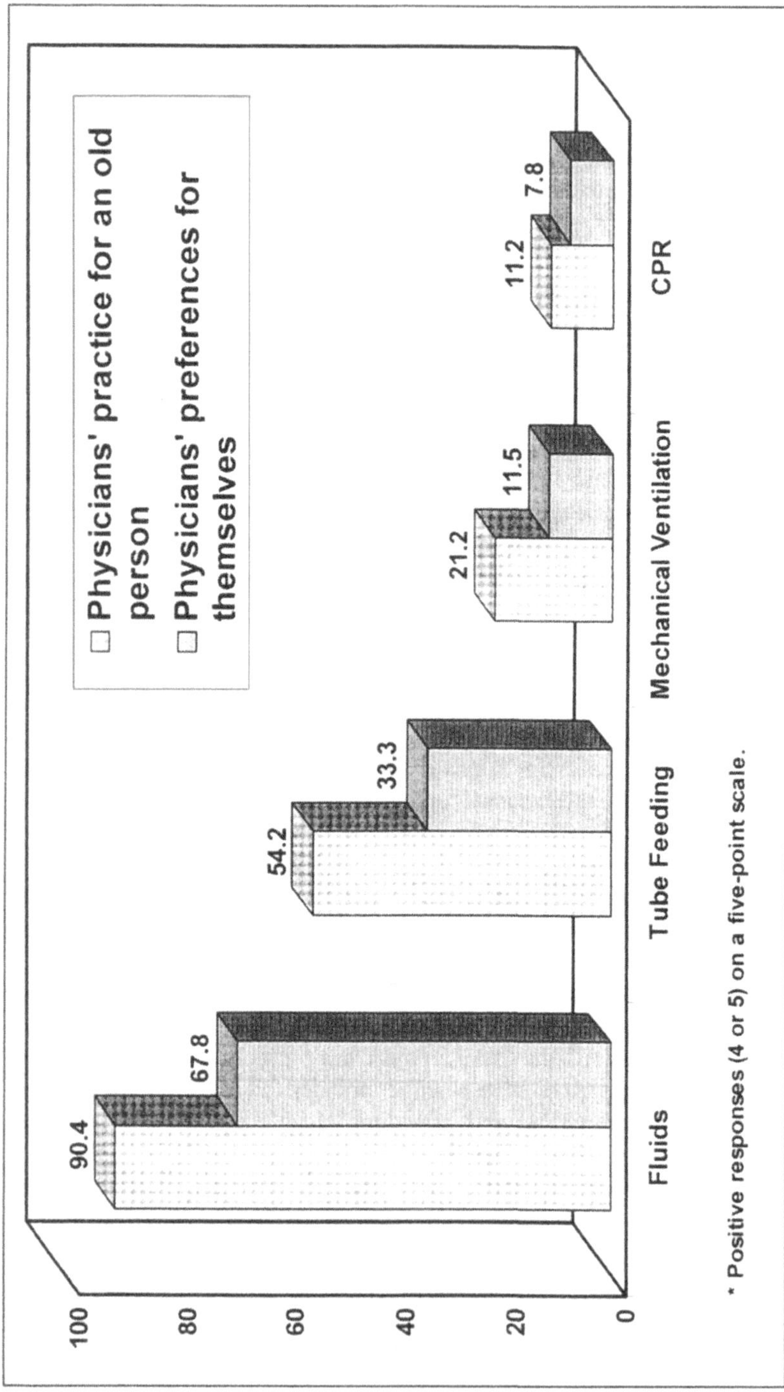

Figure 2. The use of life-sustaining treatments in a metastastic cancer condition: a comparison of physicians' practice and their wishes for themselves, in percents (*n* = 443).

and withdrawing treatment. Therefore, while withholding LST is quite common in Israel, withdrawing such treatments is rare even in ICU units (Eidelman et al., 1998). The scope of both practices is unknown because systematic documentation of such practices rarely exists in Israeli hospitals.

Subcultural Differences

Cultural and subcultural differences in preferences regarding the use of LST at the end of life are conspicuous among elderly Israelis. In the study of the elderly Jews, we found that the more religious people were, and the less educated they were, the more they desired the prolongation of their lives in the severe-illness conditions. In addition, men wanted the use of LST significantly more than women, and severely ill people wanted them less than their healthier counterparts (Carmel & Mutran, 1997a). Ethnic background was not found to be a significant predictor of preferences for LST in a model that included the fear of death and dying and the will to live (Carmel & Mutran, 1997b). A comparison between this sample of Israeli Jews and a sample of 130 Israeli Christian Arabs, aged 65+, who responded to the same questionnaire, revealed significant differences between them. While among the Jews, 21% to 31% wanted any LST in the presented severe-illness conditions, the percentages among the Arabs were unexpectedly high (66% to 78%). These discrepancies were mainly explained by the significant differences in the levels of education and religiosity that exist between the two subcultures (Churi, Werner, & Carmel, unpublished).

Religiosity was also found to be the best predictor of physicians' attitudes and practices regarding EOLC (Wenger & Carmel, 2005). For example, although religiosity was not related to withholding LST, very religious physicians, compared to moderately religious and secular physicians, were much less likely to believe that LST should be withdrawn from suffering terminally ill patients, to approve of prescribing pain medication that might hasten death, and to agree with active euthanasia.

In other countries, religiosity and gender were also reported as important factors in EOLC-related beliefs and behaviors. It thus appears that these factors and other sociocultural characteristics of patients and doctors should be considered in EOLC (Wenger & Carmel, 2005). Another factor, which is often mentioned by physicians as problematic in advanced planning of EOLC, is the instability of patients' expressed preferences for EOLC.

Stability of Preferences

One of the solutions to disagreements between doctors and their patients is enabling people to plan their EOLC in advance while they are still mentally competent and asking physicians to comply with their patients' wishes. Physicians, however, often argue that patients tend to change their preferences. We found that 70% of our elderly participants were consistent in their preferences over the course of two years. Another approximately 20% changed their minds toward preferring less treatment than they originally requested, and 10% reconsidered receiving more treatment. The most stable group was composed of people who originally wanted to forego treatment, among them 86% did not change their attitudes. Our results, therefore, indicate that elderly people not only have quite stable preferences regarding EOLC, but with time, more of them tend to prefer less use of LST in difficult health conditions (Carmel & Mutran, 1999). These levels of stability are very similar to those reported in two longitudinal studies of elderly people performed in the United States and the Netherlands (Danis, Garrett, Harris, & Patrick, 1994; Sullivan, Ormel, Kempen, & Tymstra, 1998), indicating that in general, elderly people of different cultural backgrounds respond similarly when facing the same EOLC problems. Furthermore, if preferences for EOLC are influenced by religiosity and level of education, similarities across nations between similar social groups may be greater than among different social groups within societies.

Active Euthanasia

Although active euthanasia is illegal in most countries, positive attitudes toward this medical practice are quite common. In our Israeli study, 52% of the elderly reported that they would want active euthanasia committed by doctors should their health condition deteriorate to one of the described illness conditions; 34% rejected it, and only 14% were indecisive. Sixty-five percent of the participants held the same preferences regarding active euthanasia after a period of two years. These findings indicate that elderly people in Israel have quite definitive and stable preferences regarding the practice of active euthanasia.

In the study of physicians, presented above, the percentage who in principle approved of active euthanasia was relatively high (44%). However, only 22% of the physicians reported that they would be ready to perform it themselves. It is important to note that the attitudes and practices of physicians in Israel, where no legal directives for EOLC existed, and withdrawing treatments after they have been started was forbidden, were similar to those reported in countries where investment in legal solutions was made and withdrawing LST is legal. Furthermore, despite the religious and legal prohibitions, Israeli physicians, like their American and Australian colleagues, also admit that they do commit voluntary as well as involuntary active euthanasia (Carmel, 1996; Douglas et al., 2001; Meier et al., 1998). Such phenomena can be understood against the background of the current contradictory social messages intertwined in the traditional paternalistic approach that causes physicians to be very careful, and often to withhold or withdraw LST in secrecy, without consulting the patient or the family, or even including a report about their action in the patient's medical chart (Carmel, 1996). In Israel, these silent behaviors are probably also influenced by physicians' deeply rooted belief that Israeli patients and families would want to receive the maximal care in all situations, which considering our findings, appears to be incorrect in regard to severe illness conditions.

The Family's Role

Often the families rather than the patients are the more involved party in medical decisions made at the end of life. Although the family has no formal or legal status in this regard, physicians regard them to be the best surrogates. They do so because family members are considered to be the closest people to the patient and to have his or her best interests in mind, they are usually involved in the patient's treatment and stay at the patient's bedside. Our findings indicate that this approach is also acceptable by the Israeli elderly respondents, 83% of whom said that if they were to become incompetent to make rational decisions, they would prefer their families to make the medical decisions for them rather than the doctors (Carmel, 1999b). Thus, the family plays a central role in medical decisions at the end of life, mainly because physicians feel uncomfortable discussing such issues with the patients when they are still able to make such decisions for themselves and to prepare some oral advance directive. However, similar to findings in other Western countries, only a small percent of families in Israel are involved in decisions to withhold treatments (Sonnenblick, Gratch, Raveh, Steinberg, & Yinnon, 2003), and significant discrepancies exist between family members' decisions regarding the withholding of life-support treatments and the patients' preferences (Sonnenblick, Friedlander, & Steinberg, 1993).

In view of the reported discrepancies between patients and doctors, and patients and their families, open communication, which includes exchange of feelings, knowledge, and preferences, among all three parties seems to be the suitable measure for reducing disagreements and making end of life more tolerable to all.

Communication on End-of-Life Care

The paternalistic model of doctor/patient relations, which was dominant in Israel until recent years, still prevails, especially with regard to people with low levels of education and elderly persons. In trying to prevent emotional suffering in elderly patients, physicians and families often do not inform them about a life-threatening diagnosis or an approaching death. This occurs despite our findings indicating that most of the doctors acknowledge the patient's right to be the chief influence in EOLC decision making and the Patient's Rights Law (Carmel, 1999b). However, a large proportion of the Israeli elderly people (approximately 70%) prefer to receive information about their condition even if terminal and to be involved in the decision-making process (Carmel & Lazar, 1997). These gaps can be explained by the substantial percentage of doctors and nurses who report having difficulties with treating dying patients in general, and in communicating with them on EOLC issues in particular. Medical teams in Israel also express the need for clearer directions on the treatment of dying patients and a desire for more conversation on these issues among the members of the medical staff within the hospital departments. Such requirements, mainly expressed by young physicians and nurses, are not met in most Israeli hospital departments (Carmel, 1996, 1999b; Werner et al., 2004).

Difficulties in EOLC communication among medical teams are also reported in other countries. This problem is prevalent even in countries where the patterns of communication are more open, and people are asked to sign forms, which include instructions for resuscitation (DNR), as part of standard hospitalization procedure. For example, the large scale U.S. SUPPORT study, which encompassed five central medical centers and focused on a controlled intervention intended to improve doctor/patient communication at the end of life, showed no improvement in communication after two years of intervention. The researchers of this study concluded that it is extremely difficult to change working patterns of a medical team (Connors et al., 1995). Over time, however, changes do occur. The number of physicians who report feeling quite at ease when speaking with their patients on limiting treatment is increasing (Goetzler & Moskowitz, 1991). Training programs in physician/patient communication can contribute to improving these skills (Gordon & Tolle, 1991).

Many explanations have been given to physicians' difficulties in maintaining open communication about EOLC with terminally ill patients. Among them are the classical western medical orientation, which focuses on defeating disease and saving lives, and the dominant propensity of western societies to deny death.

The denial of death is common in all western cultures. It prevents physicians from revealing their patients' preferences for care at the end of their lives and prevents patients from sharing openly death-related worries with their doctors and family members. The lack of communication even further increases the stress of the dying process for all involved parties. This phenomenon is expressed in our studies, which show that elderly people, the public, and medical personnel mainly fear the dying process rather than death itself (Carmel, 2001; Carmel & Mutran, 1997b).

Despite an increase in the awareness of these problems in recent years, and the advances in palliative care and special services for terminal patients, medical education does not prepare doctors to deal with EOLC-related problems, and programs on comprehensive supportive care for dying patients and their families are lacking in Israeli medical schools.

SUMMARY AND CONCLUSIONS

Significant percentages of patients and physicians in Israel approve of passive and active euthanasia, when it is voluntary and performed by physicians. However, similar to findings from other countries, many Israeli physicians who in principle support the different types of passive and active euthanasia are not ready to carry them out, even if legalized. In practice, physicians are less likely to withhold LST than desired by elderly persons, and to an even lesser extent than what they would want for themselves. Elderly patients are thus not treated according to their preferences. Although, in principle, there is general agreement between elderly people and physicians on the legitimacy of withholding the use of LST in severe illness conditions, there are substantial discrepancies between the two parties as to the application of these practices. The gaps are noticed in the extent of use of LST, in the differentiation among the illness conditions in which treatment should be prevented, and in the differentiation among the types of LST that should be avoided. For many doctors, it is difficult to withdraw treatment after it was started, because they perceive this action as causing immediate death. Physicians are also more reluctant than the elderly to view euthanasia as a solution for suffering at the end of life, and even when they support it in principle, a large percentage of them are unwilling to actively perform it.

The existing discrepancies between physicians and the public indicate social embarrassment caused by societal exposure to new situations that have no clear behavioral norms. The old norms are no longer fitting, and new social norms have not yet been developed. The positive attitudes of most of the public regarding passive and active euthanasia and the fear of dying reflect the public's worries about the use of futile medical treatments that only prolong the dying process.

In view of the revealed underlying disagreements, and the intense fear of dying, open doctor/patient communication seems to be a solution. Open communication is, however, problematic in Israel. Most of the elderly people want open communication about EOLC, but medical personnel, although aware of the importance of dying patients' involvement in the decision-making process at the end of life, tend to avoid it. Therefore, physicians often withhold and withdraw treatment at the end of life without the patient's knowledge. Family members, more than the patients themselves, are involved in EOLC decision making, especially in cases of elderly patients, even though their preferences are often different from those of the patients.

Since our findings are similar to those found in other countries, it is suggested that elderly people tend to have definite and quite stable preferences for medical care at the end of their lives, and that EOLC problems and solutions have become a worldwide phenomenon. Practical solutions to this problem, however, have been delayed in Israel for a long period of time. Considering the current end-of-life-care-related distress, our findings of high frequencies of fear of dying and the lack of agreement regarding EOLC practices, Israel, similar to many other nations, must address this social problem by introducing considerable changes in a number of areas: (A) Promote palliative care by increasing investment in research and services, and systematically provide information to the public about the existence of palliative care, and its effectiveness in reducing the agony of dying; (B) Invest in educating the public on EOLC alternatives and the effectiveness of the various LST; (C) Clarify to all the parties involved what is acceptable and what is prohibited by formulating clear guidelines for medical treatment and by legalizing mechanisms for advanced planning; (D) Change the approach to death by initiating channels of open communication and requiring doctors to hold discussions with patients in order to elicit their values and preferences for EOLC and reduce their fear of dying; (E) Introduce educational and training programs for professional caregivers on how to treat dying patients and their families, and how to communicate with patients about EOLC.

Although all of these changes should be addressed by many of the societal institutions—medical, political, and legal—we feel that it is the medical profession that should take the leading role in activating the recommended changes in EOLC. This includes promoting appropriate programs in medical schools and continuing education, and increasing societal knowledge about EOLC and awareness of the needed changes.

REFERENCES

Anderson, G. F., & Antebi, S. (1991). A surplus of physicians in Israel: Any lessons for the United States and other industrialized countries? *Health Policy, 17*, 77-86.

Asai, A., Fukuhara, S., & Lo, B. (1995). Attitudes of Japanese and Japanese-American physicians toward life-sustaining treatment. *The Lancet, 346*, 356-359.

Asch, D. A., Hansen-Flaschen, J., & Lanken, P. N. (1995). Decisions to limit or continue life-sustaining treatment by critical care physicians in the United States: Conflicts between physicians' practices and patient's wishes. *American Journal of Respiratory Critical Care Medicine, 151*, 288-292.

Brodsky, J., Shnoor, Y., & Be'er, S. (2004). *The elderly in Israel: Statistical abstract 2003*. Jerusalem, Israel: Mashav—National Database, JDC—Brookdale Institute & ESHEL.

Carmel, S. (unpublished). *Physicians' preferences for end of life care for themselves and their practice for elderly patients in Russia and the Ukraine.*

Carmel, S. (1996). Behavior, attitudes, and expectations regarding the use of life-sustaining treatments among physicians in Israel: An exploratory study. *Social Science & Medicine, 43*, 955-966.

Carmel, S. (1999a). Life-sustaining treatments: What doctors do, what they want for themselves and what elderly persons want. *Social Science & Medicine, 49*, 1401-1408.

Carmel, S. (1999b). *Behavior, attitudes and expectations regarding the use of life-sustaining treatments among physicians in Israel.* Science Report to the Israeli Ministry of Health, 3628.

Carmel, S. (2001). Fear of death and fear of dying scales: Structure and psychometric properties. *Gerontology: Journal of the Israeli Gerontological Society, 28*, 133-153.

Carmel, S., & German, L. (unpublished). *Doctors' practices and elderly patients' wishes regarding the use of life sustaining treatments at the end of life in the Ukraine.*

Carmel, S., & Lazar, A. (1997). Giving bad news: To what extent do elderly persons want to know, and to participate in the process of medical decision making. *Harefua—Journal of the Israeli Medical Association, 133*, 505-509.

Carmel, S., & Mutran, E. (1997a). Preferences for different life-sustaining treatments among elderly persons in Israel. *Journal of Gerontology: Social Sciences, 52B*(2), S97-S102.

Carmel, S., & Mutran, E. (1997b). Wishes regarding the use of life- sustaining treatments among elderly persons in Israel: An explanatory model. *Social Science & Medicine, 45,* 1715-1727.

Carmel, S., & Mutran, E. (1999). Stability of elderly persons' expressed preferences regarding the use of life-sustaining treatments. *Social Science & Medicine, 49,* 303-311.

Churi, G., Werner, P., & Carmel, S. (unpublished). *Attitudes towards life-prolonging treatments among Arab Christians, aged 65 and over.*

Connors, A. F., Dawson, N. V., Desbeins, N. A., Fulkerson, W. J., Goldman, L., Knaus, W. A., Lynn, J., & Oye, K. (1995). A controlled trial to improve care for seriously ill hospitalized patients. *Journal of the American Medical Association, 274,* 1591-1598.

Danis, M., Garrett, J., Harris, R., & Patrick, D. L. (1994). Stability of choices about life-sustaining treatments. *Annals of Internal Medicine, 120,* 567-573.

Douglas, C. D., Kerridge, I. H., Rainbird, K. J., McPhee, J. R., Hancock, L., & Spigelman, A. D. (2001). The intention to hasten death: A survey of attitudes and practices of surgeons in Australia. *Medical Journal of Australia, 175,* 511-515.

Eidelman, L. A., Jakobson, D. J., Pizov, R., Geber, D., Leibovitz, L., & Sprung, C. L. (1998). Foregoing life-sustaining treatment in an Israeli ICU. *Intensive Care Medicine, 24,* 162-166.

Glick, S. M. (1997). Unlimited human autonomy—A cultural bias? *The New England Journal of Medicine, 336,* 954-956.

Goeztler, R. M., & Moskowitz, M. A. (1991). Changes in physician attitudes towards limiting care of critically ill patients. *Archives of Internal Medicine, 151,* 1537-1540.

Gordon, G. H., & Tolle, S. W. (1991). Discussing life-sustaining treatment. A teaching program for residents. *Archives of Internal Medicine, 151*(3), 567-570.

Lynn, J., & Childress, J. F. (1986). Must patients always be given food and water? In J. Lynn (Ed.), *By no extraordinary means* (pp. 47-60). Bloomington, IN: Indiana University Press.

Mashav National Database. (2004). *The elderly in Israel: Statistical abstracts 2003.* JDC-Brookdale Institute & Eshel.

Mechanic, D. (1972). Response factors in illness: The study of illness behavior. In E. G. Jeco (Ed.), *Patients, physicians and illness* (pp. 128-140). New York: The Free Press.

Meier, D. E., Emmons, C. A., Wallenstein, S., Quill, T., Morrison, S. R., & Cassel, C. K. (1998). A national survey of physician-assisted suicide and euthanasia in the United States. *New England Journal of Medicine, 338,* 1193-1201.

Micetich, K., Steinecker, P., & Thomasama, D. (1986). An empirical study of physician attitudes. In J. Lynn (Ed.), *By no extraordinary means* (pp. 39-43). Bloomington, IN: Indiana University Press.

Miyashita, M., Hashmoto, S., Kawa, M., & Kojima, M. (1999). Attitudes towards terminal care among the general population and medical practitioners in Japan. *Nippon Koshu Eisei Zasshi, 46,* 391-401.

Murphy, D. J., Burrow, D., Santilli, S., Kemp, A. W., Tenner, S., Kreling, B., & Teno, J. (1994). The influence of the probability of survival on patients' preferences regarding cardiopulmonary resuscitation. *New England Journal of Medicine, 330,* 545-549.

Rosen, B. (1987). *The health of the Israeli people: An international comparison based on the World Health Organization's "Quantitative indicators for the European region."* Jerusalem, Israel: Brookdale Institute of Gerontology and Adult Human Development.

Sehgal, A. R., Weisheit, C., Miura, Y., Butzlaff, M., Kielstein, R., & Taguchi, Y. (1996). Advance directives and withdrawal of dialysis in the United States, Germany, and Japan. *Journal of the American Medical Association*, *276*, 1652-1656.

Shalev, C. (2000). Paternalism and autonomy in end-of-life decision-making: The Israeli normative ambivalence. In Y. Dinstein (Ed.), *29th Israeli yearbook on human rights*, 29 (pp. 121-136). The Netherlands: Kluwer Law International.

Sonnenblick, M., Friedlander, Y., & Steinberg, A. (1993). Dissociation between the wishes of terminally ill parents and decisions by their offspring. *Journal of the American Geriatrics Society*, *41*, 599-604.

Sonnenblick, M., Gratch, L., Raveh, D., Steinberg, A., & Yinnon, A. (2003). Epidemiology of decision on life sustaining treatment in the general internal medicine division. *Harefua—Journal of the Israeli Medical Association*, *142*(10), 650-653.

Steinberg, A. (1994). The terminally ill—Secular and Jewish ethical aspects. *Israel Journal of Medical Sciences*, *30*, 130-135.

Sullivan, M., Ormel, J., Kempen, G. I. J. M., & Tymstra, T. J. (1998). Beliefs concerning death, dying, and hastening death among older, functionally impaired Dutch adults: A one-year longitudinal study. *Journal of the American Geriatrics Society*, *46*, 1251-1257.

Wenger, N. S., & Carmel, S. (2005). Physicians' religiosity and end-of-life care attitudes and behaviors. *The Mount Sinai Journal of Medicine*, *71*(5), 335-343.

Werner, P., Carmel, S., & Zeidenberg, H. (2004). Nurses' and social workers' attitudes and beliefs about involvement in life sustaining treatments. *Health & Social Work*, *29*(1), 27-35.

World Health Organization. (2004). *World health report: Changing the history*. Geneva: Author.

Zborowsky, M. (1952). Cultural components in response to pain. *Journal of Social Issues*, *8*, 16-30.

CHAPTER 10

The Dying Patient: Israeli Attitudes and Proposals

Avraham Steinberg

The moral, sociocultural, religious, and legal aspects of the treatment of the dying patient are among the most difficult and widely discussed topics in modern medicine, encompassing tens of books, hundreds of declarations, directives, laws and judgments, and thousands of professional and nonprofessional articles within the realm of medicine, philosophy, law, sociology, and religion.

Although the approach to the dying patient has been one of the most prominent problems within medicine since time immemorial, the dilemma has been intensified in the past few decades. This is due to the enormous advances in medicine and technology, the change in the patient/physician relationship from a paternalistic to an autonomous approach, the massive involvement of various professionals in the treatment of the dying patient, and the economic and cultural changes in recent years.

Israeli society, like any other Western society, has been struggling with this dilemma for many years. Various policies (official and non-official), court cases, and declarations have been proposed and acted out, but so far no law has been enacted.

The actual behavior of health-care professionals in Israel toward dying patients is unknown. There are only a few sporadic studies from specific units and hospitals in Israel concerning DNR orders. One study from an Intensive Care Unit in Jerusalem reported that in 13.5% of the patients in the Unit a DNR order was administrated. The order included only withholding further life-support treatment but not withdrawal of treatment. Antibiotic treatment as well as food and fluid were continued. The average time of death after the order was three days (Eidelman, Jakobson, Pizov, Geber, Leibovitz, & Sprung, 1998). Another study conducted in an Internal Medicine Wing of one medical center in Jerusalem demonstrated significant ethical problems in the decision-making process concerning DNR orders. According to this study, a DNR order was administrated in 8.8% of the admissions to the departments. In no case was the patient himself consulted about the decision; in only 29% was the decision reached together with family members; and in 26% the decision was made by a junior house-physician alone (Sonneblick, Gratch, Raveh, Steinberg, & Yinnon, 2003). It is unknown, however, if these conducts represent the behaviors of other medical centers in Israel. There seems to be a confused situation, where different physicians act in different ways, very often without discussing the specific issues related to particular patients, neither with the patients themselves or even with their next of kin, or with other health-care professionals. Decisions concerning matters of life and death are not reported or documented.

On February 20, 2000 the minister of health appointed Professor Avraham Steinberg, a Medical Ethicist and a Pediatric Neurologist, to head a national committee for enacting a law that will regulate all matters concerning the dying patient in Israel. The trigger for the establishment of this committee was the case of Itai Arad in 1998, an Israeli pilot who suffered from amyotrophic lateral sclerosis (ALS), was intubated, and requested to withdraw the respirator. A local ethics committee disapproved the act, but a judge at the district court of Tel Aviv approved this request. For the first time in Israel, a respirator was withdrawn from a respirator-dependent patient in an overt and open manner. The patient died within several hours. A heated debate followed in the *Knesset* (Israeli parliament) and in the media.

Since the attitude toward the dying patient is a highly loaded issue, and since there are many varied and opposing approaches to this matter, it was decided to establish a wide committee that will represent all the relevant aspects. It was also decided to establish a strictly professional committee with no political or media influences. The idea was to enable professionals from every relevant field to freely express their standpoint, with no hesitations based on being politically correct or fear of exposure to the media.

Following is a brief summary of the mode of function of the Committee and of the major principles of the law which was proposed by the Committee.

The Committee was composed of 59 people, probably the largest committee ever established in Israel for a specific issue. There were 45 men and 14 women; 56 members were Jewish, one Christian, one Muslim, and one Druze. Of the Jewish members, 34 were secular, 17 were Orthodox-religious, 3 were Ultra-Orthodox, one Conservative, and one Reform. All members of the Committee were experts, high-ranking professionals in relevant fields. All relevant disciplines were represented. These members represented the entire spectrum of relevant views in Israel. None of them were a political or otherwise interested appointment. During almost two years (April, 2000 to January, 2002) intense debates took place. Every opinion and viewpoint was freely expressed and seriously discussed with great mutual respect. All debates and discussions were closed to the media, and indeed during the entire period of formulating the proposed law, there was no leak to the media. This was an important step in order to enable totally free communication and expression of opinions. There was a serious attempt by all members to reach as wide a consensus as possible despite the very difficult and emotionally loaded issues at stake.

The Committee was divided into four sub-committees: 1) *A medical/scientific subcommittee* composed of 26 members, including physicians, nurses, social workers and sociologists. The physicians represented all relevant fields of medicine which deal with dying patients (intensive care, palliative medicine, cardiology, geriatrics, anesthesiology, psychiatry, pediatrics, neonatology, rehabilitation, oncology, neurology and hospital management). 2) *A philosophical/ethical subcommittee* composed of 12 members, including philosophers, medical ethicists, and clergy from different religions (Jewish Reform and Conservative, Christian Greek-Orthodox, Islam, and Druze). 3) *A legal subcommittee* composed of 13 members, including judges, lawyers, professors of law, and legal advisors of relevant ministries. 4) *A halakhic (Jewish law) subcommittee* composed of 7 members, including Rabbis and physicians that are well-versed in matters of medicine and *halakhah*.

Each subcommittee discussed all relevant matters from their professional standpoint. They convened 35 times. More than 20 scientific papers were submitted by members of the Committee in order to better understand relevant facts and positions.

The entire committee convened three times to discuss the proposed law. There were six full drafts before the final version was presented to the Minister of Health on January 17, 2002. The minister endorsed the entire proposal.

The proposed law is a detailed document of principles and practical applications, which represent a balance between opposing values and positions. This balance is appropriate for the current culture and society of Israel, which is based upon Jewish and democratic values.

Despite the inherent complexity of the subject from medical, moral, philosophical, religious, legal, sociocultural, and psychological aspects, and despite the deep differences of opinion between members of the Committee, based upon their diverse backgrounds and philosophical and ethical stand-points, the Committee managed to reach a wide consensus on most issues related to the dying patient. Eighty percent of the members agreed on all the paragraphs of the proposed law; 100% of the members agreed on 95% of the paragraphs. The only significant dissenting opinion was on the issue of withdrawing continuous treatment from a dying patient. Although in principle there remains a disagreement on this issue, with a minority opinion accepting the principle that there is no difference between withholding and withdrawing any therapy, the Committee managed to minimize the practical disagreement by accepting the idea of a timer attached to a respirator.

Hence, it gives great satisfaction to note that the Committee was successful in reaching a wide consensus on the most difficult issue in medical ethics. It came about due to a serious debate, openly expressed views, with no publicity during the discussions, and particularly due to good intentions and strong determination by all members of the Committee to reach a workable and balanced solution to a very difficult issue.

The basic assumptions of the proposed law are that the majority of people do not want to die. On the other hand, the majority of people do not want to suffer at the end of life, and they do not want their lives to be prolonged artificially without purpose.

Another basic assumption of the proposed law is that decisions should be based only upon the medical condition of the patient, his wishes, and his suffering. No other considerations should matter when deciding how to treat the dying patient, including race, sex, age, economic status, mental status, lifestyle, and the like, unless bearing upon the wishes of the patient or his medical condition.

From a philosophical and moral point of view there is a need to determine an appropriate balance between various opposing values and principles such as the value of life, quality of life, personal autonomy, beneficence, nonmaleficence, distributive justice, slippery slope, and others. The proposed law sanctions life by prohibiting any action that intentionally shortens life, even if these acts were requested autonomously by the patient. They include active euthanasia, physician-assisted suicide, withdrawal of a continuous treatment such as a pacemaker or a respirator with the knowledge that these acts will cause the patient's death, and starving or dehydrating a patient to death. On the other hand, the proposed law respects an autonomous decision of a patient to withhold any treatment directly related to the dying process. This includes the withholding of any active intervention to prolong life such as intubation, ventilation, surgery, chemotherapy, and the like. It also includes the withholding of further intervention by intermittent treatments, such as dialysis or chemotherapy, even after they were initiated. The proposed law also requires providing palliative care to the patient and to his family. This includes palliative treatment that might unintentionally shorten life, based on the principle of double effect.

All members of the Committee were in full agreement concerning the prohibition of active euthanasia, and all members except for one were in full agreement concerning the prohibition of physician-assisted suicide. All members of the Committee were also in full agreement concerning the permission to withhold life-prolonging treatment in a situation of a dying patient. However, a minority of members disagreed with the prohibitions to withdraw continuous treatment and to withhold food and fluid.

Since almost no one advocates acceptance of an extreme and absolute position concerning either the value of life (i.e., prolonging *any* life by *all* means at *all* times, even when it adds only pain and suffering) or the principle of personal autonomy (i.e., accepting autonomous wishes for active euthanasia of healthy people or even of nonterminally ill patients), there is an obvious need to strike a balancing line between these values. However, any distinguishing boundary line is strongly arguable. Hence, the majority of the Committee chose to strike the balancing line between commission and omission, whereas the minority suggested striking the line between treatment and nontreatment. There are no practical differences between the two groups concerning almost all forms of treatment. Both of theses groups agree that in the case of an intermittent treatment, such as dialysis, it is permissible to withhold further treatment, either because withdrawal is permissible or because such treatment is viewed as omitting the next treatment rather than committing an act of withdrawal. However, there is an applied practical difference between these positions concerning the withdrawal of a respirator. Since it is a continuous form of treatment, there needs to be an act to stop it; hence, it is unacceptable by the majority's position. In order to minimize the differences of opinion, the Committee suggested accepting the changing of the ventilator from a continuous form of treatment to an intermittent form of treatment. This can be achieved by connecting the respirator to a timer (Ravitsky, 2005). As to withholding food and fluid from the dying patient, the minority opinion advocated the acceptance of such an act if that is the patient's wish, because it fulfills the principle of autonomy; it is a form of treatment and should be regarded the same way as any other life-sustaining treatment; and it might add suffering and complications. The majority opinion regarded food and fluid as a basic need of any living being, including the dying patient, rather than merely a form of treatment; socially and emotionally there is a fundamental difference between food and fluid and other life-sustaining treatments; dying of starvation and dehydration is an indignity to life; withholding food and fluid is unrelated to the dying process and hence should be regarded as a form of euthanasia; medical complications of nutrition and hydration should be considered individually and appropriately, not as an unfounded slogan. According to the majority opinion, the balance between respect for the value of life and respect for autonomy should be as follows: A currently competent dying patient who refuses food and fluids should be encouraged to change his mind, but should not be forced against his wishes; thus, the respect for dignity is preserved and overrides the respect for value of life. On the other hand, a currently incompetent dying patient should be sustained with food and fluid, because the value of life in such situation overrides the currently unknown autonomous wishes of the patient.

From a Jewish/religious point of view, there is a need to determine the boundaries of responsibility to prolong life versus the avoidance of unjustifiable suffering. The value of life, according to Judaism, is one of the most important values. However, according to relevant *halakhic* principles and actual rulings of some of the most prominent Rabbis, it is not an infinitive or an absolute value. Hence, any act that shortens life is *halakhically* considered as murder, even at the very end of life. Therefore, active euthanasia, physician-assisted suicide, the withdrawal of a continuous treatment such as a pacemaker or a respirator, and starving or dehydrating a living person to death is absolutely forbidden. On the other hand, there is no obligation to actively prolong the pain and suffering of a dying patient. Hence, it is permissible to withhold any treatment directly related to the dying process, including the withholding of intermittent treatments, such as dialysis or chemotherapy, even after they were initiated. Moreover, there is a Jewish/theological requirement to alleviate pain and suffering as best as possible; hence, palliative care is sanctioned. The *halakhic* arguments and sources relevant to this proposed legislation have been summarized elsewhere (Steinberg, 2003).

From a medical/scientific point of view, there is a need to define various medical situations and treatments as well as to execute the legal directions and decisions. Therefore, the proposed law requires appointing a senior physician as the responsible person to analyze all the relevant facts together with all the relevant experts and decision makers, to formulate a detailed plan of commissions and omissions, and to document all the decisions in a clear and overt manner. The decisions ought to be made on firm medical grounds as well as upon the patient's wishes, stated directly or indirectly in an accepted manner.

From a social/cultural point of view, there is a need to resolve issues concerning both competent and incompetent patients, relate to various decision makers, and establish problem/solution mechanisms for a variety of situations. Therefore, the proposed law establishes a hierarchy of decision makers: in case of a competent dying patient, his wishes take precedence over any other mode of decision making; in case of an incompetent dying patient, the decisions ought to be made according to advanced medical directives or a surrogate appointed by the patient while competent. The Committee proposed detailed ways of verifying that the advanced medical directives are indeed the calculated wishes of the now-incompetent dying patient, including the establishment of a national pool of advanced medical directives. The administrative personnel of the pool will send reminders every five years to the owners of the advanced directives to verify whether or not they have changed their minds about the directives. The pool will also serve as a source of information whenever an incompetent patient is admitted to a hospital, and it is unknown whether or not he has advance directives. Testimonies about the incompetent dying patient's wishes by family members or friends known to be emotionally closely related to the patient are also acceptable.

The Committee proposed to establish institutional ethics committees as a problem-solving mechanism. The Committee also proposed to establish a national ethics committee with the mandate to solve more difficult problems as well as establishing policies whenever needed.

It is beyond the scope of this summary to deal in-depth with the details of the proposed law. Suffice it to say that the proposed law contains definitions, determinations, and solutions to all the above-mentioned issues and many more, and that there are innovative solutions to difficult problems related to the dying patient.

The proposed law of the Committee was accepted by the Israeli government on May 23, 2004, and hence became the official governmental proposition of the Act Concerning the Dying Patient, 2004. In December 2005, the Knesset voted to accept the proposed law, and it was accepted with a great majority. The new Act of the Dying Patient, 2005 will become effective in December 2006.

REFERENCES

Eidelman, L. A., Jakobson, D. J., Pizov, R., Geber, D., Leibovitz, L., & Sprung, C. L. (1998). Foregoing life-sustaining treatment in an Israeli ICU. *Intensive Care Medicine, 24*(2), 162-166.

Ravitsky, V. (2005). Timers on ventilators. *British Medical Journal, 330,* 415-417.

Sonneblick, M., Gratch, L., Raveh, D., Steinberg, A., & Yinnon, A. M. (2003). Epidemiology of decision on life-sustaining treatment in the internal medicine division. *Harefua, 142*(10), 650-653.

Steinberg, A. (2003). The *halakhic* basis for the proposed law on the dying patient. *Assia, 25,* 71-72.

CHAPTER 11

Advance Directives

Jiska Cohen-Mansfield

HISTORY AND DEFINITIONS

Advance directives are documents in which people can record their wishes for health-care decisions in the event that they lose the ability to make or communicate decisions in the future. In these documents, people may designate a proxy who would make health-care decisions for them, or they can describe their preferences concerning health-care decisions under specific future conditions. The purpose of advance directives is to allow individuals control over their own care when they are no longer able to make such decisions. By preparing for an unknown situation with specific instructions, advance directives allow, at least in theory, people to live and die in the ways they want to, within the limits of clinical boundaries as well as social and legal constraints. This chapter briefly describes the history and definitions of advance directives, the theories underlying the concept, research findings regarding the execution of advance directives, their content and their usage in end-of-life decision making and the policy implications of the United States' experience with advance directives.

The history of advance directives in the United States has followed several steps: development of public awareness, enactment of laws recognizing advance directives, the Patient Self-Determination Act, and subsequent evaluations of the impact of these legal instruments. Luis Kutner initially suggested advance directives in 1969. Public awareness about the issue of decision making for persons who cannot speak for themselves grew in the 1970s and the 1980s following highly publicized legal cases. One such case involved a request by the family of Karen Ann Quinlan, who had been in a persistent vegetative state after ingesting tranquilizers and alcohol, to remove life support. Another controversial case involved a request by the parents of Nancy Cruzan, a 25-year-old woman left in a persistent vegetative state after a 1983 car accident, to discontinue artificial feeding. These cases highlighted issues regarding health-care costs and increased legislative suggestions for eliminating futile care through possible uses of advance directives. As a result of the public debate following these cases, states accepted advance directives as legal mechanisms to dictate future care in the event of diminished decision-making ability.

Two general types of advance directives are used: the durable power of attorney and the living will. The durable power of attorney is a document in which a person designates another person named "the attorney in fact," "agent," "proxy," or "surrogate," to make future decisions in case of inability to make or express such decisions. It is assumed that future decisions will be made on the basis of knowledge of the patient's beliefs and on the specifics of future clinical scenarios. The living will is a document in which individuals communicate their desires for medical treatments in a hypothetical future scenario in which they will not be able to actively make decisions during a terminal illness.

In addition to the general types of advance directives, specific directives relating to treatments have become common, and forms and formats have been developed to document and assess advance directives. Examples of advance directives relating to specific treatments include Do Not Resuscitate (DNR) or Do Not Hospitalize. Such specific orders can be complex or conditional, such as "hospitalize only for comfort care" (Cohen-Mansfield, Libin, & Lipson, 2003). Advance directives in the nursing home often include directions about resuscitation, hospitalization, nutrition, hydration, and medication.

Forms to document preferences in advance directives include a myriad of legal forms as well as the Medical Directive (Emanuel & Emanuel, 1989) and the Preferences for Life-Sustaining Treatment Questionnaire (PLSTQ) (Cohen-Mansfield et al., 1991). Ideally, advance-directive decisions and documents would be reviewed frequently to assure that the directives correspond correctly to any changes in medical condition and to any subsequent changes in opinion. In a study of nursing home residents, 11% of participants were not completely satisfied with their advance directives (Lurie, Pheley, Miles, & Bannick-Mohrland, 1992). The authors suggest that people are hesitant to formalize their advance-care plans because they recognize that their opinions might change over time. Thus, the authors believe that advance directives should be reviewed regularly to assure the relevancy of decisions.

While the intent of the term "advance directives" is to have the patient specify the conditions under which life-sustaining treatments would not be provided, the actual use of the term has been extended in several ways. Currently, when an individual responsible for health-care decisions for another person—either through an advance directive, a court order, or by default (being the closest relative in the absence of documentation)—makes decisions in advance of the actual care situation, it is also called an "advance directive." In fact, many of the DNR directives in nursing homes were enacted by relatives of cognitively impaired persons rather than by the patients themselves. Another extension of the term is that advance directives are used not only to limit care but also to instruct responsible parties to provide maximal levels of care.

The Patient Self-Determination Act (PSDA) was established under the Omnibus Reconciliation Act (U.S. Government, 1990), which came into effect in December, 1991. This act states that under Medicare and Medicaid laws, health-care facilities, including skilled nursing facilities, hospitals, and clinics, "must maintain written policies and procedures regarding the patient's right to participate in and direct health-care decisions affecting the patient," and individuals admitted to health-care facilities must be informed of their rights to execute an advance directive. This act, therefore, mandates offering patients the use of advance directives as a means to control medical care.

Following disappointing results (see below) in utilization of advance directives and in their impact, more recent years have seen a shift in emphasis from the use of advance directives to advance care planning and to a focus on accessibility of palliative services. Advance care planning refers to ongoing discussions between patients and their health-care providers that clarify their values and wishes concerning end-of-life care, rather than specifying preferences for specific scenarios. Presumably, such ongoing discussions will enable the care team to best address the patient's wishes in a fashion that fits both the patient's values and desires as well as the specific clinical situation in which he or she is unable to make decisions. The shift to making palliative care, including pain management and hospice care, more available is based on findings that for elderly persons, hospitalization was dependent on regional availability of alternative treatments such as hospice, rather than on the preferences and needs of patients (Lynn, 1997).

THEORY

The frameworks that have been used to examine the issues underlying advance directives can generally be classified as those concerned with ethics, values, and decision-making processes. From an ethics perspective, the initial drive toward enacting advance directives presented a shift in conceptualizing the core principles of medical decision making. The principle of autonomy—the right to self-determination in medical decisions—gained primacy over the previous paternalism, in which the physician is considered an expert who should make medical decisions on behalf of patients using the principle of beneficence (determination of what is best for the patient). However, while real autonomy requires that patients make the decisions, this is often impossible because they cannot predict all potential scenarios of incapacity. Therefore, substitute autonomy is used. In executing substitute autonomy, surrogate decision makers are expected to exercise substitute judgment, that is, to make decisions from the point of view of the patient. However, the extent to which surrogates are able to provide accurate substitute judgment, and the extent to which they use substitute judgment over beneficence, has been questioned. Despite these practical limitations, however, the concept of advance directives is consistent with the values of individualism and self-determination that are prevalent in American society.

From a public-policy point of view, an examination of values must include the principle of justice in addition to those of autonomy and beneficence. Justice pertains to the distribution of resources in society and may thus limit the system's ability to provide patients with the option of making choices that have high costs. Furthermore, from a societal point of view, development of a system that mandates the offering, documentation, enactment, and follow-through of advance directives is a use of resources that needs to be evaluated in light of alternative demands on these resources.

A framework that examines values underlying advance directives relates the decision to limit future life-sustaining treatments with an underlying value of quality of life, whereas decisions that either mandate or do not limit such treatments endorse the extension of life over quality of life. Using the Quality of Life Values Inventory, Cohen-Mansfield, Droge, and Billig (1991a) found that the pattern of preferences for life-sustaining treatments corresponded to hospital patients' reported values. Those who favored quality of life over prolongation of life were more likely to refuse most treatments and vice versa. Life values were also examined by Schonwetter, Walker, Solomon, Indurkhya, and Robinson (1996) in a study of 132 adults aged 63 and over who were living independently. They reported five factors that influenced potential directives: quality of life, capacity/autonomy, family relations, physical comfort, and treatment philosophy. According to Schonwetter et al. (1996), including a values history in advance planning would enhance patient understanding about future medical care. These guidelines would also make it easier for family members serving as proxies to act in accordance with their relatives' wishes.

Many more considerations may enter the decision-making process, as illustrated in Figure 1. These considerations are organized as those relating to medical practice, system issues, substitute judgment sources, and values regarding preservation and quality of life. Some of these, such as the futility of certain treatments under given circumstances (e.g., persistent vegetative state) and cost of treatments, were among the forces that stimulated the creation of advance directives. More recently, however, the concerns reversed. With a growing body of research documenting the futility of certain treatments, such as resuscitation or use of permanent tube feeding for nursing-home residents, concerns are voiced that advance directives promote rather than limit futile treatments by offering them as valid options.

Finally, advance directives are tools for medical decision making. In cases where there is a loss or impairment of decision-making ability, the medical decision can be a complex process involving interplay between medical and nursing personnel, relatives (or other surrogate decision makers), and advance directives (Figure 2). Both the medical and nursing team and the surrogate decision makers can be influenced by any of the concerns detailed in Figure 1.

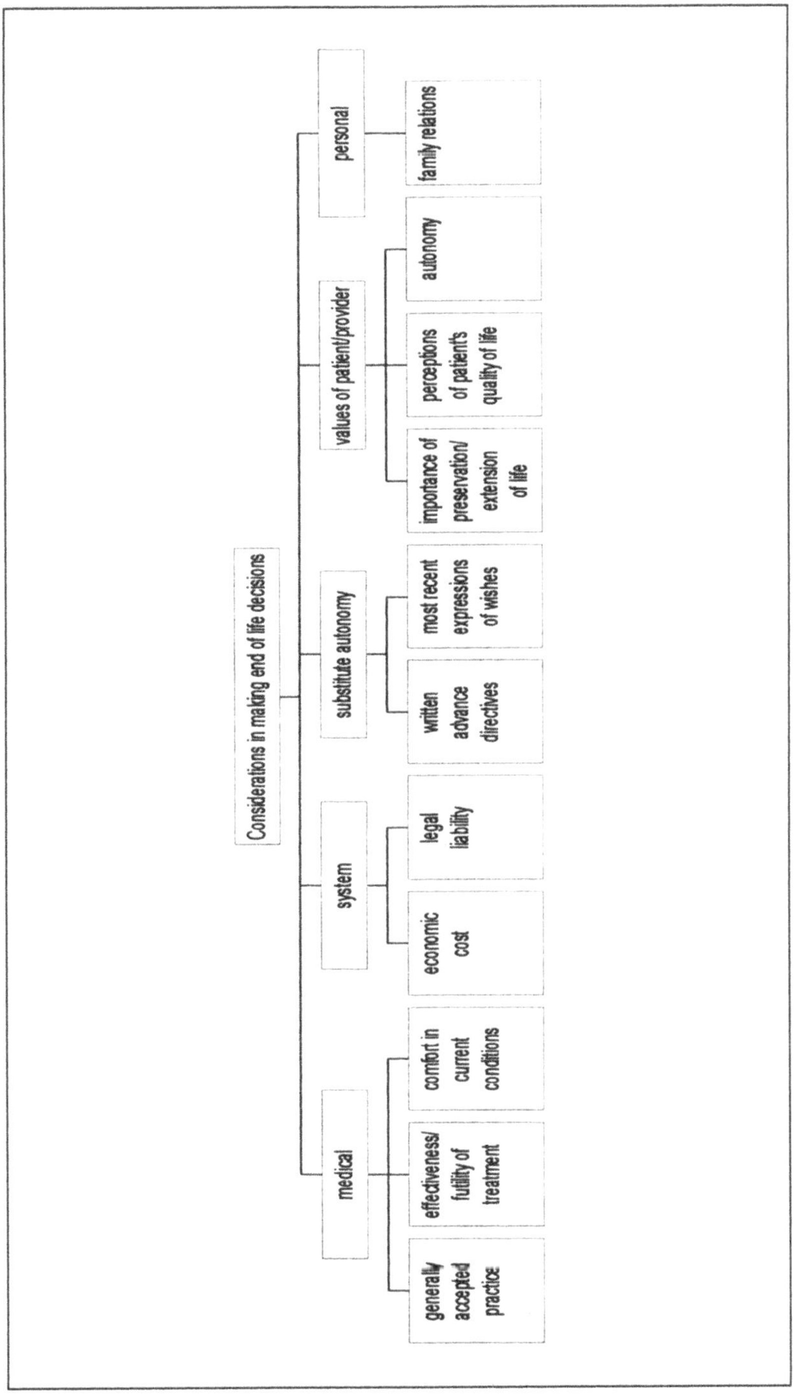

Figure 1. Consideration in making end-of-life decisions.

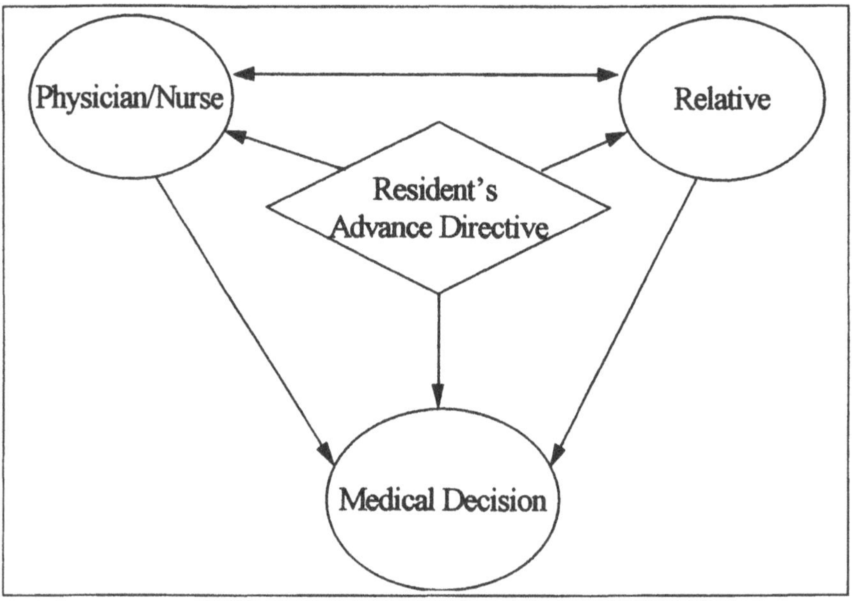

Figure 2. Interplay between resident, medical/nursing staff, and relative in medical decision process for a severely cognitively impaired resident (Cohen-Mansfield, & Lipson, 2003). Copyright © *The Gerontological Society of America*. Reproduced by permission of the publisher.

PRACTICE

Execution of Advance Directives

The prevalence of execution of advance directives varies by setting, population, and degree of effort used to encourage their utilization. Overall estimates are that less than 20% of the population has completed advance directives (Orlander, 1999), and most nursing-home residents do not have living wills or orders to forego hospitalization, nutrition, or hydration (Teno et al., 1997b). Among nursing-home residents, Dobalian (2004) found that 3% had Do Not Hospitalize orders. Even among those who are severely or terminally ill, less than 50% have an advance directive in their medical record (Kass-Bartelmes, Hughes, & Rutherford, 2003), and only 12% of patients with an advance directive developed it with input from their physician (Teno et al., 1997a).

In a study of nursing-home residents, Cohen-Mansfield, Rabinovich, et al. (1991) found that although most study participants had definite preferences for advance care planning and choice of a proxy, they had yet to discuss their preferences with anyone. Most of the other nursing-home residents were too cognitively impaired to participate in this study, and consequently may have been too cognitively impaired to execute advance directives. In a similar study in the hospital setting, Cohen-Mansfield, Droge, and Billig (1991b) found that more than half of the cognitively intact participants had not discussed their feelings about health-care decisions with anyone.

Characteristics of Those Who Execute Advance Directives

Several studies compared patients who executed advance directives with those who did not, finding that those who execute such directives may need to use one sooner, are less likely to have relatives who would make decisions in the absence of a directive, and are more aware of their utility than nonusers, as demonstrated in the following examples. In a study of community-dwelling adults aged 18 and above, those who executed advance directives tended to be older, had more prior experience with illness, and were more educated about advance directives than nonexecutors (Havens, 2000). Another study of older adults living in the community found that Caucasians, unmarried persons, and younger adults made advance care plans more often than their counterparts (Kahana, Dan, Kahana, & Kercher, 2004). Among nursing-home residents, those who executed a durable power of attorney were less likely to want life-sustaining treatment and had fewer living children in comparison to those who did not execute a durable power of attorney. It is possible that individuals who had more children assumed that the children would make decisions, and that those with an interest in limiting treatment may have felt more of a need for executing an advance directive (Cohen-Mansfield, Rabinovich et al., 1991). Completing an advance directive was associated with higher levels of education, higher levels of cognitive functioning, and higher income status (Cohen-Mansfield, Droge, & Billig, 1991b).

In contrast to the above study that found a greater tendency of older persons to execute advance directives, Lurie et al. (1992) found that younger nursing-home residents were more likely to have formal advance directives, while older residents were more likely to report that their level of involvement in the decision-making process was too great. Younger residents were also more likely to have talked to a physician or family member about advance care planning. This discrepancy between the old-old residents and the young-old residents may stem from disease severity or age-cohort differences concerning acceptance of "physician paternalism."

THE CONTENT OF ADVANCE DIRECTIVES

Interviews with 97 hospitalized patients were asked whom they would appoint as an agent for health-care decisions, how this person was related to them, and why they chose this person. Most patients (65%) chose their closest relative because the agent had desired personality traits, knew the patient best, was the closest relative, and was most geographically accessible (Cohen-Mansfield, Droge, & Billig, 1991b).

Preferences Regarding Use of Life-Sustaining Treatments

In studies of nursing home residents and hospital patients, most patients were more likely to want treatment if they expected to be cognitively intact than when a future condition involved impaired cognition or a comatose state (Cohen-Mansfield, 2002; Cohen-Mansfield et al., 1991). In a study of hospitalized patients aged 64 to 97, 66% had a treatment pattern that was cognitive dependent (i.e., requesting more treatment in a future state of better cognitive functioning), 36% did not want any treatment under most conditions, and others (16%) wanted treatment under most future conditions. The absence of a definite pattern was related to lower levels of education and higher levels of depressive symptoms. Patients indicated that personal values, religion, and experiences with the illnesses of others were most significant in the development of their treatment preferences (Cohen-Mansfield, Droge, & Billig, 1991a).

In addition to considering the quality of life in a prospective health state, patients take into account the invasiveness and length of treatment in making treatment decisions. Therefore, they are more likely to accept short-term or simple treatments, such as antibiotics, rather than long-term or invasive treatments. Patients' preferences show consistent patterns so that if a patient refuses a treatment under a prospective health state, the patient is likely to refuse a more intensive treatment under that state or the same treatment under a more severe prospective health condition (Cohen-Mansfield, 2002). Therefore, if patients' preferences are identified for a number of potential conditions and treatments, physicians and surrogates can often use this information to extrapolate values, goals, and preferences toward other treatments and conditions.

The relationship between personal characteristics and content of advance directives was investigated in several studies. Those who chose to execute DNR orders were less functionally independent and more ill than those who did not (Torian, Davidson, Fillit, Fulop, & Sell, 1992). Kellogg and Ramos (1995) found that DNR orders in the nursing home were associated with older age, dementia diagnosis, and white race. Among hospitalized patients, Caucasians were more likely to prefer no treatment than African American patients (Cohen-Mansfield, Droge, & Billig, 1991a).

Among the possible advance directives, orders regarding cardiopulmonary resuscitation (CPR) tend to be the most common, though directives concerning hospitalization were the most needed, according to the residents' physicians. Discussion of any advance directive was highest among those patients with cancer or chronic obstructive pulmonary disease (COPD), diseases in which death seems more imminent. However, discussions regarding CPR among patients with dementia occurred in less than one-third (29%) of the study group (Ghusn, Teasdale, & Jordan, 1997).

Advance care planning with physicians increased visit satisfaction among patients aged 50 years and over (Tierney et al., 2001). Discussions with physicians can catalyze discussions with family members. This is significant as it relates to the finding that surrogates who discussed advance directives with patients reported more confidence in their ability to exercise substitute judgment (Ditto et al., 2001).

Several papers discuss barriers to execution of advance directives, and these can be divided into physician-based barriers, patient-based barriers, and system- and culture-based barriers. Emanuel, Barry, Stoeckle, Ettelson, and Emanuel (1991) found that lack of physician-initiated discussion was the most often cited barrier, and that nearly one third (29%) of patients would discuss advance care planning if their physicians initiated such a conversation. Physician-based barriers were also investigated by Morrison, Morrison, and Glickman (1994), who found that physicians who knew how to formulate advance directives initiated more conversations with patients. Physicians' belief that advance directives were relevant for all patients was also related to increased conversation initiation. Similarly, Morrison (1998) notes that physicians are trained to treat pain and therefore find it difficult to initiate conversations that may elicit the pain caused by emotional stress. In addition, doctors may feel helpless or guilty for not being able to cure the patient (Morrison, 1998). Patient-based barriers are exemplified in a study of persons with end-stage renal disease, for whom physical difficulties may have resulted in denial or avoidance of thinking about death, thus preventing them from initiating advance directives (Cohen, McCue, Germain, & Woods, 1997). The barriers experienced by family members to enacting advance directives were explored by Forbes, Bern-Klug, and Gessert (2000) and included lack of information, lack of a consistent medical provider, and need for emotional support in the process.

THE UTILITY OF ADVANCE DIRECTIVES

Can Surrogates or the Medical Team Provide Substitute Judgment?

The extent to which surrogates know patients' preferences has been questioned (Coppola, Ditto, Danks, & Smucker, 2001). As described above, most patients do not discuss their preferences with anyone. Similarly, it is unclear whether surrogates make decisions using substitute-judgment principles rather than beneficence or other guiding principles. Diamond, Jernigan, Moseley, Messina, and McKeown (1989) demonstrated that there are inconsistencies between proxies' perceptions and the actual wishes of patients, as 27% of proxy preferences disagreed with those expressed by patients. Similarly, Uhlmann, Pearlman, and Cain (1988) found that spouses and physicians of elderly outpatients did not accurately assess patients' preferences regarding resuscitation. Across six scenarios, physicians correctly reported patient preferences in 65% of cases, while spouses were slightly more accurate at 69% agreement. In a study designed to compare the abilities of hospital-based and primary care physicians to predict patients' treatment wishes, a control group of family surrogates was more successful than both hospital-based and primary care physicians, predicting wishes with 74% accuracy (as compared with 64% and 66% for physicians, respectively). Family surrogate errors tended to be overestimates of the patient's request for treatment (Coppola et al., 2001). Furthermore, even when surrogates know preferences, they are often not present to make decisions or are too distressed to opt for a decision.

Are Advance Directives Followed?

The reported rates of the extent to which advance directives are followed vary depending on the methodology used. Most often, studies have retrospectively examined the treatment provided and the advance directives and reported the rates of treatment that contradicted advance directives. For example, Danis et al. (1991) examined the impact of advance directives in the nursing home. The analysis of 96 outcome events showed that the care delivered was consistent with previously expressed wishes 75% of the time. Consistency of care with the advanced directives was actually lower in those cases in which the advance directive was placed in the medical record. Danis et al. (1991) state that of these care inconsistencies, 75% resulted in less aggressive care than specified and 25% with more care than requested. However, the reasons for consistency in care may have nothing to do with the directives. Most often the treatment discussed in the directive (e.g., do not resuscitate) has nothing to do with the decision at hand (e.g., sending the person to the hospital), therefore resulting in no inconsistency.

Studies in the hospital support the notion that even if advance directive instructions are given, they are not necessarily followed. The SUPPORT (Study to Understand Prognoses and Preferences for Outcomes and Risks of Treatments) study concentrated on improving patient/physician communication as a means to improve patients' knowledge of advance directives and physicians' adherence to them. The 9,105 seriously ill patients in the study were treated in five teaching hospitals over the course of 4 years, beginning 2 years prior to the implementation of the PSDA (Teno et al., 1997a). The results found that the presence of advance directives neither enhanced patient knowledge nor influenced decision making about resuscitation. An increase in the frequency of execution of advance directives did not improve the care of dying patients, which contradicts the very purpose of advance care planning. The SUPPORT study is of particular importance because it included a randomized control group, with the additional intervention of a nurse to facilitate communication between patients, surrogates, and doctors, and to encourage completion of advance directives. With the implementation of the PSDA, all medical facilities were required to inform patients of their rights to complete advance directives. The second phase of the SUPPORT study took place at the very beginning of the implementation of the PSDA. Its timing allowed for comparison of those who received the regular government-suggested information and those who participated in the enhanced intervention. This study then demonstrated that the enhanced-communication intervention had no actual influence on patient care. Similarly, Schneiderman, Kronick, Kaplan, Anderson, & Langer (1992) did not find a difference in resource utilization prior to death or in use of CPR between a group of patients who were offered the opportunity to complete an advance directive and a group who received routine care.

Two studies provide evidence suggesting that advance directives may decrease hospitalizations. Using data from the Medical Expenditures Panel Survey, Dobalian (2004) found that residents with a Do Not Hospitalize order were hospitalized approximately half as often as those without this order. In another study, an educational program regarding advance directives was administered to staff in Canadian nursing homes and resulted in fewer hospitalizations in the intervention nursing homes in comparison to those in the control group (Molloy et al., 2000). In contrast to these studies, a study that examined the actual decision-making process of physicians at the time of status change events in the nursing home found that advance directives had a very small role in making decisions because they often did not apply to the situation at hand, were not available, or were changed at the time of decision making (Cohen-Mansfield & Lipson, 2002).

Many barriers contribute to the limited impact of advance directives. A study by Teno et al. (1997a) showed that despite the efforts of the PSDA, many patients remain unaware of their options. This study found that one-third of seriously ill hospital patients did not know about living wills, and less than one half were aware of durable powers of attorney as they relate to health care. One in four patients had advance directives, a small increase from the pre-PSDA numbers (Teno et al., 1997a). In addition, there are inconsistencies in the documentation of advance directives (e.g., the directives described inside the medical chart are at times different than those on the chart cover), and both vary from those indicated on the Minimum Data Set (MDS) (Cohen-Mansfield, Libin, & Lipson, 2003). It is therefore not surprising that physicians are unaware of advance directives for a substantial proportion of patients. Among cancer patients who had advance directives, 76% of their interviewed physicians were unaware of these orders (Virmani, Schneiderman, & Kaplan, 1994). Many older individuals who do complete advance directives provide little or no specific guidance to their families or care providers other than the refusal of "extraordinary measures." As a result, in order to make medical decisions, staff caregivers and relatives are forced to reconstruct the now incapacitated resident's preferences for medical treatment based on conversations, notions, or presumed values. Language in the directive is often too general to guide specific treatment decisions. Especially difficult is the decision as to when treatment should be stopped. Even when advance directives are in place and known to physicians, they are usually not considered applicable until very late stages of a patient's disease.

Some of these barriers to utilization of advance directives are illustrated in a study by Happ et al. (2002), who found that advanced-care planning in the nursing home was conducted by social workers during the admission process, rather than by physicians who use the information. The social workers did not focus on the most relevant topics for nursing home residents, as evidenced by their concentration on CPR. In addition, directives were only reviewed following a medical crisis. The forms used vague and at times inconsistent language concerning the conditions under which the advance directives were to be implemented.

Should Advance Directives Be Offered or are Certain Treatments Futile?

In 1983, the President's Commission set the standard of mandated CPR unless otherwise specified without consideration of its success rates. Studies of CPR show significant decrease in survival rate for patients over the age of 85, as well as for those with chronic conditions (Kane & Burns, 1997). Thus, when an elderly resident of a nursing home experiences cardiopulmonary failure, the survival rate is exceedingly low. One study conducted at a military long-term-care facility showed no improvement in the outcome of CPR, even when performed by an ACLS trained, physician-led team (Awoke, Mouton, & Parrott, 1992). Of the 45 residents who underwent CPR, none survived to hospital discharge, leading the authors to conclude that in a long-term-care facility, CPR is both expensive and ineffective. This study and others with similar results emphasize the necessity for reevaluating the policy for mandated CPR and the use of feeding tubes. Advance care planning for CPR is often done without clear background information. According to Ackerman (1997), uninformed patients greatly overestimate the efficacy of CPR. Once accurate data are supplied, the percentage of patients requesting this intervention declines. Additionally, CPR is a relatively uncommon intervention, and therefore an increase of DNR on residents' charts will have little effect on the actual care they receive. Therefore, decisions about medical care may need to be based upon patients' preferences as well as the likelihood of successful treatment.

POLICY

The story of advance directives in the United States offers a fascinating case study of the interplay between philosophy, theory, economic considerations, public policy, and actual clinical practice. Advance directives have emerged as a way for individuals to express their preferences for medical care should they become unable to do so in the future, with the aim of increasing patient autonomy and decreasing costs. Forms of advance directives vary from specific formal ones, such as living wills and durable power of attorney, to more informal ones such as advance-care planning. Some previously controversial forms of advance directives have become legal in all U.S. states following debates over the use of life-sustaining treatments and have subsequently been promoted by the Patient Self-Determination Act. Advance directives are therefore potentially useful tools to express one's wishes in the event of future incapacitation, an event that is quite common in the nursing home. However, how advance directives are discussed and when they are implemented are also influential factors in their efficacy. Although rates of execution of advance directives have increased over the years, they remain relatively low. The original intent of advance directives was to enhance autonomy and decrease utilization of futile life-sustaining treatments. Over the years, they have been extended to include family decisions regarding the future use of life-sustaining treatments for cognitively incapacitated individuals. The ability of family members to provide substitute judgment of patients' preferences is, however, limited. The medical team's effort to provide substitute preferences has also been found to be skewed. Finally, research has questioned the actual impact of advance directives on care in the hospital and in the nursing home.

As demonstrated in the SUPPORT study, receiving information about advance directives does not ensure that the directed terms are carried out. And although the PSDA necessitates keeping record of presence or absence of advance directives, it does not specify which directives are to be used. There are a number of advance directive instructions varying in form and content. Some directives are more detailed, giving specific instructions of what to do in certain situations. But most directives tend to cover a few specific conditions, such as Do Not Resuscitate or No Intubation, without regard for the current medical condition. The multitude of forms used, together with their often irrelevant content, result in information that is inconvenient at best and frequently inconsistent with the needs for information at the time of decision making.

Arguably, there is no reason for anyone not to have advance directives. Yet, despite the PSDA increasing the opportunity for advance care planning at all nursing facilities, most residents do not take advantage of the offer. Teno et al. (1997b) demonstrated that from 1990 to 1993, chart documentation of living wills increased from only 4% to 13%. The same study found a dramatic increase in Do-Not-Resuscitate orders, but no increase in orders not to hospitalize or to forgo more specific treatments such as artificial nutrition and hydration.

What lessons does the U.S. experience have for public policy in other countries? On the one hand, advance directives are a reasonable means for alleviating concerns about potential future use of life-sustaining treatments in the face of extreme incapacitation. However, their use has been associated with multiple risks that need to be taken into consideration in the development of public policy. Most notably, a major risk is the development of expectations that these instruments can be used not only to limit treatment but also to dictate treatment even when it is futile. Similarly, the decision-making process is often conducted in the absence of an understanding of treatments, their risks, and potential benefits. Furthermore, despite the original intent of enhancing patient autonomy, these documents are often used to dictate proxies' wishes when the patient is incapacitated and often do not approximate the patient's wishes. These observations suggest that legislation regarding advance directives must proceed cautiously, taking these considerations into account.

More important than the limitations in the content of the directives themselves is the mounting evidence of their limited utility in actual decision making. These consistently disappointing results across studies suggest that the cost/benefit of the investment of resources in enacting and regulating the Patient Self-Determination Act is questionable at best. Indeed, it is not clear that advance directives are a high priority in comparison with other patient needs. For example, in a study of families of terminally ill cancer patients, Kristjanson (1989) found that the most important patient-care issues were relief of pain and prompt, attentive, and thorough medical care. Similarly, Kayser-Jones (2002) found that factors affecting the dying experience included insufficient staffing levels, lack of sufficient and adequate communication between nursing staff and residents and families, loss of dignity, and lack of meaningful activities. As a result of a better understanding of the importance of these factors, there is a growing perception that the key to improving end-of-life care lies in the provision of quality terminal care rather than the promotion of advance directives, and interest in hospice and palliative care has increased. In the face of models of excellence in end-of-life care, the perception of need for advance directives may also diminish.

Shared decision making is an important value that must be promoted, either by accepted practice guidelines or by legislation in cases where it is appropriate. Whitney, McGuire, and McCullough (2004) organize medical decisions along two axes—risk and certainty—that call for four types of decisions. They contend that shared decision making is most appropriate in situations in which there are two clinically viable routes. If the decision also contains significant risk, informed consent may also be necessary. When there is only one reasonable option, information sharing is the appropriate route. This framework is appealing, yet it calls for additional information relating to advance directives In other words, can advance directives assist in such shared decision making for elderly persons in hospitals and nursing homes? In their current form as used in the United States, the utility of advance directives seems limited. A better understanding of the context in which shared decisions are called for, considering what decisions are made and the patient's cognitive functioning level, may help determine an improved format for advance directives.

REFERENCES

Ackerman, T. F. (1997). Forsaking the spirit of the letter of the law: Advance directives in the nursing home. *Journal of the American Geriatrics Society, 45*(1), 114-116.

Awoke, S., Mouton, C. P., & Parrott, M. (1992). Outcomes of skilled cardiopulmonary resuscitation in a long-term-care facility: Futile therapy? *Journal of the American Geriatrics Society, 40*(6), 593-595.

Cohen, L. M., McCue, J. D., Germain, M., & Woods, A. (1997). Denying the dying: Advance directives and dialysis discontinuation. *Psychosomatics, 38,* 27-34.

Cohen-Mansfield, J. (2002). Development of a framework to encourage addressing advance directives when resources are limited. *Journal of Ageing and Health, 14*(1), 24-41.

Cohen-Mansfield, J., Droge, J. A., & Billig, N. (1991a). Factors influencing hospital patients' preferences in the utilization of life-sustaining treatments. *The Gerontologist, 32*(1), 89-95.

Cohen-Mansfield, J., Droge, J. A., & Billig, N. (1991b). The utilization of the durable power of attorney for health care among hospitalized elderly patients. *Journal of the American Geriatrics Society, 39,* 1174-1178.

Cohen-Mansfield, J., Libin, A., & Lipson, S. (2003). Differences in presenting advanced directives in the chart, in the Minimum Data Set, and through staff's perceptions. *The Gerontologist, 43*(3), 302-308.

Cohen-Mansfield, J., & Lipson, S. (2002). Which advance directive matters? An analysis of end-of-life decisions made in the nursing home. *Journal of the American Geriatrics Society, 50*(4), S56.

Cohen-Mansfield, J. & Lipson, S. (2003). Medical staff's decision-making process in the nursing home. *J Gerontol Med Sci.* 58A:271-278.

Cohen-Mansfield, J., Rabinovich, B. A., Lipson, S., Fein, A., Gerber, B., Weisman, S., & Pawlson L. G. (1991). The decision to execute a durable power of attorney for health care and preferences regarding the utilization of life-sustaining treatments in nursing home residents. *Archives of Internal Medicine, 151*, 289-294.

Coppola, K. M., Ditto, P. H., Danks, J. H., & Smucker, W. D. (2001). Accuracy of primary care and hospital-based physicians' predictions of elderly outpatients' treatment preferences with and without advance directives. *Archives of Internal Medicine 161*(3), 431-440.

Danis, M., Southerland, L. I., Garrett, J. M., Smith, J. L., Hielema, F., Pickard, C. G., Egner, D. M., & Patrick, D. L. (1991). A prospective study of advance directives for life-sustaining care. *The New England Journal of Medicine, 324*(13), 882-888.

Diamond, E. L., Jernigan, J. A., Moseley, R. A., Messina, V., & McKeown, R. A. (1989). Decision-making ability and advance directive preferences in nursing home patients and proxies. *The Gerontologist, 29*(5), 622-626.

Ditto, P. H., Danks, J. H., Smucker, W. D., Bookwala, J., Coppola, K. M., Dresser, R., Fagerlin, A., Gready, R. M., Houts R. M., Lockhart, L. K., Zyzanski, S. (2001). Advance directives as acts of communication: a randomized controlled trial. *Archives of Internal Medicine, 161*(3), 421-430.

Dobalian, A. (2004). Nursing facility compliance with do-not-hospitalize orders. *The Gerontologist, 44*(2), 159-165.

Emanuel, L. L., & Emanuel, E. J. (1989). The medical directive: A new comprehensive advance care document. *Journal of the American Medical Association, 261*(22), 3288-3293.

Emanuel, L. L., Barry, M. J., Stoeckle, J. D., Ettelson, L. M., & Emanuel, E. J. (1991). Advance directives for medical care—A case for greater use. *The New England Journal of Medicine, 324*(13), 889-895.

Forbes, S., Bern-Klug, M., & Gessert, C. (2000). End-of-life decision making for nursing home residents with dementia. *Journal of Nursing Scholarship, 32*(3), 251-258.

Ghusn, H. F., Teasdale, T. A., & Jordan, D. (1997). Continuity of do-not resuscitate orders between hospital and nursing home settings. *Journal of the American Geriatrics Society, 45*(1), 465-469.

Happ, M. B., Capezuti, E., Strumpf, N. E., Wagner, L., Cunningham, S., Evans, L., & Maislin, G. (2002). Advance care planning and end-of-life care for hospitalized nursing home residents. *Journal of the American Geriatrics Society, 50*, 829-835.

Havens, G. A. D. (2000). Differences in the execution/nonexecution of advance directives by community dwelling adults. *Research in Nursing & Health, 23*, 319-333.

Kahana, B., Dan, A., Kahana, E., & Kercher, K. (2004). The personal and social context of planning for end-of-life care. *Journal of the American Geriatrics Society, 52*(7), 1163-1167.

Kane, R. S., & Burns, E. A. (1997). Cardiopulmonary resuscitation policies in long-term care facilities. *Journal of the American Geriatrics Society, 45*(2), 154-157.

Kass-Bartelmes, B. L., Hughes, R., & Rutherford, M. K. (2003). Advance care planning: Preferences for care at the end of life. Agency for Health Care Research and Quality. *Research in Action, 12*, 1-19.

Kayser-Jones, J. (2002). The experience of dying: An ethnographic nursing home study. *The Gerontologist, 42* (special issue III), 11-19.

Kellogg, F. R., & Ramos, A. (1995). Code status decision-making in a nursing home population: Processes and outcomes. *Journal of the American Geriatrics Society, 43*(2), 113-121.

Kristjanson, L. J. (1989). Quality of terminal care: Salient indicators identified by families. *Journal of Palliative Care, 5*(1), 21-30.

Kutner, L. (1969). Due process of euthanasia: The living will, a proposal. *Indiana Law Journal, 44*, 537-554.

Lurie, N., Pheley, A. M., Miles, S. H., & Bannick-Mohrland, S. (1992). Attitudes toward discussing life-sustaining treatments in extended care facility patients. *Journal of the American Geriatrics Society, 40(12)*, 1205-1208.

Lynn, J. (1997). Hospitalization of nursing home residents: The right rate? *Journal of the American Geriatrics Society, 45*(3), 378-379.

Molloy, D. W., Guyatt, G. H., Russo, R., Goeree, R., O'Brien, B. J., Bedard, M., Willan, A., Watson, J., Patterson, C., Harrison, C., Standish, T., Strang, D., Darzins, P. J., Smith, S., & Dubois, S. (2000). Systematic implementation of an advance directive program in nursing homes: A randomized controlled trial. *Journal of the American Medical Association, 283*(11), 1437-1444.

Morrison, M. F. (1998). Obstacles to doctor-patient communication at the end of life. In M. D. Steinberg & S. J. Younger (Eds.), *End-of-life decisions: A psychosocial perspective* (pp. 109-136). Washington, DC: American Psychiatric Press.

Morrison, R. S., Morrison, E. W., & Glickman, D. F. (1994). Physician reluctance to discuss advance directives: An empiric investigation of potential barriers. *Archives of Internal Medicine, (154),* 2311-2318.

Orlander, J. D. (1999). Use of advance directives by health care workers and their families. *Southern Medical Journal, 92*(5), 481-484.

Schneiderman, L. J., Kronick, R., Kaplan, R. M., Anderson, J. P., & Langer, R. D. (1992). Effects of offering advance directives on medical treatments and costs. *Annals of Internal Medicine, 117*(7), 599-606.

Schonwetter, R. S., Walker, R. M., Solomon, M., Indurkhya, A., & Robinson, B. E. (1996). Life values, resuscitation preferences, and the applicability of living wills in an older population. *Journal of the American Geriatrics Society, 44*(8), 954-958.

Teno, J. M., Lynn, J., Wenger, N., Phillips, R. S., Murphy, D. P., Connors, A. F., Desbiens, N., Fulkerson, W., Bellamy, P., & Knaus, W. A. (1997a). Advance directives for seriously ill hospitalized patients: Effectiveness with the Patient Self-Determination Act and the SUPPORT intervention. *Journal of the American Geriatrics Society, 45*(1), 500-507.

Teno, J. M., Branco, K. J., Mor, V., Phillips, C. D., Hawes, C., Morris, J., & Fries, B. E. (1997b). Changes in advance care planning in nursing homes before and after the Patient Self-Determination Act: Report of a 10-state survey. *Journal of the American Geriatrics Society, 45*(8), 939-944.

Tierney, W. M., Dexter, P. R., Gramelspacher, G. P., Perkins, A. J., Zhou, X., & Wolinsky, F. D. (2001). The effect of discussions about advance directives on patients' satisfaction with primary care. *Journal of General Internal Medicine, 16*(1), 32-40.

Torian, L. V., Davidson, E. J., Fillit, H. M., Fulop, G., & Sell, L. L. (1992). Decisions for and against resuscitation in an acute geriatric medicine unit serving the frail elderly. *Archives of Internal Medicine, 152*, 561-565.

Uhlmann, R. F., Pearlman, R. A., & Cain, K. C. (1988). Physicians' and spouses' predictions of elderly patient's resuscitation preferences. *Journal of Gerontology, 43*(5), M115-121.

U.S. Government. (1990). Omnibus Budget Reconciliation Act of 1990. Public Law 101-508. Washington, DC: Author.

Virmani, J., Schneiderman L. J., & Kaplan, R. M. (1994). Relationship of advance directives to physician-patient communication. *Archives of Internal Medicine, 154*(8), 909-913.

Whitney, S. N., McGuire, A. L., & McCullough, L. B. (2004). A typology of shared decision making, informed consent, and simple consent. *Annals of Internal Medicine, 140*(1), 54-60.

CHAPTER 12

Resources, Autonomy, and Lack of Focus on the Common Good: End-of-Life Decision Making for Older Patients in the United States

Neil S. Wenger and James W. Davis

The United States is a study in contrasts in end-of-life care for older individuals. Broad availability of medical technology, an affluent health-care system, a population enamored with medical breakthroughs, and an unparalleled focus on individual autonomy has generated widespread use of aggressive and expensive care for the old and very old in the United States. The precipitant of death in an older person is commonly the purposeful cessation of life-sustaining treatment (Angus et al., 2004). The compression of morbidity, discomfort with the "way that people die," and difficulty with letting go has led to the United States also being the leader in the development of mechanisms and instruments to enhance decision making to facilitate removal of life-sustaining treatment at the end of life (Field & Cassel, 1997). Advance-care planning, advance directives, and policies on removal of life-sustaining care are well advanced in the United States. Ethics Committees and ethics consultation also play a substantial role in end-of-life decisions. Because the combination of factors that promoted the development of advance-care planning in the United States is becoming common in other countries, the experience of the United States may serve to foreshadow what might soon be expected elsewhere.

FACTORS RELATED TO AGGRESSIVE CARE TOWARD THE END OF LIFE

End-of-life care for older people in the United States is largely influenced by the wide availability of unprecedented technology to maintain life, combined with a strong cultural valuation of the autonomous preference. This results in Americans receiving unparalleled aggressive care to permit survival in old age despite the failure of organs and functional incapacity. However, such a landscape also produces, in some circumstances, substantial amounts of time spent in poor health states (Support Principal Investigators, 1995). In part, this is related to the worldwide phenomenon of the "squaring" of the aging curve. People in their 60s in the United States have a substantial life expectancy. Woman aged 65 can expect to live another 20 years on average, while men can expect to live another 16 years. The "old-old" also can look forward to quite a bit of additional life. Women aged 85 have a life expectancy of 6.9 more years, while men's life expectancy is 5.6 additional years at this age (Arias, 2002). Some of the remaining years, however, are likely to be spent in a state of reduced function due to disease and declining health. Alzheimer's disease, cerebrovascular disease, and cardiovascular disease all produce significant disability during the later years of life.

The availability of resources in the United States has made the provision of life-sustaining treatments and life-saving surgeries available even for patients in the old and very old age groups. Use of hemodialysis for patients 85 and older is common. Increasing numbers of aggressive cardiovascular procedures such as coronary artery bypass graft surgery and valve replacements for patients in the 85 and over age group have spawned a series of investigations demonstrating that these procedures can be successful in selected very old patients (Bacchetta et al., 2003). Expanding the age limits of available care has led to a general perception that, irrespective of prognosis, there is no resource limit on what care can be instituted, and that if a care modality exists, it might be used, regardless of a patient's physiologic age or how close a patient is to death. Contrary to wrestling with whether a treatment is "indicated" in a particular situation, commonly toward the end of life a specific decision *not* to employ aggressive care must be enunciated. This care paradigm influences much of the care received by older patients at the end of life and has important implications for the communication patterns between providers, patients, and families that shape care for dying older patients.

Yet when aggressive care is applied with inadequate regard for underlying prognosis, adverse health states commonly result. Such medical care may produce a barely responsive older individual, living in a nursing home, kept alive by feeding provided through a percutaneous gastrostomy tube. Similarly, the combination of available resources and a cultural focus on autonomy results in some older individuals spending their final days receiving prolonged intensive care aimed at a tiny chance of recovery. Consider the following case:

> Mr. X was the 97-year-old patriarch of a large family. He had been generally well with controlled hypertension and mild heart failure until 7 years earlier when he had a stroke. At that time he lost function of his right leg and

had some speech impairment, which partially resolved. His wife died soon thereafter; his children insisted that he live with them, and he split his time between his two sons' houses. He also had two daughters. One, who had her own family, would visit him often. The other was mildly developmentally disabled and unmarried. She was always at his side and dependent upon her father for support.

Despite close attention and careful medical care, Mr. X had several subsequent strokes with associated cognitive decline and diminished ability to complete daily activities. He was hospitalized several times for heart failure exacerbations and each time was discharged to a nursing home where his omnipresent family was visibly unhappy with the level of care. They were distressed that his kidney function, which was failing, was not checked often enough and that his myriad medications were not always given on schedule. Physicians, during hospitalizations and in the nursing facility, attempted on numerous occasions to outline for the patient a plan of care with a palliative bent, but were met with resistance and anger. Attempts to speak with the patient about goals for care were thwarted by the patient's cognitive impairment and his family's view that the physicians should communicate only with them.

The patient became short of breath in the nursing home and was transferred again to the hospital. He was found to have had a myocardial infarction and was in heart failure. The patient's heart status and blood pressure were unstable despite medical therapy; the family asked that an angiogram be performed so that the patient might receive angioplasty or perhaps a bypass surgery. The cardiologists were very reluctant because they felt that the patient was unlikely to benefit from the procedure and because he would be dialysis-dependent after the procedure. The heart surgeons declared that Mr. X was not a surgical candidate. The family pressed for the patient to be moved to the intensive care unit, receive dialysis, and be taken for the cardiac procedure. Believing that they could not refuse, the physicians complied with the family's wishes. Two weeks later, the patient died— after a resuscitation attempt—in the intensive care unit.

There are many underlying factors that contribute to the behaviors illustrated in this case. In addition to the broad availability of resources for clinical care and the strong focus on autonomy evident in the United States, market forces play a role. Decades of rewarding increased expenditure have imprinted practice patterns on providers and health systems. Patients enjoyed the push for more care and contributed to the momentum. More recently, direct marketing of medication and procedures to the public has also increased the demand for the newest products (Rosenthal, Berndt, Donohue, Frank, & Epstein, 2002). Sensational news coverage of new developments in medical technology and preliminary release of research findings before their full implications are understood also reinforce the zeal for the latest in medical technology (Peterson, 2001). Medical insurance is yet another factor driving utilization and a focus on receiving all available care. For many patients, there is little or no out-of-pocket expenditure for enormously expensive procedures. While this serves to provide excellent access to these services, it removes the economic realities of medicine from many patient-level decisions and creates a psychology of unlimited resources in the patient/physician/hospital relationship. This creates an unusual situation in which consideration of proportionality can be lost. Embarking on a course of care that will cost $5000 per day and occupy a prized ICU bed in order to attempt to salvage a 1% or 2% chance of benefit is not considered extraordinary.

This widespread availability of medical care for those with health insurance contrasts sharply with the millions of Americans who have no health insurance coverage at all. The uninsured population in the United States has severely compromised access to timely routine care and prevention (Hadley, 2003). Yet, it is remarkable that even for such individuals without insurance, in the setting of need for life-sustaining care, there again are no limits. A homeless individual who could not secure adequate food and shelter and who was never vaccinated against pneumococcal infection (let alone receive medical attention for his chronic conditions) will be admitted to an ICU to receive weeks of mechanical ventilation and other therapies in an attempt to save him from respiratory failure from pneumonia. In death, this uninsured individual may receive care worth hundreds or thousands of times what was expended to help him live.

A further factor, and a byproduct of the strength of autonomy in the United States, is the lack of consideration of what is best for the community in the making of individual decisions. The fact that three more unnecessary days in an intensive care unit prior to death will use resources that could instead support dozens of prenatal visits or purchase hundreds of vaccine doses is not lost on clinicians and trainees providing the ICU care. But there is no direct way to translate resource savings in one area to good works in another. It is not clear who will take responsibility for the general good (Hiatt, 1975). One state, which attempted to take an organized approach to resource allocation, was thwarted in its effort (Bodenheimer, 1997). Stewarding resources at the end of life—if it means an earlier death that is contrary to the expressed wishes of the patient or family—is considered "rationing," a politically unacceptable word in the United States.

Certainly, not all patients toward the end of life receive all possible technological care. Many patients, families, and physicians work together to craft a care plan so that care matches prognosis, and to ensure that the focus is on dignity and comfort at the end of life. However, this is not the case often enough—and cases such as that described above are common enough—that the advance-care planning movement was spurred forward in the United States. As a result, the United States has highly developed laws concerning advance directives, communication about end-of-life care is taught in medical schools and residency training programs, and hospitals have policies about withholding and withdrawing care.

ADVANCE CARE PLANNING

The end-of-life movement in the United States draws its roots from the civil and women's rights movements, the consumer movement, and a backlash against physician paternalism. It was propelled by the Karen Ann Quinlan and Nancy Cruzan legal cases in which the women's families petitioned that the patients, who would never awaken, be allowed to die. In the area of research ethics, the movement prompted the advent of institutional review boards. The President's Commission for the Study of Ethical Problems in Medicine and Biomedical Research (1983) and the Hastings Center Guidelines (1987) in the 1980s advanced the practical application of patient autonomy into the clinical setting. Advance-directive legislation began at the state level to compel physicians to follow patients' wishes to terminate life-sustaining treatments. The federal Patient Self-Determination Act in 1990 required health-care providers to inform patients of their rights to make health-care decisions and to execute advance directives.

The theory behind advance-care planning is that care can continue to reflect a patient's preferences toward the end of life when many patients have lost the ability to participate in care decisions. This method maintains the U.S. focus on autonomy as the compelling principle guiding care and does not necessarily incorporate community or resource allocation concerns, except as they affect the individual. Preserving preferences or decision making can avoid or curtail aggressive care at the end of life in favor of care focusing on comfort. If the health-care system default is to always promote longevity, then advance-care planning can coordinate care to instead reflect preferences that may aim toward different goals.

Advance-care planning is carried out through conversations with patients. Theoretically, this would best be accomplished within the context of a continuous clinical relationship during a time of clinical stability. The physician should be able to discuss with the patient the relevant clinical information, and the patient can understand his or her prognosis and possible care options. Patients should have social support present during the discussion as well as individuals whom they would involve in making important medical decisions. Two general types of information can be elicited from the patient: preferences concerning care and potential surrogate decision makers.

Preferences can involve many different aspects of care and various sorts of decisions. Decisions may focus on care modalities to be employed (such as whether a patient would want to receive tube feeding, mechanical ventilation, or cardiopulmonary resuscitation) or venue of care. One can also focus the conversation on specific health states, such as what sort of care the patient would want if he or she were to be permanently comatose (Pearlman et al., 1993). Based on our experience, and recommended by others (Doukas & McCullough, 1996; Lo, Quill, & Tulsky, 2001), it is better to focus on patient's values and goals. Goals can be placed into a clinical context for patients, and then recommendations can be made to the patient concerning the types of treatment modalities that will achieve the patient's goals.

Another strategy, which can be adjunctive to preference elicitation, is to identify someone to make decisions in the patient's stead when the patient becomes incapable. This is a canonization of the usual practice of turning to the family when a patient cannot make decisions. However, the surrogate need not necessarily be a relative, and the goal is for this individual—the legally designated "agent"—to reflect the patient's values or preferences in making decisions for the patient. If advance-care planning is successful, the agent will be able to follow a patient's previously specified wishes in guiding treatment with the physician and be informed by the patient's values in making decisions that could not have been discussed with the patient in advance. This is demonstrated in the following case:

> An 85-year-old man was seen for a routine clinic visit. He was generally healthy with well-controlled hypertension and diabetes. And he was fit; he rode his bicycle to doctor's appointments. The physician knew that the patient lived alone and on this visit asked the patient who would help to make decisions for him if he were too ill to participate in decision making. The patient noted that this was a good question because he had no relatives. The physician should turn to his landlord. They had been close friends for 40 years, and the patient relied on his landlord for help in making all important decisions. However, when the physician asked about goals for care, the patient had no ready answers. The patient explained that he had always assumed he would die in his sleep, as had both of his parents; he never had considered that decisions would be needed. Further discussion, which required the remainder of the office visit, revealed that the patient perceived that he enjoyed a high quality of life and, that if he became ill, he desired medical care that would return him to a state in which he could continue to care for himself and interact with others. He loved to argue politics and enjoyed playing cards. "If I can't do those things and need help to eat and pee, I'd rather be dead." These wishes were documented in the patient's medical record, and an advance directive was completed noting his preferences and agent. He took the document home to discuss it with his landlord. Several years later, the discussion, advance directive and landlord guided care.

Advance directives come in various forms and can be chosen according to their desired function. If one desires to specify only preferences, an "instruction directive" (also termed a living will, among others) can be completed. Usually these documents delineate that in certain future health states the patient desires specific types of care and less commonly the precise types of treatments that a patient would want. In order to designate a surrogate decision maker, a Durable Power of Attorney for Health Care is usually completed. This document commonly also allows for specification of alternate surrogates and in some cases can even indicate who cannot make decisions and whether the authority of the agent would begin at a time other than decisional incapacity of the patient. Physicians who follow the advance directive are immune to legal action for allowing a patient to die. If a physician cannot carry out the patient's requests because of a disagreement of conscience, care must be transferred to another physician. In general, in the United States these documents are combined; both preferences and agent are specified in the advance directive. This makes sense because the surrogate should be guided by the patient's values and preferences. Many Americans have their attorney formulate advance directives for them at the time of estate planning. However, these documents are widely available in health-care facilities, often from one's physician, and also on the Internet. Completion of an advance directive need not involve a lawyer.

The advance-directive discussion and the document should involve a patient's surrogate and physician in most cases. This is because the document and related discussions will be applied to clinical decisions. The physician can provide the clinical context so that discussions between the patient and the surrogate (and other family) can focus on goals of care and at times on particularly relevant treatment decisions. Such interaction can help to avoid unhelpful instructions such as "do everything." A surrogate saddled with such a preference (often stated in the setting of aggressive treatment for severe illness and at times even documented in an unfortunate advance directive) is placed in an untenable position in which preferences do not match the clinical options. For advance-care planning to be valuable (rather than destructive), it must retain a clinical context.

Optimally, it should be the physician who interprets the patient's goals in light of the clinical circumstances and prognosis in order to translate goals into care-guiding order recommendations that will be presented to the patient or family to form a plan for care or to stimulate further discussion. Most U.S. hospitals have policies that permit withholding and withdrawing of treatment modalities, including food and fluids under the proper circumstances. In all cases, care must focus on respect for the patient and maintenance of comfort and dignity. Some nursing homes permit similar care decisions, and many states and municipalities have provisions to document No CPR decisions in the outpatient setting.

APPROACHES TO FAILED ADVANCE-CARE PLANNING

Studies since the passage of the Patient Self-Determination Act have revealed only a modest increase in use of advance directives. Except in unusual communities (Hammes & Rooney, 1998), it appears that less than one in three older community-living patients in U.S. inpatient and outpatient settings have completed advance directives (Burg, McCarty, Allen, & Denslow, 1995; Hopp, 2000). Many factors conspire against the success of advance-care planning, including inadequate physician education, the time needed to carry out the task, Americans' discomfort with death and desires not to discuss end-of-life issues (Hoffman, 1997), and concerns about the validity of prior decisions to direct later care. As illustrated in the case beginning this chapter, advance-care planning may be obstructed by families. Furthermore, the practice may promote filial autonomous decision making that contradicts what appears to be the socially appropriate use of health-care resources. At one academic medical center, during one year, more than one ICU-bed year was devoted to care that clinicians at the institution felt was unnecessarily aggressive (Ross & Wenger, 1994). This can include patients with miniscule (but nonzero) chances of survival receiving maximal intensive care unit support as well as patients in permanent coma receiving life-sustaining treatments (such as dialysis or ventilatory support). Experts have suggested renewed efforts at communication with families under such circumstances (Goold, Williams, & Arnold, 2000; von Gunten, Ferris, & Emanuel, 2000).

When there is disagreement about what treatment should be provided toward the end of life in U.S. hospitals, ethics consultants or ethics committees commonly are consulted. Ethics consultants are usually physicians or lawyers or health-care workers with additional training in clinical ethics. Ethics committees—distinct from institutional review boards or Helsinki committees that review ethical aspects of research—are usually hospital-based interdisciplinary groups of health-care providers and others who consider ethical dilemmas arising in the hospital as well as develop policies and carry out education (McGee, Caplan, Spanogle, & Asch, 2001). A variety of mechanisms are used to facilitate decision making, ranging from a medical consultative model, in which the committee provides a suggested clinical approach, to mediation (Dubler & Liebman, 2003; Ross, Glaser, Rasinski-Gregory, Gibson, & Bayley, 1993). Many ethics-consultation approaches focus on enhancing the "process" of ethics in which goals and prognosis clarification occurs in the context of compassionate interdisciplinary communication. A recent attempt to target prospective ethics consultation demonstrated a small reduction in aggressive-care utilization at the end of life (Schneiderman et al., 2003).

Developing regional or hospital policies to preclude patient or family "autonomous" decisions for expenditures of health-care resources inconsistent with societal need has been a common theoretical topic of discussion in U.S. ethics committees and the medical literature. "Futile care," in which health-care providers and hospitals do not need to provide treatments requested by families, has been defined variously as care that cannot achieve the goals of medicine (Council on Ethical and Judicial Affairs (American Medical Association), 1999), care that could not ever be meaningful to the patient, or care with a tiny chance of success (Schneiderman, Jecker, & Jonsen, 1996). Such policies have been rarely implemented, and when they have, appear to have had a minimal impact (Fine & Mayo, 2003).

CONCLUSION

Care of the older patient toward the end of life in the United States includes a combination of factors that promote the availability of remarkable care for older patients that can dramatically extend individuals' independence and vitality. But these same factors also create a situation in which such care can pose inordinate burdens on patients and the health-care system. These factors have spurred development of advance-care planning, which attempts to permit autonomous decision making to guide care toward the end of life. However, these methods are not always successful, and many patients die after receiving inordinately aggressive, and expensive, care. In the United States, little of this conversation focuses on how health-care resources should be used to promote the good of society. As these technologies disseminate throughout the world, efforts to merge autonomy with community interest will be critical to creating models of end-of-life care that best serve both older patients and society.

REFERENCES

Angus, D. C., Barnato, A. E., Linde-Zwirble, W. T., Weissfeld, L. A., Watson, R. S., Rickert, T., & Rubenfeld, G. D. (2004). Robert Wood Johnson Foundation ICU End-of-Life Peer Group. Use of intensive care at the end of life in the United States: An epidemiologic study. *Critical Care Medicine, 32*, 638-643.

Arias, E. (2002). United States life tables, 2000. *National Vital Statistics Reports*. Vol. 51, No. 3. Hyattsville, MD: National Center for Health Statistics.

Bacchetta, M. D., Ko, W., Girardi, L. N., Mack, C. A., Krieger, K. H., Isom, O. W., & Lee, L. Y. (2003). Outcomes of cardiac surgery in nonagenarians: A 10-year experience. *Annals of Thoracic Surgery, 4,* 1215-1220.

Bodenheimer, T. (1997). The Oregon Health Plan—Lessons for the nation. *New England Journal of Medicine, 9*, 651-655 & *10*, 720-723.

Burg, M. A., McCarty, C., Allen, W. L., & Denslow, D. (1995). Advance directives. Population prevalence and demand in Florida. *Journal of the Florida Medical Association, 12*, 811-814.

Council on Ethical and Judicial Affairs, American Medical Association. (1999). Medical futility in end-of-life care. *Journal of the American Medical Association, 10*, 937-941.

Doukas, D. J., & McCullough, L. B. (1996). A preventive ethics approach to counseling patients about clinical futility in the primary care setting. *Archives of Family Medicine, 10*, 589-592.

Dubler, N. N., & Liebman, C. B. (2003). *Mediating bioethical disputes: Seeking consensus in conflict*. New York: United Hospital Fund.

Field, M. J., & Cassel, C. K. (1997). *Approaching death: Improving Care at the end of life*. Washington, DC: National Academy Press.

Fine, R. L., & Mayo, T. W. (2003). Resolution of futility by due process: Early experience with the Texas Advance Directives Act. *Annals of Internal Medicine, 9*, 743-746.

Goold, S. D., Williams, B., & Arnold, R. M. (2000). Conflicts regarding decisions to limit treatment: A differential diagnosis. *Journal of the American Medical Association, 283*(7), 909-914.

Hammes, B. J., & Rooney, B. L. (1998) Death and end-of-life planning in one Midwestern community. *Archives of Internal Medicine, 4*, 383-390.

Hadley, J. (2003). Sicker and poorer—The consequences of being uninsured: A review of the research on the relationship between health insurance, medical care use, health, work, and income. *Medical Care Research and Review, 2*(Supplement), 3S-75S, 76S-112S.

Hastings Center. (1987). *Guidelines on the termination of life-sustaining treatment and the care of the dying*. Briarcliff Manor, NY: Hastings Center.

Hiatt, H. H. (1975). Protecting the medical commons: Who is responsible? *New England Journal of Medicine, 5*, 235-241.

Hofmann, J. C., Wenger, N. S., Davis, R. B., Teno, J., Connors, A. F., Desbiens, N., Lynn, J., & Phillips, R. S. (1997). Patient preferences for communication with physicians about end-of-life decisions. *Annals of Internal Medicine, 127*, 1-12.

Hopp, F. P. (2000). Preferences for surrogate decision makers, informal communication, and advance directives among community-dwelling elders: Results from a national study. *Gerontologist, 4*, 449-457.

Lo, B., Quill, T. E., & Tulsky, J. (2001). Discussion palliative care with patients. In L. Snyder & T. E. Quill (Eds.), *Physician's guide to end-of-life care*. Philadelphia: American College of Physicians—American Society of Internal Medicine, 3-18.

McGee, G., Caplan, A. L., Spanogle, J. P., & Asch, D. A. (2001). A national study of ethics committees. *American Journal of Bioethics, 1*, 60-64.

Pearlman, R. A., Cain, K. C., Patrick, D. L., Appelbaum-Maizel, M., Starks, H. E., Jecker, N. S., & Uhlmann, R. F. (1993). Insights pertaining to patient assessments of states worse than death. *Journal of Clinical Ethics, 4*, 33-41.

Petersen, A. (2001). Biofantasies: Genetics and medicine in the print news media. *Social Science and Medicine, 8*, 1255-1268.

President's Commission for the Study of Ethical Problems in Medicine and Biomedical Research. (1983). *Deciding to forgo life-sustaining treatment*. Washington, DC: U.S. Government Printing Office.

Ross, J. W., Glaser, J. W., Rasinski-Gregory, D., Gibson, J. M., & Bayley, C. (1993). *Health care ethics committees: The next generation*. San Francisco, CA: Jossey-Bass.

Ross, J. W., & Wenger, N. S. (1994). Institutional ethics: Hospital practices and policies for denying life-sustaining treatment. *Whittier Law Review, 15*, 33-49.

Rosenthal, M. B., Berndt, E. R., Donohue, J. M., Frank, R. G., & Epstein, A. M. (2002). Promotion of prescription drugs to consumers. *New England Journal of Medicine, 7*, 498-505.

Schneiderman, L. J., Jecker, N. S., & Jonsen, A. R. (1996). Medical futility: Response to critiques. *Annals of Internal Medicine, 8*, 669-674.

Schneiderman, L. J., Gilmer, T., Teetzel, H. D., Dugan, D. O., Blustein, J., Cranford, R., Briggs, K. B., Komatsu, G. I., Goodman-Crews, P., Cohn, F., & Young, E. W. (2003). Effect of ethics consultations on nonbeneficial life-sustaining treatments in the intensive care setting: A randomized controlled trial. *Journal of the American Medical Association, 290*, 1166-1172.

Support Principal Investigators. (1995). A controlled trial to improve care for seriously ill hospitalized patients. The study to understand prognoses and preferences for outcomes and risks of treatments. *Journal of the American Medical Association, 274*, 1591-1598.

von Gunten, C. F., Ferris, F. D., & Emanuel, L. L. (2000). The patient-physician relationship. Ensuring competency in end-of-life care: Communication and relational skills. *Journal of the American Medical Association, 23*, 3051-3057.

CHAPTER 13

Palliative Care for the Aged Community: An Australian Perspective

Linda J. Kristjanson, Jayne Walton, and Christine Toye

> You matter because you are you, and you matter until the last moment of your life. We will do all we can, not only to help you die peacefully, but also to live until you die (Dame Cicely Saunders, 1993, p. vii).

The philosophical beliefs and attitudes that a society holds regarding death and dying and palliative care are pertinent to how care is provided to older persons at the end of life. As well, attitudes toward the elderly influence the extent to which care services are provided and the quality and types of services offered. Given Western society's obsession with youth and beauty and pursuits of excellence, it is not surprising that older persons in our society, and particularly those facing the end stages of their lives, are relatively neglected, may feel less valued, and may not always receive optimal health care.

Most research on dying has been undertaken with younger populations despite the fact that death occurs more commonly in older persons. The largest study of hospital death in the United States had a median age of 66, while the median age of death in the United States is 77 (Support Principal Investigators, 1995). Some studies suggest that older patients receive fewer burdensome life-prolonging interventions irrespective of baseline functional measure (Perls & Wood, 1996). This difference may be due to de facto rationing based on age rather than emphasis on individualizing the goals of care.

In Australia the term "residential aged-care facilities" is used to refer to nursing homes and hostels that care for most of Australia's frail citizens. Many people who become residents in these care settings will die there. In the year 2000, 81% of permanent residents died. Of the remainder leaving permanent care, 5% returned to the community, 6% moved to another residential aged-care facilities, and 7% were discharged to hospitals (1% were not reported) (Australian Institute of Health and Welfare, 2002). It is unknown how many of these residents received a palliative approach in the end stages of their life. However, a North American study found that individuals with advanced dementia who were transferred to acute settings generally had their palliative care plans abandoned (Wenger et al., 1996). It is plausible that this might also be the case in Australia. Additionally, the proportion of residents that might have benefited from a palliative-care approach, but did not have access to this type of support, is unknown. And although death may occur more often in a residential aged-care facility compared with other residential locations, specific attention to the needs of terminally ill individuals in nursing homes and care hostels is likely uneven across Australia.

One of the challenges of providing a supportive palliative approach to these individuals arises from the broader social context within which death and dying are understood. In most Western societies, in recent times the discussion of death and dying creates discomfort. This distancing response to death and dying is reflected in poor communication about the topic, limited resources directed to this specialty area, and minimal education about how to provide supportive end-of-life care. These barriers may make it more difficult for nurses, family, doctors, and other allied health professionals to provide care for dying residents. And health-care providers who endeavor to adopt a palliative approach to care for older persons may feel challenged to overcome some of the death denying attitudes pervasive in the wider culture. This chapter will first define palliative care and related terms and discuss when and where a palliative approach to care may be offered in an aged-care context. Key issues associated with a palliative approach to care for older persons facing a progressive or terminal illness will then be outlined, building on the results of the Australian Palliative Residential Aged Care Study, which developed the Guidelines for a Palliative Approach in Residential Aged Care (Australian Government Department of Health and Ageing, 2004). These issues include physical symptom management, psychological support, cognitive changes, family support, and palliative needs of Indigenous Australians. The chapter concludes by outlining some of the barriers to palliative aged care and offers some direction regarding changes to the Australian aged-care health system that hold particular promise.

WHAT IS PALLIATIVE CARE?

The World Health Organization (2003) defines palliative care as:

> An approach that improves the quality of life of individuals and their families facing the problem associated with life-threatening illness, through

> the prevention and relief of suffering by means of early identification and impeccable assessment and treatment of pain and other problems, physical, psychosocial, and spiritual.

The WHO document further states that palliative care aims to:

- Provide relief from pain and other distressing symptoms
- Intends neither to hasten nor postpone death
- Integrates the psychological and spiritual aspects of resident care
- Offers a support system to help patients live as actively as possible until death
- Offers a support system to help the family cope during the patient's illness and in their own bereavement
- Uses a team approach to address the needs of patients and their families including bereavement counseling, if appropriate
- Will enhance quality of life and may also positively influence the course of illness
- Is applicable early in the course of illness, in conjunction with other therapies that are intended to prolong life, such as chemotherapy or radiation therapy, and includes those investigations needed to better understand and manage distressing clinical complications

This recent definition and description of palliative care asserts that, contrary to earlier definitions of palliative care, individuals with diseases other than cancer that have a terminal phase and are progressive in nature would benefit from the philosophical underpinning of the palliative approach. Underlying the philosophy of palliative care is a positive and open attitude towards death and dying.

THREE FORMS OF PALLIATIVE CARE

In considering palliative care for older persons facing the end of life, it is important to distinguish between a *palliative approach, specialized palliative-care-service provision* and *end-of-life* or *terminal care* (Kristjanson, Toye, & Dawson, 2003).

A palliative approach. The person's condition is not amenable to cure and the symptoms of the disease require effective symptom management. Provision of active treatment for the person's disease may still be important and may be provided concurrently with a palliative approach. However, the primary goal of a palliative-care approach is to improve the ill person's level of comfort and level of function.

Specialized palliative-service provision. This form of palliative care involves referral to a specialist palliative-care team or health professional. This form of palliative care does not replace a palliative approach. Rather, involvement of a specialized palliative-care service augments a palliative approach with focused, specific input as required usually in two ways:

- assessment and treatment of complex symptoms experienced by the person, or
- information and advice to aged-care staff about complex issues (e.g., ethical dilemmas, family issues, or psychological or existential distress).

End-of-life (terminal) care: This form of palliative care is appropriate when the individual is in the final days or weeks of life and care decisions and goals are focused on the dying person's physical, emotional, and spiritual comfort and support for the family.

WHEN SHOULD PALLIATIVE CARE BE OFFERED?

Terminal illness is a clinical category used by doctors to identify the status of a person's condition to guide an appropriate plan of care. However, this classification is the opinion of the doctor and is not a definitive clinical category. Prognosis, survival time, and terminal care are profoundly linked, yet the methods used to identify survival time have limitations in accuracy and precision.

There is usually no sharp delineation between curative care and the acceptance that the goal of management is palliation. Unlike people who are dying of cancer, palliative-care recipients in aged-care facilities generally have a gradual decline in functional ability. Therefore, a palliative approach should be offered according to the needs of the individual, regardless of the clinical stage, and for those with incurable nonmalignant conditions as well as people with progressive malignancies.

Timely recognition by the health team of the need for a change in focus from curative or rehabilitative care to a palliative-care approach provides an opportunity for improved symptom control and tailored support for the older person and family. Some elders (and/or their family) may accept palliation much earlier in a disease trajectory than others. Alternatively, a person may not be able or willing to decide on one course of action over another, which leads to a decision to keep curative or rehabilitative options open in addition to receiving palliative support.

Families' concerns about good end-of-life care are usually centered on controlling pain and communicating effectively with staff members about the prognosis, trajectory of the condition, and care and treatment decisions that need to be made. Lack of clarity among the health-care team or lack of openness with residents and families may lead to conflict and confusion regarding care goals. Hanson, Danis, and Garrett (1997) interviewed 461 families whose older relative had died from a chronic disease. The aim of the study was to describe family perceptions of treatment decision, treatment intensity, and symptom relief and to determine their priorities to improve end-of-life care. Family members were generally satisfied with the treatment decisions made during their relative's care. However, 23% of family members did not recall a discussion of treatment decisions, irrespective of whether there had been a living will in place for that relative.

WHERE PALLIATIVE CARE SHOULD BE PROVIDED

The principles of palliative care can be applied in any setting, and a palliative care approach can be provided wherever people who require this approach reside (e.g., home, hostel, nursing-home setting). Depending upon the availability of family support and home hospice care, the older person's home may be an ideal setting for end-of-life palliative care. As well, if aged-care staff are trained and resources are available to support the resident, residential aged-care facilities can provide appropriate palliative care in an informal, home-like atmosphere. The implementation of palliative care in residential aged-care facilities can reduce the potential distress to residents and their family caused by a transfer to an acute-care setting.

One study conducted in South Australia found that of 151 nursing-home settings surveyed, 71 (47%) were providing a palliative approach to approximately 10% of their residents (29). However, provision of a palliative approach in rural residential aged-care facilities may be more difficult. One study found that rural terminally ill cancer patients were less likely to receive a palliative approach (59% compared with 71% in urban settings) (Hunt, Fazekas, Luke, & Roder, 2001). Access to medications for symptom control may be a problem in some remote settings.

Physical Symptom Management

Older individuals coping with a progressive or chronic illness may experience a range of physical symptoms that require prompt attention. The prevalence of symptoms associated with the palliative-care phase of an illness remains the same for those in a residential aged-care facility as other palliative-care populations. Fatigue, pain, shortness of breath, constipation, and anorexia are the five most common symptoms reported in older palliative-care patients. Mental confusion and incontinence, however, are more frequent in the older palliative-care population than in the younger palliative-care group.

Data on treatment of pain in old age suggest that older patients receive less pain medication than younger persons for chronic and acute pain. Nearly 30% of older persons with cancer living in long-term-care facilities did not receive pain medication, despite daily complaints of pain, and another 16% received only mild analgesics; these percentages increased with age and minority ethnicity (Bernabi et al., 1998). Older patients with hip fractures also received inadequate pain control, particularly if suffering from cognitive impairment.

Chronic pain syndromes such as arthritis, low back syndrome, and other musculoskeletal problems affect 20% to 50% of the community-dwelling older and are also typically under-treated (AGS Panel on Chronic Pain in Older Persons, 1998).

Several studies have found that pain management in residential aged-care facilities has not been addressed well. A study conducted in the United States reported that nearly one-sixth of residents had pain daily (Teno, Bird, & Mor, 1999). Bernabi and colleagues (1998) reported that residents over 85 years of age were more likely to receive no analgesics than were younger residents. One Australian study found that 22% of residents who reported pain had no medication recorded in the medical record, and 16% did not have analgesics ordered (McLean & Higginbotham, 2002). Some of the reasons for this inattention to pain have been attributed to inadequate assessment tools, especially for those with cognitive impairment who cannot articulate their care needs. Some doctors' and nurses' knowledge of pain assessment and management is notably deficient because many have little formal pain management education. The literature citing these deficiencies calls for a collaborative approach between doctors and nurses to manage pain consistently and well in the aged-care setting.

Poor care practices, difficulties in prescribing adequate and appropriate medication, or not having ready access to medications, especially in some rural and remote regions have also been cited as possible reasons for suboptimal pain control. In response to the reports of the presence of persistent pain among nursing home residents, changes in practice have been initiated. These changes have included improved education of doctors and nurses about pain assessment and prescribing, development of more responsive assessment tools, improved treatment strategies, and better monitoring practices of residents' pain levels (AGS Panel on Chronic Pain in Older Persons, 2002). There is evidence indicating that residents receiving the support of a palliative-care team have better analgesic management of daily pain than residents in aged-care facilities without access to this type of expertise (Miller, Mor, Wu, Gozalo, & Lapane, 2002).

Psychological Support

Studies of physical frailty in older persons reveal that frailty does not only refer to physical well-being, but has psychological and social dimensions as well. Similarly, a palliative approach focuses not only on physical symptoms, but also involves the psychological changes and needs of patients and family members. Psychological care is concerned with the older person's and family's psychological and emotional well-being, including issues such as self-esteem, and insight into and adaptation to either the illness and/or the residential aged-care environment.

Psychological distress is the term applied predominantly to anxiety, phobic, and depressive symptoms. The most common psychological problems for residents requiring palliative care are depression, confusion, and anxiety, with depression being one of the most prevalent psychiatric problems among older adults. Changes in the resident's emotional and cognitive abilities reflect both psychological and biological effects of the person's medical condition and its treatment. As well, psychological distress may be associated with greater physical distress. For instance, individuals suffering from depression may experience increased physical or somatic pain and compromised immune function. Therefore, the interactive effects of psychological and physical well-being need to be carefully considered.

Depression and anxiety are generally considered to be reactions to losses and threats associated with end-of-life illnesses. Confusion can also be a complicating factor at this time. Residents experiencing confusion may appear forgetful, disoriented to time and place, and exhibit changes in mood or behavior. The two main clinical syndromes associated with confusion are delirium, which is potentially reversible, and dementia, which is usually permanent. It can be difficult to distinguish between confusion, dementia and delirium, and depression; and comprehensive assessment of the resident should be made by a trained health professional. There is a risk that this type of symptom, if not properly assessed, may be dismissed as a "normal part of aging" and be undertreated.

Advanced Dementia

Advanced dementia is a neurological condition characterized by severe cognitive decline of an irreversible nature that is associated with poor prognostic factors such as swallowing disturbance, weight loss, anorexia, bowel and bladder incontinence, and often results in the person being bedridden. The progression from diagnosis of advanced dementia to death is usually three years. This prognosis sounds very sweeping given the variation known to occur. Thus, dementia is a progressive degenerative condition that is life limiting, and a palliative approach to care should be offered as this condition evolves (Hurley, Volicer, & Volicer, 1996).

The number of people living to an age when the likelihood of developing a dementing illness is highest is increasing. According to a recent report, more than 162,000 Australians had dementia in 2002, and it is anticipated that 500,000 people will have dementia by the year 2040 (Giles, Cameron, & Crotty, 2003). Approximately half of those diagnosed with dementia live in a residential aged-care facility. Overall, residents in low-care facilities (hostels) diagnosed with dementia were approximately 30% of the population, and approximately 60% resided in high-care facilities (nursing homes). Only 10% of nursing-home residents have no cognitive impairment (Gibson, Benham, & Racic, 1999). However, this figure was based upon a documented diagnosis, leading to a likely underestimation of the prevalence of the condition.

One study conducted in the United Kingdom found that the symptoms most commonly identified in the last year of life were confusion (83%), urinary incontinence (72%), pain (64%), depressed mood (61%), constipation (59%), and poor appetite (57%) (McCarthy, Addington-Hall, & Altmann, 1997). Symptoms of people with dementia were compared to people with cancer and it was found that people dying from dementia have symptoms and health-care needs comparable to those dying from cancer. However, the study showed that people with advanced dementia have less contact with the General Practitioner, and their family carers were less satisfied with the assistance received from the doctor than people dying from cancer. There is evidence to suggest that a palliative-care approach benefits both the person and the family. The features of a palliative approach most helpful to the family caregiver are continual follow-up evaluation by the primary carers and the emphasis on avoiding hospitalization. Underlying a palliative approach philosophy is the assumption that all individuals with advanced dementia should be thoroughly assessed with a view to managing all treatable causes of confusion.

One of the most difficult issues for staff members caring for the cognitively impaired is assessing whether or not the resident is experiencing pain. One study conducted in the United States compared cognitively intact residents' and their nursing staffs' ratings of the residents' pain intensity (Weiner, Peterson, & Keefe, 1999). This study reported disagreement between residents' and their nursing staffs' perceptions of pain-related behaviors, raising concerns about the abilities of nurses to correctly assess the pain of residents who would be unable to communicate. However, it has also been noted that members of the aged-care team who have cared for a resident for some time may be the first to detect changes in the resident's condition (Australian Government Department of Health and Ageing, 2004).

Several tools have been developed to assist staff members in determining pain in residents with dementia. Yet, many of these tools are too complex and subsequently are not used well in the aged-care setting. At present, the Pain Assessment in Advanced Dementia Scale (PAINAD) is used in Australia for residents with advanced dementia (Warden, Hurley, & Volicer, 2003). Until now there has been little research undertaken to validate the tool, and further testing is warranted.

Most recently, a new tool, specifically developed for people with late-stage dementia, is the Abbey Pain Scale (Abbey et al., 2004). The scale has been trialed in residential aged-care facilities in various states of Australia, and reasonable validity estimates have been reported. Although further substantiation of this scale is required, given its brevity and promising preliminary validity estimates, the tool has merit and may be useful following further testing.

People with advanced dementia who are admitted to hospital with acute illness while under the care of a palliative-care team often have their palliative care abandoned. The limitations of this study included a small sample size and the possibility that the research team intervened in treatment plans by their mere presence. However, the study highlights the need to prioritize goals of treatment before a person is sent to the hospital when there is less urgency to make life and death decisions. The extent of disruption on the resident is not beneficial, and it is appropriate for health-care providers to shift the paradigm from cure to comfort care.

Family Support

The palliative-care approach generally refers to the family as the "unit of care." However, such a view is often tied to the more traditional Western society view of the family as a nuclear entity based on biological or marital ties. Modern society does not always reflect this traditional view of the family, and therefore, notions of family must be much broader and more inclusive. A family member can be considered as any person who is part of the central core in the support network of an individual. A commonly used definition of family from a palliative-care context is those closest to the patient in knowledge, care, and affectation. Based on this definition, family could include friends, neighbors, or care workers and extends the boundaries beyond biological and legal relationships.

Research undertaken to evaluate the effectiveness of palliative care has suggested that it may be at least of equal and often even more value to the family than the resident (Kristjanson, Sloan, Dudgeon, & Adaskin, 1996). The evidence suggests that families value not only technically competent physical care, but also regard emotionally sensitive care as especially important. Families appreciate good communication with staff members, affirmation from the staff members that their input is valued, and permission to withdraw at times from the caregiving situation. Families describe the importance of time with staff members, being kept informed about the resident's condition, and being treated as if they have an active and equal role in the care planning process.

Specific palliative-care interventions found to be helpful to families include:

- Access to twenty-four hour medical and nursing advice
- Use of family conferences to obtain and share information
- Attention by the health-care team to the patient/resident as a "whole person"
- Competent pain management and comfort measures (Kristjanson et al., 1996).

The role of the family in decision making focuses on the need for individualized care and providing a link to the community, personal history, and the resident's preferences. The role of family members as advocates for highly dependent nursing-home residents may be limited by the weak position that family carers may have in the organization and the complexity of their relationships with staff members.

Health deterioration and death of the resident may also impact upon the physical and emotional health of family members. Family caregivers may also be elderly and have pre-existing health problems of their own. Caregiver burden has been found to be heaviest on spouses, followed by daughters, other relatives, and then sons. Some spouses, especially when their partner has severe cognitive impairment, report feeling like a "married widow."

A number of studies report the difficulties that families experience when coping with changes in mental status of their relative. Management of agitated delirium is a frequent source of conflict between families and health-care staff members (Waltrowicz, Ames, McKenzie, & Flicker, 1996). Kristjanson et al. (1996) found that family members of confused or unconscious patients had higher expectations of health-care staff than did family members of patients who were lucid.

Families who witness a difficult or poorly managed death may experience more grief, guilt, and regret in the bereavement period. For example, poorly managed pain or shortness of breath is extremely distressing for family members to witness, and they may feel guilt later if they believe that the patient suffered a difficult death.

Many families also mourn the loss of relationship with the person with a cognitive impairment and may require support in dealing with this "double death." People with dementia have often been termed "the living dead" and family members, in particular spouses, find the progressive degeneration difficult to watch, and the grieving process is often protracted and painful. Residential aged-care facilities that have a dementia support group in place where issues of grief and loss are addressed may help provide families with the support they require. One study found that support groups for bereaved seniors enhanced satisfaction with support given, diminished feelings of loneliness, and positively increased their emotional affect (Vickio & Cavanaugh, 1985).

ABORIGINAL AND TORRES STRAIT ISLANDER ISSUES

The values underpinning both a palliative approach and aged care in Australia are strongly grounded in the nonindigenous culture that dominates health and social services. Noticeably absent from the literature on aged care or palliative care is information related to the perspectives of indigenous Australians. A review of age distributions within Australia reveals that slightly more than half of the residents in states and territories in aged-care facilities at June 30, 2001 were aged 85 and older. The exception was in Northern Territory where 28% of residents were 85 years and over. There are fewer residents over the age of 65 because of the higher proportion of indigenous Australians in the Northern Territory and the lower life expectancy of this group of Australians. Therefore, aged-care planning for Aboriginal and Torres Strait Islanders is based upon the anticipated needs of people 50 years and older due to their poorer health outcomes (Australian Institute of Health and Welfare, 2002). Despite the fact that Aboriginal and Torres Strait Islanders have poorer health outcomes and a shorter life expectancy, attention to the palliative-care needs of this group of Australians has been almost nonexistent.

A recent study on terminal illness in rural Aboriginal communities found that indigenous participants were aware of the availability of health services (Willis, 1999). However, they preferred care to be provided by their family for as long as possible, as dying in their home country had considerable spiritual significance. Some indigenous people believed that if they were to die in the city, their spirit would never return to their homeland. Clearly the site of death for indigenous people is an important consideration as to where and how palliative care is provided, particularly for those in rural and remote areas (Ramanathan & Dunn, 1998).

Eckerman and colleagues (1992) warn about transporting simplistic views of traditional values into rural and urban settings. Traditional Aboriginal culture is far from simple. Adopting a standard view of Aboriginal culture and expecting it to "fit" every indigenous person does not do justice to understanding a complex culture. Indigenous populations are not, of course, a homogenous group of people. Indigenous Australians live in a wide spectrum of ecological zones, speak several hundred languages, and have varying religious and healing practices, diets, family traditions, political structures, and economic strategies. Eckerman takes this even further with an exhortation to be aware of differences within cultural groups and see Aboriginal people as individuals.

In March 2002, the Commonwealth Department of Health & Ageing commissioned a study into the palliative-care needs of indigenous Australians (Sullivan et al., 2002) This study has identified significant issues in the delivery of a palliative approach to Aboriginal and Torres Strait Islander people. Results from this study helped to shape recommendations for a palliative approach to residential aged care, including the importance of respectful attention to the individual needs of Indigenous residents, taking into account beliefs regarding illness, healing, comfort, care practices, location of care, and death and dying (Australian Government Department of Health and Ageing, 2004).

BARRIERS TO PROVISION OF PALLIATIVE CARE

In most instances, residential aged-care facilities in Australia endeavor to provide a high standard of palliative care. However, residential aged-care facilities are predominantly staffed with personal-care assistants who have no formal palliative-care training and registered nurses with varying levels of palliative-care expertise (Australian Department of Health and Ageing, 2004). The issues of limited staff training and a lack of time to be with dying residents are practical difficulties that many facilities face. Lack of adequate staffing may be a barrier to the provision of palliative care in many nursing homes. Additional barriers may include limited funding and environmental factors, such as unsuitable premises, a lack of single rooms/space, and limited privacy for residents and their family.

Despite these barriers, there is anecdotal evidence that many residential aged-care facilities attempt to provide a palliative approach to care rather than transfer residents to an acute setting when end-of-life care becomes a particular challenge. One study found that family members reported greater satisfaction with the care their relative received if the family members perceived that either they or their relative had control of care decisions, such as where they would die and who would care for them (Johnson, Morton, & Knox, 1992). Dying with dignity involves the right of the dying resident to choose where they wish to be cared for and/or die and whom they wish to care for them.

CONCLUSION

Unique and challenging issues emerge when providing palliative care for older persons. The illness trajectory may be prolonged and is highly likely to involve co-morbidity and cognitive and communicative impairment. Institutional care may be required because of the often severe and long-term nature of functional incapacity and the frailty of older family carers.

Palliative-care practices directed to the care of older persons are still in their infancy, and there is an expressed need within the aged-care literature for guidelines for care of the older person by nonspecialist palliative-care teams.

Traditional models of palliative care have tended to focus on the care of patients who have cancer. Although cancer is, for the most part, a disease of older people, these models do not necessarily meet the palliative-care needs of the wider population of elders. The question is, therefore, how to provide the best possible palliative care for this population.

Health-care staff working in residential aged-care facilities, the community, hospitals, and hospices all have a role in providing palliative care for older people, although episodes of care in hospitals or hospices may only be brief. There is a need to develop a blend of gerontological and palliative-care expertise in all these staff.

For this blend of expertise to evolve, palliative-care education and training is required across a range of settings where gerontological experience already exists, and vice versa. The most pressing priority, however, is that high quality, long-term, palliative care for elders must be easily accessible, avoiding the scenario of distressed relatives desperately searching for a suitable long-term placement or home-care services for a relative nearing the end of life.

In answer to this challenge, the Australian Department of Health & Ageing recently commissioned the development of guidelines for a palliative approach to care in residential aged-care facilities. The project has also involved the development of competencies for aged-care staff based upon the guidelines and the design of educational programs for all staff in these settings. The work undertaken has potential to provide an innovative and forward-thinking charter of care that promotes best practice palliative care for the residential aged-care sector. Ultimately, the allocation of resources and support for better end-of-life care for the aged-care population depends upon how a society values and cares for its most vulnerable citizens.

ACKNOWLEDGMENTS

The authors gratefully acknowledge the funding support of the Australian Department of Health & Ageing for the development of the *Guidelines for a Palliative Approach in Residential Aged Care* (Australian Government Department of Health and Ageing, 2004) and the research career support to the first author from The Cancer Council of Western Australia.

REFERENCES

Abbey, J., De Bellis, A., Easterman, A., Parker, D., Giles, L. A., & Lowcay, B. (2004). The Abbey pain scale: A 1-minute numerical indicator for people with end-stage dementia. *International Journal of Palliative Nursing, 10*(6), 6-13.

AGS Panel on Chronic Pain in Older Persons. (1998). The management of chronic pain in older persons. *Journal of the American Geriatrics Society, 46*, 635-651.

Australian Institute of Health and Welfare & Commonwealth Department of Health and Ageing. (2002). *Older Australia at a glance* (3rd ed.). AIHW Catalogue No. AGE 25. Canberra, Australia: Australian Government Printing Office.

Australian Government Department of Health and Ageing. (2004). *Guidelines for a palliative approach in residential aged care.* Canberra, Australia: Rural Health and Palliative Care Branch, Australian Government Department of Health and Ageing.

Bernabi, R., Gambassi, G., Lapane, K., Landi, F., Gatsonis, C., Dunlop, R., Lipsitz, L., Steel, K., & Mor, V. (1998). Management of pain in elderly patients with cancer. *Journal of the American Medical Association, 279*, 1877-1882.

Eckerman, A., Dowd, T., Martin, M., Nixon, L., Grav, R., & Chong, E. (1992). Binangoonj. *Bridging cultures in Aboriginal health.* Armidale, NSW: University of New England Press.

Gibson, D., Benham, C., & Racic, L. (1999). *Older Australia at a glance* (2nd ed.). Canberra, Australia: Australian Institute of Health and Welfare.

Giles, L. C., Cameron, I. D., & Crotty, M. (2003). Disability in older Australians: Projections for 2006-2031. *Medical Journal of Australia, 179*(3), 130-133.

Hanson, L. C., Danis, M., & Garrett, J. (1997). What is wrong with end-of-life- care? Opinions of bereaved family members. *Journal of the American Geriatrics Society, 45*(11), 1339-1344.

Hunt, R. W., Fazekas, B. S., Luke, C. G., & Roder, D. M (2001). Where patients with cancer die in South Australia, 1990-1999: A population-based review. *Medical Journal of Australia, 175*(10), 526-529.

Hurley, A. C., Volicer, B. J., & Volicer, L. (1996). Effect of fever-management strategy on the progression of dementia of the Alzheimer type. *Alzheimer Disease & Associated Disorders, 10*(1), 5-10.

Johnson, J. A., Morton, M. K., & Knox, S. M. (1992). The transition to a nursing home: Meeting the family's needs. *Geriatric Nursing, 13*(6), 299-302.

Kristjanson, L. J., Sloan, J. A., Dudgeon, D., & Adaskin, E. (1996). Family member's perceptions of palliative cancer care: Predictors of family functioning and family members' health. *Journal of Palliative Care, 12*(4), 10-20.

Kristjanson, L. J., Toye, C. T., & Dawson, S. (2003). New dimensions in palliative care: A palliative approach to neurodegenerative diseases and final illness in older people. *Medical Journal of Australia, 179*(Supplement 6), S42-44.

McCarthy, M., Addington-Hall, J., & Altmann, D. (1997). The experience of dying with dementia: A retrospective study. *International Journal of Geriatric Psychiatry, 12*(3), 404-409.

McClean, W. J., & Higginbotham, N. H. (2002). Prevalence of pain among nursing home residents in rural New South Wales. *Medical Journal of Australia, 177,* 17-20.

Miller, R. D., Mor, V., Wu, N., Gozalo, P., & Lapane, K. (2002). Does receipt of hospice care in nursing homes improve management of pain at the end of life? *Journal of the American Geriatrics Society, 50*(3), 507-515.

Perls, T., & Wood, E. (1996). Acute care costs of the oldest old: They cost less, their care intensity is less, and they go to non-teaching hospitals. *Archives of Internal Medicine, 156,* 754-760.

Ramanathan, S., & Dunn, P. (1998). Terminal illness in rural Aboriginal communities. *Aboriginal & Islander Health Worker Journal, 22*(5), 23-26.

Saunders, D. C. (1993). Palliative care. In D. Doyle, G. W. C. Hanks, & N. MacDonald (Eds.), *Oxford textbook of palliative medicine* (1st ed., p. 7). New York: Oxford University Press Inc.

Sullivan, K., Johnston, L., Colyer, C., Beale, J., Willis, J., Harrison, J., & Welsh, K. (2002). *Indigenous palliative care needs study—Final report.* Canberra, Australia: Commonwealth of Australia.

Support Principal Investigators. (1995). A controlled trial to improve care for seriously ill hospitalized patients. The study to understand prognoses and preferences for outcomes and risks of treatments (SUPPORT). *Journal of the American Medical Association, 274,* 1591-1598.

Teno, J., Bird, C., & Mor, V. (1999). *The prevalence of pain in United Sates nursing homes.* Providence, RI: Center for Gerontology and Health Care Research, Brown Medical School.

Vickio, C. J., & Cavanaugh, J. C. (1985). Relationships about death anxiety, attitudes toward ageing, and experience with death in nursing home employee. *Journal of Gerontology, 40*(3), 347-349.

Waltrowicz, W., Ames, D., McKenzie, S., & Flicker, L. (1996). Burden and stress on relatives (informal carers) of dementia sufferers in psychogeriatric nursing homes. *Australian Journal on Ageing, 15*(3), 115-118.

Warden, V., Hurley, A. C., & Volicer, L. (2003). Development and psychometric evaluation of the pain assessment in advanced dementia (PAINAD) scale. *Journal of the American Medical Directors Association, 4,* 9-15.

Weiner, D., Peterson, B., & Keefe, F. (1999). Chronic pain-associated behaviors in the nursing home: Resident versus care giver perceptions. *Pain, 80*(3), 577-588.

Wenger, N. S., Oye, R. K., Desbiens, N. A., Phillips, R. S., Teno, J. M., Connors, A. F. J., Liu, H. L., Zemsky, M. F., & Kussin, P. (1996). The stability of DNR orders or hospital readmission. *Journal of Clinical Ethics, 7*(1), 48-54.

Willis, J. (1999). Dying in country: Implications of culture in the delivery of palliative care in Indigenous Australian communities. *Anthropology & Medicine*, *6*(3), 423-435.

World Health Organization. (2003). WHO definition of palliative care. Retrieved August 11, 2003, from http://www.who.int/cancer/palliative/definition/en/print.html.

Epilogue

It's now fairly well-known that much of the world's population is growing older and experiencing increased life expectancy. However, the unique challenges facing various nations around the world have been less understood. Global aging is a universal phenomenon, but it affects nations differently. This volume examines three countries and focuses on three central topics: Caregiving, family care, and the end of life; and explores the unique and universal issues arising from these topics that may face nations in the developed and the developing world. Israel, Australia, and the United States are different from each other in many ways, including size, geography, democratic systems, history, and geopolitical relationships with each other and with other nations. Thus, how they respond to the aging of their populations and the care provided to older adults also differs. Yet, the three also face commonalities in terms of interests, problems, conflicts, and potential solutions. Their differences and commonalities are instructive lessons for global aging.

CHALLENGES

Examining the challenges facing Israel, Australia, and the United States raises a host of concerns that require action and resolution, some in the short term and others over a longer period of time. Israel, as Iecovich describes, is facing the dilemmas of changing family structure while its population ages and becomes more diverse. Central to its efforts in assisting caregivers is the changing notion of "filial responsibility." The problem of rising divorce rates and greater numbers of single-parent families creates a more problematic set of relationships in determining who is responsible for the care of an older adult. Yet, Israel's immigrant groups arrived in that country with traditional notions of filial responsibility: The family carries that responsibility. In time, though, like Australia and the United States, even those immigrant groups acculturate and face changing family structures. Israel's government has passed laws and incorporated public policies that provide formal caregiving supports, but the question of filial obligations to one's own and the extent to which it can be mandated or supplanted by government will increasingly dominate public policy there.

Benjamin brings forth one model that seeks to address this dilemma: Consumer directed care, wherein the client decides how he or she wishes to be taken care of. This case study of empowerment in which the individual can use state funds to pay a family member or hire a formal caregiver is one option. Tilse, Wilson, and Setterlund present another set of choices in describing the reform and restructuring of residential aged-care services in Australia. Ultimately, however, as each nation addresses family obligations, there will be an escalating need, as Galinsky describes, for greater numbers of professionals trained in gerontology and geriatrics.

One overriding issue in the art of caring for older adults is the continued prevalence of women as the predominant, informal workforce in family care. Morse, Lau, and Raveis highlight the crucial role that women perform and the pressures they face in caring for chronically and terminally ill patients. Caring for an elderly cancer patient requires tremendous time, energy, and compassion; and families—women, in particular—shoulder those complex demands, often at a cost to their own emotional, physical, and financial well-being. Raveis refers to one attempt by the United States to legislate support for family members through the National Family Care Givers Support Program. Whether this relatively small program can make a difference for the many women and families involved in caregiving remains to be seen. For now, all three nations rely to some extent on their immigrant and minority populations as nonfamily caregivers to fill in for family members who are unavailable or unable to care for their own. This use of culturally diverse groups as a source of caregivers able and willing to perform this noble duty with minimal compensation demonstrates one benefit of diversity but also raises additional questions about filial obligations.

Eventually, all humans reach the end of their life stages and face the inevitable, yet sobering reality that they will die. Death and dying becomes the ultimate social, political, and personal issue facing an aging society. How we prepare, respond to, and accept this inevitability provides a barometer for the overall values of a particular community and country for its most vulnerable citizens. Aberdeen describes the difficult process that family members and caregivers must face in following a "pathway" of letting go and allowing their loved ones to move into a more formal and institutional facility better able to handle a terminal illness. Tulloch examines the bioethics and end-of-life issues facing the United States, England, the Netherlands, and Australia, and the "feminist" concerns of male-oriented practices for an aging world where women predominate. The practice of voluntary euthanasia and the need for informed consent and decision making when faced with impaired rationality point out the emotional, social, and legal complications in addressing the art of letting go. Cohen-Mansfield describes an increasingly accepted legal and policy tool—advance directives—as a way for individuals to express their wishes for their end-of-life.

Carmel uses Israel's experience to describe a patient's right to forego medical treatment, the legal developments in enabling individuals to die with dignity, the problematic role of the family in end-of-life decision making, and discrepancies in end-of-life care between elderly persons' preferences and physicians' practices. Kristjanson, Walton, and Toye, as well as Cohen-Mansfield, Carmel, and Tulloch advocate palliative care as an essential component in addressing death and dying. Yet, as Steinberg and Cohen-Mansfield illustrate, these end-of-life issues are further complicated by diverse and often opposing values brought on by secular, religious, and sociocultural views and norms in the approach to death and dying. Advances in medical technology, as Wenger and Davis point out, create further complexity by lengthening the time we must ponder this difficult issue.

Each country in this study—Israel, the United States, Australia—is grappling with the art of caregiving, family care, and letting go; and each has developed different approaches to differing dilemmas. Yet, there are universal lessons to be gleaned from their experiences.

LESSONS LEARNED

What is it that most nations in an aging world might have in common with the experiences of Israel, Australia, and the United States? And what are the issues that require a response if the world is to prepare for its demographic revolution? Foremost, of course, are the nature of longevity and the continued rise of life expectancy. With a few notable exceptions (e.g., Russia, some African countries), most nations are seeing the life spans of their citizens increase. This longevity, while an unprecedented success for humankind, also creates formidable challenges. The changing population pyramid occurring in the United States, Australia, and Israel also faces most other nations. We are witnessing a shift from a demographic pyramid, with young people forming the larger base, middle-aged people in the midsection, and elderly at the top, to a rectangle and, in extreme cases (e.g., Japan), an inverted pyramid. In these scenarios, the elderly will compose an ever increasing portion of the population, and the ratio of young and middle-aged persons will drop, leading to fewer workers supporting more retirees. Already in Western Europe, we see some dramatic manifestations of this changing pyramid. Italy, France, and Germany have workers shouldering greater responsibility for the productivity and taxes needed to support larger numbers of retirees, a support system aided in part by generous pension and welfare policies. This has led to resentment by workers, efforts to downsize the social welfare system, and insecurity by retirees. The United States, Australia, and Israel, however, have an escape valve: Immigration and higher fertility rates among their indigenous and minority populations. This diversity keeps their nations relatively young, providing workers, taxpayers, and caregivers. Yet, it also leads to an "age/race stratification," whereby the elders and retirees are of one homogenous characteristic, and the workers and caregivers represent a diverse set of immigrant and racial groups. This trend lends itself to tensions and conflicts. These three nations can, if they resolve this stratification and achieve a healthy multicultural society, provide lessons for other parts of the world.

The question of who is responsible for the care of older adults raises another universal conundrum. These three nations struggle with the dilemma of which sector—public, private, voluntary, nonprofit, religious, or corporate—should play a role in assisting individuals and families with caregiving and in responding to the growing expectations and demands by the elderly for formal benefits and services. As mentioned earlier, traditional societies, including each nation's immigrant and refugee populations, still hold to an answer that, to some degree, puts that responsibility squarely on the family. But that solution becomes untenable in modern, Western, democratic, and capitalistic societies and forces governments to contribute with financing, public benefits, laws, and programs. Yet, each nation has robust, nonprofit, voluntary, private, and religious sectors; and each is facing pressures to play a role, whether through charitable care, volunteers, church support, or market driven solutions. Most nations of the world will find that their government alone and their traditional societies will not be able to fully shoulder this burden. The costs, complexities, and overwhelming needs of aging populations will require a mix of sector involvement in most cases. How and in what way the public and private sectors interact and share that responsibility will be a source of lively debate in the coming years. These three nations are already engaged in this debate and provide lessons for global aging.

Alongside the question of which sector, and in what mix, should assume responsibility for the care of older adults lies the issue of organizing such services. All three nations face a vexing dilemma of coordinating and integrating the proliferation of programs, services, benefits, and policies that have developed over the last decades. The good news is that each nation wants to serve older adults, their families, and caregivers, but the nature of their democratic system often leads to fragmented overlapping, disjointed and categorical laws, financing, and services. Each country, in turn, is emphasizing the concepts of "continuity of care," coordinating among services and linking such programs to the informal system of caregiving, volunteer activities, and charitable supports. "Care managers" and case management are such vehicles where a person or an agency oversees the coordination and development of "one stop" points of entry. Despite this seeming inefficiency, such a multiple system of programs, laws, and benefits can, under the best case scenario, foster competition, innovation, and involvement among the various sectors of society.

An ancillary dilemma is where to place and house those with the highest levels of dependency. The United States of America has historically chosen institutional care and has put the bulk of their public financing in nursing homes and hospitals. Yet, the public overwhelmingly prefers home- and community-based systems for care that gives families the choice of how to care for their own. Israel and Australia, to a greater extent, promote home- and community-based systems of long-term care, yet institutional care will remain an important component of this continuum of long-term care. Achieving that balance will be one more organizational challenge for all nations as they respond to the aging of their populations.

Ultimately, how each nation and the world respond to longevity will reflect their values about aging and caring for older adults. And herein lies another source of tension, conflict, and even opportunity. In many respects, caregiving is the great equalizer in societies divided by class, income, education, race, ideology, partisanship, and religion. Caring for older adults and the disabled will eventually confront all families and individuals. Someone will be needed to help someone who can no longer be fully independent. The values of compassion, dignity, filial obligation, and even love should permeate how governments, individuals, and families respond to the care of older adults. Yet, we see in the lessons learned from these three nations that another set of values is emerging—values often cloaked in "choices." Increasingly, older and disabled persons, whether they are healthy, impaired, or terminally ill, are asking for choices in how they help themselves and are assisted by others. These emerging values are couched in the language of "empowerment," "dignity," "control," "choice," and even "power." They reflect the desires of individuals and families to not be helpless and "subject" to the whims and vagaries of fate and circumstance or the expertise of professional and formal support systems. Increasingly, we may find in an aging world that other nations will have a constituency of elders, families, and caregivers who want a say in how they respond to age, caregiving, and death and dying and may even want to influence the formal governmental responses to aging.

These elements of "choice" are raised in the legal debates over advance directives, euthanasia, and how individuals plan for death and dying. Each country grapples with the philosophical, ethical, emotional, and political debate over who should decide how one ages and dies. Each of the countries studied in this volume finds that issues such as euthanasia bring to the surface visceral and competing values and norms over who should exercise such intimate decisions. The debates over abortion and actions related to death and dying will force governments and individuals to confront both the traditional values and notions about caregiving and emerging desires for control, choice and empowerment.

How this plays out may be evident in another emerging trend that, while not explicitly addressed in this volume, may be a logical outcome of longevity: A politics of aging. In Australia, Israel, and especially the United States, there is growing advocacy on behalf of the elderly and for public policies benefiting retirees. This phenomenon of elders exercising political clout is unique in the history of humankind. With the possible exception of gerontocracies in some ancient societies, there has never been an instance of old-age lobbies. The United States has a sophisticated and widespread movement of such lobbies, notably the American Association of Retired Persons, that influences national, state, and local policymaking. Pensioners in Israel have established some political parties on the national and local levels, but their power and influence are still limited. In

Australia, the Council on Ageing is one leading organization that is increasingly making its issues known to government and being listened to. Soon, caregivers and their families will organize to promote their interests. All governments facing rising life expectancy will have to contend with new lobbies in their political worlds: Organized groups of elders. Even more traditional nations in Asia and Latin America are witnessing the emergence of old-age lobbies. Such a development will further complicate our response to caring for older adults, but it can also transform societies to be more compassionate and caring toward their elders.

A final lesson gleaned from this treatise is the "wild card" in what nations can expect as their populations age: Technological innovations and biomedical advances have the potential to dramatically alter the aforementioned lessons and scenarios. As seen in these three nations, technology, medicine, pharmaceuticals, and biological developments are already changing the equation of how someone will age and who will experience a longer life span. The advent of public health and medicine has made for a healthier and longer-lived population. Drugs and sophisticated medical treatments and interventions have prolonged the life span and kept individuals alive when, historically, they would not have lived as long. Biomedical advances have the potential to cure such curses as dementia, cancer, arthritis, and incontinence—the very attributes of aging that lead to disabilities, mobility limitations, dependence, and premature death. Advances and "magic bullets" in any of these areas could dramatically alter the need for caregiving and long-term care. Technological and biomedical advances are the great unknown for global aging and they argue for increased investments in research and development. The three nations studied here, in particular, benefit from well-funded and sophisticated research and development, largely through their universities and the private sector. What they learn can be shared and will benefit the world.

THE FUTURE OF GLOBAL AGING

The future of global aging bodes well. We can all enjoy the added years that destiny and human endeavors have bestowed on us. With few exceptions, all nations of the world will live longer and will have unprecedented numbers of older adults. This assumes, however, that we continue to use existing definitions of being old. Most countries use some version of age 60 or 65 years of age to denote who has reached that magic threshold of becoming elderly. Yet, the reality is that as we strive to care for older adults and address issues such as caregiving, family care, and end-of-life, the very foundation and paradigm of how individuals perceive their old age is changing. In advanced nations such as the United States, Australia, and Israel, we see a redefinition of how individuals label themselves in the aging process. To be old and to be viewed, officially at least, as a senior citizen, is increasingly falling into the later ranges of a 100-year life span. Individuals in their 70s and 80s are by and large active, healthy, and involved, while those in their 60s no longer see themselves as older adults. With more of us likely to be centenarians, we may want to rethink who is old and how we define aging. In short, with the blessings of longevity, more individuals are living longer, healthier, and "younger."

This does not mean, however, that there will not be greater numbers of persons who will face the challenges and problems of old age: Chronic illnesses, disabilities, and impairments. And many will still face the problems even as early as their 50s. The challenge of all nations is to address the problems facing older adults at whatever age while acknowledging the true benefits of longevity and healthy aging.

This volume, by necessity, focuses on the central challenges of individual and population aging and may unintentionally give a somber tone to increasing life spans. We do not want to detract from the positive side of aging, but we do want to insure that all sectors of society assume a measure of responsibility for the needs of caregivers, caregiving, and those in need. Finding that balance—assisting older adults while celebrating the freedoms of successful aging—will be the measure by which nations are judged to effectively respond to the art of caring.

The two volumes of this series draw from the experiences of only three nations, but by doing so we hope that most other countries will draw lessons that help them to be innovative, compassionate, and bold in addressing this demographic revolution.

Glossary

Active euthanasia: Refers to intentional active measures taken in order to end the life of another person. This category is divided into two different types of actions: The first one is a direct act of giving or injecting a lethal dose of medication to a terminally ill patient. The second one is physician-assisted suicide, which refers to assisting a person to commit suicide by writing a prescription for a lethal dose of medication.

Activities of daily living (ADL): Multidimensional functional assessment based on six activities of daily living: Eating, dressing, bathing, toileting, transferring in and out of a bed/chair, and walking (see also "instrumental activities of daily living").

Advance care planning: Refers to ongoing discussions between patients and their health-care providers which clarify their values and wishes concerning end-of-life care, rather than specifying preferences for specific scenarios. The purpose of this process is to enable the care team to address the patient's wishes when he or she is unable to make decisions, in a manner that fits both the patient's values and desires and the specific clinical situation.

Advance directives: Documents in which people can record their wishes for health-care decisions in the event that they become incompetent to make or communicate their wishes. In these documents, people may designate a proxy to make health-care decisions for them, or they can specify their preferences concerning health-care decisions under specific future conditions, or both.

ATSI people: Australian Aboriginals and Torres Strait Islanders.

Bioethics: Bioethics is a branch of ethics that deals with the ethical and social implications of biotechnology and the revolutionary developments in the biological sciences.

CALD people: Culturally and linguistically diverse peoples.

Chemotherapy: Drug treatment designed to kill cancer cells.

Clinical trial: A research study that tests the success of new medical treatments or other interventions on people.

Complementary model of care: A task-specific model of care provision, in which different primary groups provide different forms of care and support for diverse needs.

Consumer-directed care: A set of approaches to organizing home-based and other services for those with chronic care needs in which the service recipient, rather than a social or health professional, makes the primary decisions about how resources are used, including which workers are hired, which services are provided, when, and how.

Continuity of care: Provision of designated health and welfare services from a variety of existing services, in a coordinative manner adjusted to the patients' varying individual needs as they change over time.

Dementia: A progressive disabling condition, primarily of older persons, affecting cognitive functions, abilities, and the personality characteristics of each individual.

Dependency: Reliance on others for receiving physical, mental, and social support.

Disability-adjusted life expectancy: A modification of conventional life expectancy that takes into account years lived with disability.

Distributive justice: Pertains to the need to consider the distribution of resources in society considering all social needs.

Double effect: Providing medications in order to relieve pain and decrease suffering, despite the knowledge that this act might hasten the patient's death.

Durable power of attorney: A document in which a person designates another person named "the attorney in fact," "agent," "proxy," or "surrogate," to make future decisions in the case of inability to make or express such decisions.

End-of-life care: Medical, nursing, spiritual, psychological, and social care provided to a patient in an incurable health condition during the last stages of his or her life.

Euthanasia: A general term used for deliberate acts of assistance in ending the life of a person who suffers from an incurable or terminal disease.

Family-based caregiving: Care provided to semi- or fully dependent older persons in activities of daily living, health needs, financial assistance, protective custodial care, or general home maintenance in their own home or the caregiver's home.

Filial commitment: Attitudes that reflect personal acceptance for the care and well-being of an elderly parent, and express family solidarity and intergenerational positive feelings.

Filial responsibility: Refers to adult children's duty to provide care for their aging parents and to ensure what appropriate behaviors are expected. This obligation stems from the perception that adult children should feel gratitude toward their parent(s) for rearing and caring for them throughout their formative development.

Futile treatment: A treatment is regarded as futile when nothing can be done to reverse the dying process and when it is merely slowing the dying process.

Hierarchical substitution model: The hierarchy of support providers involved in the service provision of formal care.

High care: Referring to residential nursing homes for the infirm aged.

Low care: Referring to hostels where residents provide their own care with access to a supervisor for assistance.

"Hospital-in-the-home": Provision of expert medical personnel services in the patient's home following an inpatient stay.

"Iceberg" phenomenon: Health issues of older people that are overlooked by medical practitioners in favor of traditional causes of morbidity, which are more likely to affect younger active adults.

Informed choice: Relating to entry decisions and lifestyle choices in residential facilities and care support.

Instrumental activities of daily living (IADL): A multidimensional functional assessment based on six activities of daily living: Eating, dressing, bathing, toileting, transferring in and out of bed/chair, walking (ADL), and on "Instrumental activities of daily living" (IADL), such as cooking, shopping, and housekeeping.

Living will: A document in which individuals communicate their desires for medical treatments in a hypothetical future scenario in which they will not be able to actively make decisions during a terminal health condition.

Managed care: A health-care delivery system that entails interventions to control the price, volume, delivery site, intensity of health provision, and the services provided. The goal of managed care is to maximize the value of health benefits and the coordination of health-care management for a covered population.

Medical model of care: Provision of forced medical and/or nursing care in physical and mental health conditions.

Metastatic, distal: Having to do with metastasis, the spread of cancer from one part of the body to another.

Morbidity: Any departure, subjective or objective, from a state of physiological or psychological well-being. In this sense, sickness, illness, and morbid conditions are similarly defined and synonymous.

Mortality: Deaths. Refers to cases of death in a population.

Out-of-pocket payment: A fee paid by the consumer of health services directly to the provider at the time of delivery.

Palliative care: Has been developed as a new medical specialty, which focuses on comprehensive treatments intended to ease the physical and psychological suffering of the severely ill and dying patients and their families.

Passive euthanasia: A term referring to two different types of acts: The withholding of treatment, such as permitting a terminally ill person to die by refraining from the use of life-sustaining treatments such as cardiopulmonary resuscitation (CPR), antibiotics, artificial feeding, and hydration. The second type of passive euthanasia is the withdrawal of treatment after it has begun, such as disconnecting a person from a ventilator. The patient may or may not die immediately as a result of these acts.

Personal care assistance: Referring to provided help with "activities of daily living" (ADL) such as bathing, dressing, and eating, and with "instrumental activities of daily living" (IADL) such as cooking, shopping, and housekeeping.

Prevention: Attempts made in order to preserve health and prevent disease and functional dependency.

Prophylactic therapy: Preventive treatment.

Radiation: High-energy radiation used in low doses to diagnose diseases and in high doses to treat cancer.

Recurrence: The return of cancer, at the same site as the original (primary) tumor or in another location, after it had disappeared.

Regional: In oncology, describes the body area surrounding a tumor.

Resident-focused care: An explicit awareness of the importance of honoring the rights of aged residents, their citizenship, and adulthood care. This approach views aged consumers as active participants in the decision-making processes about services and choices.

Voluntary vs. involuntary euthanasia: Refers to hastening a patient's death following the request or agreement of a competent adult patient versus hastening a patient's death without the permission of the person whose life is being taken.

Coeditors

JoAnn Damron-Rodriguez, LCSW, PhD, is faculty in the Department of Social Welfare, University of California, Los Angeles. She has served at the state, national, and international level to evaluate and build community health care, including the California Blue Ribbon Panel on State Nursing Homes, the U.S.A. Veterans Administration Geriatric and Gerontology Advisory Council, as consultant to the U.S. Department of Justice on the Olmstead Decision, as past president of the California Council on Gerontology and Geriatrics, and as advisor to the World Health Organization, Kobe Center for Health Development. She serves on multiple editorial boards and has published widely on eldercare issues.

Susan Feldman, MA, PhD, is a Sociologist and Senior Research Fellow and Director of the Alma Unit for Research on Ageing: Gender and Health across the Lifespan, in the Centre for Ageing, Rehabilitation, Exercise & Sport, Victoria University, Melbourne, Australia. She has researched widely on older women's issues including widowhood and intergenerational relationships.

Terence Seedsman, PhD, is a Social Gerontologist, Professor and Deputy Dean, Faculty of Human Development, Victoria University, Melbourne, Australia. His research interests include intergenerational relations and education.

Contributors

Suzanne Aberdeen, RN, BN, M Ed, Cert. Critical Care, is a Nurse Practitioner and a part-time Lecturer at Victoria University, Melbourne, Australia. She has considerable experience in training and education provision for dementia care and general health care and lectures in the Graduate Program in Aged Services Management and Dementia Care. In 2004 she was awarded formal recognition by the Australian Dementia Association for her services and expertise with dementia sufferers and their families.

A. E. Benjamin, PhD, is a Professor in the Department of Social Welfare, School of Public Affairs, University of California, Los Angeles. His interests include understanding how societies respond to the health and long-term service needs of people with various chronic conditions and diseases, the impact of consumer-direction for people needing supportive services, and strategies for addressing entry-level workforce shortages in health care.

Jiska Cohen-Mansfield, PhD, ABPP, is a Professor of Health Care Sciences and of Prevention and Community Health at the George Washington University Medical Center and School of Public Health and the Director of the Research Institute on Aging of the Hebrew Home of Greater Washington. Her interests include advanced directives, preferences regarding life sustaining treatments, medical decision making in the nursing home, agitation/behavior problems in elderly persons and other aspects well-being, such as sleep, pain, depression, and use of physical restraints.

James W. Davis, MD, is a Clinical Professor in the Division of Geriatrics at the David Geffen School of Medicine at UCLA. He has been actively caring for geriatrics patients and teaching students at all levels of training for the past 25 years.

David Galinsky, MD, is a Professor of Geriatric Medicine in the Faculty of Health Sciences, Ben-Gurion University, Israel. He is the former chief of the Geriatric Department in the Soroka University Hospital, Beer-Sheva, Israel. His interests include organization of geriatric services, geriatric education in the pre- and postgraduate levels, elderly falls, dementia, and clinical problems among elderly.

Esther Iecovich, PhD, is a Senior Lecturer and director of the Masters Program in Gerontology at the Faculty of Health Sciences, Ben-Gurion University, Beer-Sheva, Israel. She is a social worker and gerontologist, interested in policy issues in old age, services for elderly people, and boards and administration of nonprofit organizations.

Linda J. Kristjanson, RN, BN, MN, PhD, is Professor of Palliative Care Nursing and Director of the Cancer Council, Western Australia Centre for Cancer and Palliative Care. She researches on the needs of individuals facing life-threatening and progressive illnesses.

Rosalind Lau, RN, RM, NICN, BN, M Ed Studs., PhD, is a Research Fellow in the Alma Unit for Research on Ageing, Centre for Ageing, Rehabilitation, Exercise & Sport at Victoria University, Melbourne, Australia. She is a nurse and midwife, with prior interests specializing in neonatal intensive-care nursing and research in neonatology. Her current interests are in transcultural positive aging of older adults.

Victoria H. Raveis, PhD, is an Associate Professor of Clinical Sociomedical Sciences at Columbia University's Mailman School of Public Health, New York and Co-Director of the school's Center for the Psychosocial Study of Health and Illness. She is interested in the psychosocial issues facing seriously ill or dying older adults and the health-related demands and challenges confronting family caregivers in chronic illness situations.

Deborah Setterlund, BSoc Studs., GCert Ed., MSW, PhD, is a Social Worker and Senior Lecturer, School of Social Work and Applied Human Services, University of Queensland, Brisbane, Australia. Her research interests include services delivery for older people in community settings and residents' rights in aged-care facilities.

Avraham Steinberg, Clinical Associate Professor of Medical Ethics, Hadassah Medical School, Hebrew University, Jerusalem. He is the Director of the Centre for Medical Ethics and a senior pediatric neurologist. He is interested in Jewish medical ethics, general medical ethics, history of medicine, medicine and law, and pediatric neurology.

Cheryl Tilse, BSW, BA, PhD, is a Social Worker and Senior Lecturer, School of Social Work and Applied Human Services, The University of Queensland,

Brisbane, Australia. Her research is on housing options for low-income families, resident participation in residential care and assets management by older people.

Christine Toye, RN, BN, PhD, is a Lecturer in the School of Nursing, Midwifery & Postgraduate Medicine, Edith Cowan University, Western Australia. She has significant experience in the nursing care of frail elderly people and is currently President of the Western Australian Division of the Australian Association of Gerontology. Her interests include palliative care for the frail elderly.

Gail Tulloch, BA, PhD, is an Adjunct Research Fellow in the Quality of Life Research Unit, Griffith University, Brisbane, Queensland, Australia. She is the author of "Euthanasia— Choice and Death" (Edinburgh University Press, 2005) that explores end-of-life issues through case studies from America, England, The Netherlands, and Australia from a philosophical basis.

Jayne Walton, BA, is a psychologist and a Projects Manager in the National Palliative Residential Aged Care (APRAC), Edith Cowan University, Western Australia. She has considerable experience, involving stakeholders as active participants in palliative aged-care research.

Neil S. Wenger, MD, MPH, is a Professor in the Division of General Internal Medicine and Health Services Research at the David Geffen School of Medicine at UCLA. He is a practicing general internist and geriatrician and Chair of the UCLA Medical Center Ethics Committee and Director of the UCLA Health Care Ethics Center. He teaches clinical ethics at UCLA. His research interests include clinical ethics and quality of care for older patients.

Jill Wilson, BSoc Studs., MSW, PhD, is a Social Worker and Associate Professor, School of Social Work and Applied Human Services, the University of Queensland, Brisbane, Australia. Her research interests are in policy and practice issues in residential aged-care and community settings.

Index